P9-CAO-318

Learn Microsoft®
Visual Basic® 2012

Michael Halvorson

Published with the authorization of Microsoft Corporation by:
O'Reilly Media, Inc.
1005 Gravenstein Highway North
Sebastopol, California 95472

ISBN: 978-0-7356-7298-7

1 2 3 4 5 6 7 8 9 LSI 7 6 5 4 3 2

Printed and bound in the United States of America.

Microsoft Press books are available through booksellers and distributors worldwide. If you need support related to this book, email Microsoft Press Book Support at *mspinput@microsoft.com*. Please tell us what you think of this book at http://www.microsoft.com/learning/booksurvey.

Microsoft and the trademarks listed at *http://www.microsoft.com/about/legal/en/us/IntellectualProperty/ Trademarks/EN-US.aspx* are trademarks of the Microsoft group of companies. All other marks are property of their respective owners.

The example companies, organizations, products, domain names, email addresses, logos, people, places, and events depicted herein are fictitious. No association with any real company, organization, product, domain name, email address, logo, person, place, or event is intended or should be inferred.

Acquisitions and Developmental Editor: Russell Jones

Production Editor: Holly Bauer

Editorial Production: Zyg Group, LLC

Technical Reviewer: Tim Patrick

Copyeditor: Zyg Group, LLC

Indexer: Zyg Group, LLC

Cover Design: Jake Rae

Cover Composition: Zyg Group, LLC

Illustrator: Rebecca Demarest

For my brother, Jon Halvorson

Contents at a Glance

Contents

What do you think of this book? We want to hear from you!

Microsoft is interested in hearing your feedback so we can continually improve our
books and learning resources for you. To participate in a brief online survey, please visit:

www.microsoft.com/learning/booksurvey/

What do you think of this book? We want to hear from you!

Microsoft is interested in hearing your feedback so we can continually improve our
books and learning resources for you. To participate in a brief online survey, please visit:

www.microsoft.com/learning/booksurvey/

Introduction

Microsoft Windows 8 is a powerful and visually compelling operating system designed to dramatically enhance consumer productivity and offer access to a wide range of web-based products and services. A rich user experience is at the heart of Windows 8, where the new look and feel of Windows 8 applications provide rapid access to music, photos, contacts, and user settings in the Internet "cloud", and the Windows Store provides immediate access to exciting consumer applications. Windows 8 has been designed to operate on a broad spectrum of devices, from touch-enabled tablets, to laptops, to traditional desktop computers. As customers immerse themselves in hundreds of vibrant Windows 8 applications, they are given the freedom to focus on the task at hand, rather than the commands or features of the operating system.

From the perspective of the software developer, Windows 8 presents amazing opportunities; it's fast, secure, and robust, and will be installed on millions of computers worldwide, including the Microsoft Surface tablets. Windows 8 applications are exciting and easy to use, and they offer customers an interface that is content-rich and runs equally well on touch-based devices or desktop PCs. Most significantly, the Windows Store allows developers to sell their Windows 8 applications directly to the global marketplace, providing new sources of revenue and streamlining installation procedures.

This book will show you how to create compelling Windows 8 applications with Microsoft Visual Studio 2012, the newest version of Microsoft's bestselling software development suite. You will learn how to download a free version of the Visual Studio 2012 Express software (that's right—*free!*), and how to create interesting Windows 8 apps by using several of the tools and technologies within Visual Studio, including the Visual Basic programming language. By the end of this book you will have learned how to create the core features of a Windows 8 application; how to work productively in the Visual Studio Integrated Development Environment (IDE); how to design a user interface with XAML markup and Blend for Visual Studio; how to write efficient Visual Basic program code; and how to sell your own applications in the Windows Store.

One of the coolest features of this book, of course, is that every programming tool that it teaches and describes is *free*! Microsoft is offering complementary access to the Express edition of Visual Studio because it hopes that you will enjoy learning how to program with it, and that you will one day become a professional Visual Basic programmer who will build and sell great Windows applications. All you need is Windows 8 installed on a compatible computer with an Internet connection, and the desire to write Visual Basic programs.

In fact, the outlook for professional Visual Basic programmers has never been brighter. You just need to *Start Here*!

Who Should Read This Book

This is a hands-on programming tutorial for readers who enjoy learning to do new things by actually doing them. *Start Here! Learn Microsoft Visual Basic 2012* assumes no prior knowledge of Visual Studio or Visual Basic, and it focuses entirely on introductory programming concepts and procedures. You will be surprised at how much you can accomplish as a beginning programmer with Visual Studio, and you will be building your own projects in no time. I assume only that you are an intelligent student, hobbyist, or IT professional who is interested in learning how to program, and that you have no prior experience with Visual Basic or the Visual Studio software suite.

This book's content will provide you with concrete Visual Basic coding techniques as well as a broad overview of programming strategies. In addition, you will learn about the capabilities of the Windows 8 operating system, and the specific design guidelines that Microsoft recommends for Windows 8 applications, an exciting new way of creating software. The Windows 8 user interface design principles are sleek and empowering, and they encourage developers to put information-rich, web-aware applications at the center of the computing experience. Windows 8 applications present new ways of collaborating with others, as well as exciting opportunities for working with new input devices, such as built-in cameras, touchpads, accelerometers, gyros, compasses, GPS controls, and ambient light sensors.

The overall goal of *Start Here! Learn Microsoft Visual Basic 2012* is to get you to the point where you can comfortably use the development tools in Visual Studio, create your own basic Windows 8 applications, and then be ready to follow a more comprehensive Visual Basic programming book, such as my own *Microsoft Visual Basic 2012 Step by Step* (Microsoft Press, 2013).

Assumptions

This book is designed to teach readers with no programming experience how to use the Visual Basic programming language. As part of that process, readers will also learn how to use the Visual Studio 2012 Express software, which they can download for free. Chapter 1, "Getting to Know Visual Basic 2012," shows you how to download and install Visual Studio 2012 Express on your system.

The book assumes that you have purchased and are running the Windows 8 operating system, and that you want to learn how to create applications for Windows 8. These applications are simply programs that run under Windows 8, follow basic guidelines about how the user interface works, and are (or should be) designed to take advantage of the numerous resources and connections available on the web. Windows 8 applications are deeply interactive, and are designed to be downloaded by customers from the Windows Store.

To make the most of your programming practice, you will need to know a little about how to perform common tasks in Windows 8, how to work with information on the web, how to customize the Start page and user interface, and how to adjust basic system settings. If you also have Windows 8 installed on a tablet or touchpad device, all the better, because a fundamental design emphasis of Windows 8 is to make touch and gestures a natural way to manipulate content. You can build your applications on a laptop or desktop running Visual Studio 2012 and Windows 8, and then test them on your tablet or touchpad.

If you happen to be using one of the full retail versions of Visual Studio 2012, you will be able to create a wider range of application types than I describe in this book—Visual Studio Express 2012 for Windows 8 software restricts the application types you can create to just Windows 8–style applications. A more advanced book such as *Microsoft Visual Basic 2012 Step by Step* will show you how to create HTML applications for the Web, how to create console applications, how to develop software specifically for Windows Phone, and how to create desktop applications (Windows Forms projects) for Windows 8 and Windows 7.

Who Should Not Read This Book

You're going to be disappointed with this book if you're an advanced programmer and interested in learning Visual Basic as a second language. The examples in this book are relatively basic, and the explanations are kept simple. You may also be disappointed if you already have significant Visual Basic programming experience, and just want to know the new features of Visual Studio 2012. However, if you have not programmed before, or if it has been some time since you wrote programs, you will probably appreciate the thorough introduction to Visual Studio 2012 and the coverage of the fundamentals of writing Windows 8 programs with Visual Basic, tasks that involve a number of tools and methods that may be unfamiliar.

Developers who have a lot of experience will feel that I'm exploring the obvious—but what is obvious to experienced programmers often isn't obvious at all to someone who is just learning to write code. If programming is a new concept for you, this is the place to start.

Organization of This Book

Start Here! Learn Microsoft Visual Basic 2012 uses a hands-on approach to learning, in which readers actually build Windows 8 applications from scratch, one step at a time. Each chapter introduces a new tool or technique, and the book has been designed to be read sequentially, so that what you learn in one chapter is carried forward to the next. Although the core of this book involves teaching Visual Basic coding techniques, you will also learn how to use the interesting tools and features in the Visual Studio IDE, including the Toolbox, the Code Editor, XAML controls, Solution Explorer, and the debugger. You will also learn how to use Blend for Visual Studio 2012, a separate design application distributed with Visual Studio.

Collectively, the twelve chapters in this book offer you a complete introductory programming course that you can complete at your own pace. You might try to finish one or two chapters a day for a few days, and then take some time off to practice building applications on your own before moving on. Reading about new techniques, trying out what you have learned, and then pushing a bit further on your own is the best way to acquire many new skills, including how to program.

This book offers the following topics:

- **Chapter 1: Getting to Know Visual Basic 2012** What types of applications can Visual Basic programmers actually create, and how should they go about doing it? This introductory chapter answers these fundamental questions, and then introduces the Visual Studio IDE, an electronic workshop where Visual Basic applications are built from the ground up. You'll learn how to download the Visual Studio Express 2012 for Windows 8 software, how to start it, and how to get going with the Visual Studio programming tools.

- **Chapter 2: Creating Your First Windows 8 Application** In this chapter you learn how to build your first Windows 8 application, a web browser that allows you to explore web sites and record the locations that you have visited. You'll learn more about the programming tools in Visual Studio, and you'll learn what it means to test an application and prepare it for distribution to others.

- **Chapter 3: Using Controls** The controls that you use to receive input, display output, and help the user navigate your application represent a fundamental element of the user interface. In this chapter, you'll learn how to create several useful XAML controls, including *Ellipse*, *TextBlock*, *CheckBox*, *RadioButton*, and *MediaElement*.

- **Chapter 4: Designing Windows 8 Applications with Blend for Visual Studio** Your Visual Studio 2012 Express software installation includes a separate program called Blend for Visual Studio, which provides easy-to-use design tools for creating the user interface of a Windows 8 application. You'll use Blend in this chapter to construct a user interface that displays digital photographs and uses storyboards and animation effects. You'll also learn how to switch from Blend to Visual Studio, where you can write Visual Basic program code.

- **Chapter 5: Working with XAML** Windows 8 applications use the XAML markup language to define how the user interface appears on the screen, and how it presents information to the user. This chapter explores in detail the structure of XAML markup, and explains how you can customize a program's look and feel by working with XAML markup in the Visual Studio Code Editor.

- **Chapter 6: Visual Basic Language Elements** Visual Basic is an advanced programming language that allows you to control how a Windows application operates. When you create a Windows 8 application, you use Visual Basic code to define how the application manages all types of information, such as input received from the user and the results of mathematical calculations. In this chapter, you will learn the syntax and format of Visual Basic program statements, how to use variables to store information, how to use fundamental data types and constants, and how to work with formulas and operators in a program.

- **Chapter 7: Controlling Application Design, Layout, and Program Flow**   Windows 8 applications should feature compelling content and pages prepared for rich user interaction. This chapter digs deeper into Windows 8 design principles by focusing on tile-based layout and user input with the *Image* and *ListBox* controls. To help you control execution and program flow, you'll learn how to write effective decision structures, loops, and exception handlers in your applications.

- **Chapter 8: Using the .NET Framework**   As you write more sophisticated programs, you'll need to manipulate graphics, display text files, perform calculations, process strings, and retrieve information from the web. These capabilities and much more are supplied to you via the .NET Framework, an underlying programming interface that is part of the Windows operating system. This chapter explains how to learn more about .NET Framework classes using the Visual Studio Object Browser, how to use Framework methods to process strings and calculate formulas, and how to save development time by inserting ready-made Code Snippets into your project.

- **Chapter 9: Debugging Applications**   The complex nature of Window programming means that you'll run into syntax errors and other logic problems from time to time as you build your applications. This chapter introduces the programming tools in the Visual Studio IDE that help you locate and correct programming mistakes, and how to anticipate operating errors that your users may encounter in the future.

- **Chapter 10: Managing Data with Arrays and LINQ**   Because there is so much data in the world—employee records at the office, price and product information online, confidential patient records at the clinic—it makes sense that software developers are spending a lot of time thinking about how data is managed in their programs. In Visual Studio, an important technology used for accessing and managing data is known as Language Integrated Query (LINQ), and you will learn the basics of using LINQ in this chapter. You'll learn how to store information in temporary locations called arrays, how to write LINQ query expressions to retrieve data from arrays, and how to use the data in XML documents as a source for LINQ queries.

- **Chapter 11: Design Focus: Five Great Features for a Windows 8 Application**   This chapter returns to the user interface of Windows 8 applications, and offers additional instruction about how programs can be designed so that they comply with Microsoft's design guidelines for Windows 8 applications. You'll learn how to create a tile for your app on the Windows Start page, how to create a splash screen for your project, how to control application permissions and capabilities, how to use ready-made project templates, and how to add support for touch input and gestures.

- **Chapter 12: Future Development Opportunities and the Windows Store**   This last chapter provides a summary of the Visual Basic programming techniques that you have learned, and presents future development opportunities for those interested in careers in Visual Studio programming. The chapter also presents a detailed look at the final testing and packaging of applications, including a discussion of the Windows Store, an exciting new distribution point for Windows 8 applications. Also included in this chapter are web resources and books that you can use to continue your learning.

Free eBook Reference

When you purchase this title, you also get the companion reference, *Start Here!™ Fundamentals of Microsoft® .NET Programming*, for free. To obtain your copy, please see the instruction page at the back of this book.

The *Fundamentals* book contains information that applies to any programming language, plus some specific material for beginning .NET developers.

As you read through this book, you'll find references to the *Fundamentals* book that look like this:

For more information, see *<topic>* in the accompanying *Start Here! Fundamentals of Microsoft .NET Programming* book.

When you see a reference like this, if you're not already familiar with the topic, you should read that section in the *Fundamentals* book. In addition, the *Fundamentals* book contains an extensive glossary of key programming terms.

Conventions and Features in This Book

This book presents information using conventions designed to make the information readable and easy to follow:

- Step-by-step instructions help you create Visual Basic applications. Each set of instructions is listed in a separate section and describes precisely what you'll accomplish by following the steps that it contains.

- Screen illustrations show you exactly what is happening as you complete the step-by-step instructions. I have used the default colors and settings for Windows 8 to create these illustrations, and configured my screen resolution at a low setting to make the illustrations as readable as possible.

- Boxed elements with labels such as "Note" provide additional information or alternative methods for completing a step successfully. Make sure that you pay special attention to warnings because they contain helpful information for avoiding problems and errors.

- Text that you type (apart from code blocks) appears in **bold**.

- A plus sign (+) between two key names means that you must press those keys at the same time. For example, "Press Alt+Tab" means that you hold down the Alt key while you press the Tab key.

- A vertical bar between two or more menu items (such as File | Close), means that you should select the first menu or menu item, then the next, and so on.

System Requirements

You will need the following hardware and software to work through the examples in this book:

- The Windows 8 operating system. Depending on your Windows configuration, you might require Local Administrator rights to install or configure Visual Studio 2012 Express.

- An Internet connection to download Visual Studio, try out the Windows Store, and download this book's sample files.

- Visual Studio 2012 Express for Windows 8 (see Chapter 1 for installation instructions).

- A computer with 1.6 GHz or faster processor.

- 1 GB RAM (32-bit) or 2 GB RAM (64-bit).

- 16 GB available hard disk space (32-bit) or 20 GB (64-bit) for Windows 8.

- 4 GB of available hard disk space for Visual Studio 2012 Express.

- DirectX 9 graphics device with WDDM 1.0 or higher driver.

- 1024 X 768 minimum screen resolution.

- If you want to use touch for user input, you'll need a multitouch-capable laptop, tablet, or display. Windows 8 supports at least five simultaneous touch points, although not all tablets or displays do. A multitouch-capable device is optional for the exercises in this book, although one is useful if you want to understand what such devices are capable of as a software developer. Typically a programmer will develop software on a desktop or laptop computer, and then test multitouch functionality on a multitouch-capable device.

Code Samples

Most of the chapters in this book include exercises that let you interactively try out new material learned in the main text. All sample projects, in both their pre-exercise and post-exercise formats, can be downloaded from the following page:

http://go.microsoft.com/FWLink/?Linkid=271576

Follow the instructions to download the *9780735672987-files.zip* file.

Installing the Code Samples

Follow these steps to install the code samples on your computer so that you can use them with the exercises in this book:

1. Unzip the *9780735672987-files.zip* file that you downloaded from the book's website. (Name a specific directory along with directions to create it, if necessary.)

2. If prompted, review the displayed end-user license agreement. If you accept the terms, select the accept option, and then click Next.

Using the Code Samples

The code samples .zip file for this book creates a folder named "Start Here! Programming in Visual Basic" that contains 11 subfolders—one for each of the chapters in the book (except the last chapter). To find the examples associated with a particular chapter, open the appropriate chapter folder. You'll find the examples for that chapter in separate subfolders. The subfolder names have the same names as the examples in the book. For example, you'll find an example called "Web List" in the *My Documents\ Start Here! Programming in Visual Basic\Chapter 02* folder on your hard drive. If your system is configured to display file extensions of the Visual Basic project files, look for *.sln* as the file extension. Depending on how your system is configured, you may see a "Documents" folder rather than a "My Documents" folder.

Acknowledgments

The planning for this book began well before the release of Windows 8 and the first Visual Studio 2012 test releases. In early conversations with Microsoft Press and O'Reilly Media, we all realized that Windows 8 and Visual Studio 2012 presented truly revolutionary opportunities for Visual Basic programmers. The question was: how could we prepare the right learning materials for new and existing software developers so that they could get up-to-speed quickly and begin exciting Windows applications as soon as possible?

The solution we came up with was to create two original books with information about the Visual Studio software release—the book that you are holding now, my *Start Here! Learn Microsoft Visual Basic 2012*, and a second book designed for more experienced developers, my *Microsoft Visual Basic 2012 Step by Step*. These two books work together to provide a comprehensive course on Windows 8 programming with Visual Basic 2012.

Although I have written over a dozen books on Visual Basic programming in my career as a writer and software developer, this experience was one of the most rewarding and exciting, as two back-to-back book projects required significant coordination among publishing team members at both Microsoft Press and O'Reilly Media. I hope that you enjoy the results and are able to use the books to explore deeply these amazing new products. Very quickly, you'll be learning to program in Visual Basic 2012, and preparing applications for distribution in the Windows Store.

At Microsoft Press, I would like to thank Devon Musgrave for his early enthusiasm for the books, and for connecting me to team members in the Visual Studio product group. At O'Reilly Media, I would like to thank first and foremost Russell Jones, for our many conversations about Visual Basic programming, and our hope that these books will provide a complete path for new and experienced programmers to unlock the secrets of Visual Basic 2012. Tim Patrick, a talented author and Visual Basic developer in his own right, provided a thorough review of the *Start Here!* manuscript, and answered many practical questions about Visual Studio for me. Within the editorial group, I would like to thank Holly Bauer, for scheduling the editorial review and answering questions about content; and Damon Larson, for his skillful copy editing and managing the style issues that arose. Also within O'Reilly Media, I would like to thank Kristin Borg and Rebecca Demarest, and at Zyg Group, I'd like to thank Linda Weidemann, Kim Burton-Weisman, and Kevin Broccoli for their important editorial, technical, and artistic contributions.

I am also most grateful to the Microsoft Visual Studio 2012 development team for providing me with the beta and release candidate software to work with. In addition, I would like to thank the Microsoft Windows 8 team for their support, and offer my special thanks to the many MSDN forum contributors who asked and answered questions about Visual Basic and Windows 8 programming.

As always, I offer my deepest gratitude and affection to my family for their continued support of my writing projects and various academic pursuits. In particular, Henry Halvorson created impressive electronic music, electronic artwork, and a video file for Chapters 3, 7, and 11. I am so thankful for your efforts, son.

Errata & Book Support

We've made every effort to ensure the accuracy of this book and its companion content. Any errors that have been reported since this book was published are listed on our Microsoft Press site at oreilly.com:

http://go.microsoft.com/FWLink/?Linkid=271575

If you find an error that is not already listed, you can report it to us through the same page. If you need additional support, email Microsoft Press Book Support at *mspinput@microsoft.com*.

Please note that product support for Microsoft software is not offered through the addresses above.

We Want to Hear from You

At Microsoft Press, your satisfaction is our top priority, and your feedback our most valuable asset. Please tell us what you think of this book at:

http://www.microsoft.com/learning/booksurvey

The survey is short, and we read every one of your comments and ideas. Thanks in advance for your input!

Stay in Touch

Let's keep the conversation going! We're on Twitter: *http://twitter.com/MicrosoftPress*.

You can also learn more about Michael Halvorson's books and ideas at *http://michaelhalvorsonbooks.com*.

CHAPTER 1

Getting to Know Visual Basic 2012

After completing this chapter, you'll be able to

- Describe various development opportunities for Visual Basic programmers.

- Download and install Visual Studio Express 2012 for Windows 8.

- Start Visual Studio Express and explore the Visual Studio IDE.

- Open and run a Visual Basic program.

- Use Visual Studio programming tools and windows.

- Customize the Visual Studio IDE.

- Save changes and exit Visual Studio.

THIS CHAPTER INTRODUCES YOU to Microsoft Visual Basic programming and gives you the skills you need to get up and running with the Microsoft Visual Studio Express 2012 for Windows 8 Integrated Development Environment (IDE). The Visual Studio IDE is the application you use to build and run Visual Basic programs. The Visual Studio IDE is a busy place with numerous menu options, buttons, tool windows, code editors, and output windows. However, you'll discover that any general experience you may have had with Windows applications will help you a lot as you learn how to use the IDE, and you'll find that some of the tools and features are more important than others. The important thing to remember, faced with the IDE's extensive capabilities, is that you don't need to learn everything at once.

This chapter also provides an overview of the types of programs, called *applications*, that you can create with Visual Basic 2012. This was once a rather straightforward subject, because choosing to write programs in Visual Basic meant you could create great Windows desktop applications but not much more. As you'll see, however, Visual Studio now allows Visual Basic programmers to create applications in a variety of formats for many different uses. Although this book focuses on creating Windows 8 apps, it will be helpful for you to learn just how capable Visual Studio is, especially in one of the full retail versions.

Development Opportunities for Visual Basic Programmers

Visual Basic is an object-oriented computer programming language that has roots in earlier development tools such as BASIC and QuickBASIC—that is, logical and practical (though somewhat quirky) programming languages from the 1960s, '70s, and '80s.

In 1991, Microsoft released Visual Basic 1.0, which innovatively combined a sophisticated Visual Basic language compiler with an IDE that allowed developers to build Windows applications by visually arranging controls on a Windows form and then customizing the controls with property settings and Visual Basic code. Over the past two decades, Visual Basic has grown into an extremely powerful development tool, capable of creating fast and efficient Windows applications that can run on a variety of hardware platforms.

The term *Visual Basic* has come to have two meanings over the past 10 years or so. In the narrower sense, *Visual Basic* is the name of a programming language with specific syntax rules and logical procedures that must be followed when a developer creates code to control some aspect of an application's functionality. However, *Visual Basic* is also used in a more comprehensive product-related sense to describe the collection of tools and techniques that developers use to a build Windows applications with a particular software suite. In the past, developers could purchase a stand-alone version of Visual Basic, such as Microsoft Visual Basic .NET 2003 Professional Edition, but these days Visual Basic is sold only as a component within the Visual Studio software suite, which also includes Microsoft Visual C#, Microsoft Visual C++, Microsoft Visual Web Developer, and other development tools.

 More Info For more information about object-oriented computing, see Chapter 10, "Object-Oriented Programming," in the free companion volume, *Start Here! Fundamentals of .NET Programming* (Microsoft Press, 2011).

The Visual Studio 2012 development suite is distributed in several different product configurations, including Test Professional, Ultimate, Premium, Professional, Express for Windows 8, and Express for Web. Express for Windows 8 and Express for Web are currently the free editions that you can use to test-drive the software. (Express for Windows 8 is the product that you will be using in this book.) The full retail versions of Visual Studio 2012 have different prices and feature sets, with Test Professional being the most comprehensive (and expensive) development package. The Visual Studio web site (*http://www.microsoft.com/visualstudio*) explains the differences between all these versions.

You have purchased this book because you want to learn how to program in Visual Basic. This is an excellent choice; there are over 3 million Visual Basic programmers in the world developing innovative solutions, blogging on the web, and shopping for add-ons and training materials.

The programming language that you decide to learn is a matter of choice, often related to your past experiences and the requirements of the companies that you work for. Because different organizations have spent considerable time and capital building up their code bases, you'll find that they have specific language and software requirements for the teams that they employ. You may have encountered such requirements listed in hiring advertisements for programmers. Often they require that developers know more than one programming language, in addition to specific skills related to database or web development.

Microsoft has tried to satisfy a wide range of programming audiences by bundling many different software development technologies into Visual Studio, including Visual Basic, Visual C#, Visual Web Developer, and JavaScript. Visual Studio also contains some core tools that all developers use, no matter which programming language they choose. These include the various toolbox controls, the Project and Properties windows, the code editors, the debugger, the Blend Designer, various management tools, and the .NET Framework—a library of coded solutions designed to be used by applications that run on the Windows operating system.

New Development Platforms

So, what can you actually *do* with Visual Basic and Visual Studio?

In the early 2000s, Visual Basic programmers were concerned primarily with creating Windows applications that helped businesses manage data effectively. Visual Basic's ability to graphically display information and provide access to it with powerful user interface controls gained many supporters for the product. Over the past decade, the leading Visual Basic applications have been database front-ends, inventory management systems, web applications and utilities, purchasing tools, CAD programs, scientific applications, and games.

In the 2010s, however, the explosion of Internet connectivity and online commerce has dramatically changed the landscape for software developers. In the past, most Windows applications ran on a server or a desktop PC. Today, laptops, tablet devices, and smartphones are everywhere, and often the same person owns all three device types. Consumers need to move applications and information seamlessly across devices, and software developers need the tools that will allow them to create applications that work on multiple platforms, or can at least be ported easily from one device to the next.

The Visual Studio 2012 product team took the challenge of coding for diverse platforms seriously, and they have created a software suite that allows developers to leverage their existing work while also allowing developers to create a variety of different application types. The following list highlights the major development platforms and opportunities for Visual Basic programmers (some of which are supported only by the full retail versions of Visual Studio 2012):

- **Windows 8**   Visual Basic developers can create Windows 8 applications and traditional desktop applications for a wide range of Windows 8 devices, including Microsoft Surface tablets, and sell them on the Microsoft Store.

- **Windows 7 and earlier**   Visual Basic developers can create applications for earlier versions of Windows and distribute them in a variety of ways. The Visual Basic and Extensible Application Markup Language (XAML) programming techniques you learn in this book will be closest to writing Visual Basic and XAML programs for Windows Presentation Foundation (WPF).

- **Windows Phone**   Using Visual Studio and the Windows Phone software development kit (SDK), Visual Basic programmers can create applications that run on Windows Phone and take advantage of its unique features.

- **Web development**   Developers can use Visual Basic, HTML5, CSS3, or JavaScript to create applications that will run on the web and look great in a variety of browsers. A technology known as ASP.NET allows Visual Basic programmers to build web sites, web applications, and web services quickly without knowing all the details about how the information will be stored on the web.

- **Device drivers and console applications**   Visual Basic programmers can write applications that work primarily with the internal components of the operating system or run in command-line mode (the MS-DOS shell).

- **Office applications**   Visual Basic programmers can build macros and other tools that enhance the functionality of Microsoft Office applications, such as Excel, Word, Access, and PowerPoint.

- **Xbox 360**   Visual Basic programmers can write games for the Xbox using Visual Studio and Microsoft XNA Game Studio.

- **Windows Azure applications for web servers and the cloud**   Visual Basic is powerful enough to write applications that will be used on sophisticated web servers, distributed data centers, and a version of Windows designed for cloud computing known as Windows Azure.

This is an amazing list of application types! Although this list might seem daunting at first, the good news is that the fundamental Visual Basic programming skills that you will explore here remain the same from platform to platform, and there are numerous tools and techniques that help you to port work easily between them. This book provides a solid introduction to many of the core skills that you will use; you can then learn specific programming techniques related to any particular platform when you are ready.

Obtaining, Installing, and Starting Visual Studio Express 2012 for Windows 8

Before you can begin programming in Visual Basic, you need to install the Visual Studio software. If you already have Windows 8 and one of the retail versions of Visual Studio 2012, you are all set already; the teaching in this book will apply to Windows 8 and the Visual Studio software that you have. If you don't already have a version of Visual Studio, you can download a free copy of Visual Studio Express 2012 for Windows 8 directly from Microsoft. After you install that product, you'll be able to use the examples in this book to create your own Windows 8 apps.

Note This book requires that you are running Windows 8 and that you have a version of Visual Studio 2012 installed on your system. Although you can download Visual Studio Express 2012 for Windows 8 for free, you will also need a valid, installed version of Windows 8 to create the applications.

Downloading the Product

Microsoft produces a number of Express products that you can download from *http://www.microsoft.com/express/Downloads/,* but for the purposes of this book you need to download only this one:

- **Visual Studio Express 2012 for Windows 8**   This product provides the Visual Studio IDE and tools that allow you to create Visual Basic, Visual C#, Visual C++, or JavaScript applications for Windows 8. You also have to have Windows 8 installed on your computer—Windows 8 does not come with Visual Studio Express 2012.

You must have an Internet connection to install the product. The setup files for Visual Studio Express 2012 can either be installed either directly from the web or downloaded to your hard drive and then opened and installed later.

Installing Visual Studio Express 2012 for Windows 8

To download Visual Studio Express 2012 for Windows 8, complete the following steps:

1. Open a web browser (Internet Explorer or other) and go to the following web site: *http://www.microsoft.com/express/Downloads.*

2. Click Visual Studio 2012 to see a list of the Express products available for Visual Studio 2012.

 Note You must have Window 8 installed on your computer *before* you install Visual Studio Express 2012 for Windows 8.

3. Click Express for Windows 8, and follow the instructions to download and install Visual Studio Express 2012 for Windows 8.

Specify a web installation or download the product files first and then install them. You will also have an opportunity to specify the language that you will be using when using Visual Studio. (For this book, the recommended language is English.) When the Express installation is complete, you're ready to start working with Visual Studio!

Starting Visual Studio Express 2012

To start Visual Studio Express and begin working with the Visual Studio IDE, complete the following steps.

Start Visual Studio Express 2012

1. On the Windows Start screen, click VS Express for Windows 8.

    If this is the first time you are starting Visual Studio, the program will take a few moments to configure the environment. You may be prompted to get a developer license for Windows 8, which typically requires that you create a Windows Live account or enter existing account information. During the beta testing for Visual Studio 2012, developer licenses were free and valid for about a month before they needed to be renewed. You will likely encounter a similar registration scenario.

2. If you are prompted to identify your programming preferences, select Visual Basic Development Settings.

    When Visual Studio starts, you see the IDE on the screen with its many menus, tools, and component windows. (These windows are sometimes called tool windows.) You also should see a Start page containing a set of tabs with links, learning resources, news, and project options. The Start page is a comprehensive source of information about your project, as well as resources within the Visual Basic development community.

    The screen shown following offers a typical Visual Studio setup. I captured the screen at a resolution of 1024×768, which may be smaller than you are using on your computer, but I wanted you to see the content as clearly as possible. (Larger resolutions are often great to work with on screens that support them, but they don't reproduce well in books.)

    I have also chosen to use the Light color theme for the screen illustrations in this book. When you first open Visual Studio, however, you may see the Dark color theme, which displays white text on a dark background. Although the Dark color theme is restful and emphasizes the code and user interface elements of your program, it doesn't appear well in books. If you see the Dark color theme now, change to the Light theme by choosing the Options command on the Tools menu, clicking General in the Environment category, selecting Light from the Color Theme drop-down list box, and clicking OK. The following screen illustration shows the Light theme:

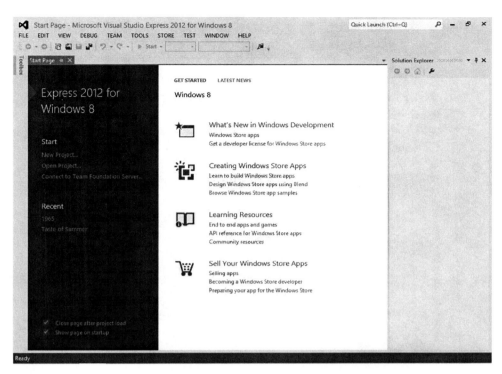

After starting Visual Studio, you're ready to explore the Visual Studio IDE.

Note The following section describes how to open and run a Visual Basic program in the IDE. If you haven't downloaded this book's sample files yet, you should do so now, because you'll be asked to open a specific program on your hard disk. (For sample code installation instructions, see the "Code Samples" section in the Introduction.) Return to this point after you have installed the code samples.

The Visual Studio Development Environment

In the Visual Studio IDE, you can open a new or existing Visual Studio project, or you can explore the many online resources available to you for Visual Basic programming.

Right now, let's open an existing Visual Studio project that I created for you, entitled World Capitals, which displays the capital of Peru in a text box. (The project is intentionally very simple right now, but you'll expand it later in the book.)

Open a Visual Basic project

1. On the Start page, on the left side of the screen, click the Open Project link.

You'll see the Open Project dialog box shown in the following illustration. (You can also display this dialog box by clicking the Open Project command on the File menu or by pressing Ctrl+Shift+O.) Even if you haven't used Visual Studio before, the Open Project dialog box will seem straightforward because it resembles the familiar Open dialog box in many other Windows applications.

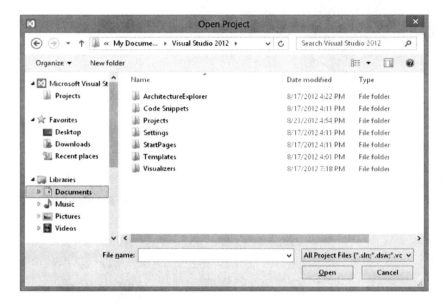

 Tip In the Open Project dialog box, you see a number of storage locations along the left side of the window. The Projects folder under Microsoft Visual Studio Express 2012 for Windows 8 is particularly useful. By default, Visual Studio saves your programming projects in this Projects folder, giving each project its own subfolder. However, this book uses a different folder to organize your programming coursework, as you'll discover following. Additional locations such as Favorites and Libraries are also made available to you through this dialog box, depending on how your computer and operating system has been configured.

2. Browse to the My Documents\Start Here! Programming in VB 2012 folder on your hard disk.

   This folder is the default location for the book's extensive sample file collection, and you'll find the files there if you followed the instructions in "Code Samples" in the Introduction. If you didn't copy the sample files, close this dialog box and copy them now.

3. Open the *Chapter 01\World Capitals* folder, and then double-click the *WorldCapitals* solution file. (If your system shows file name extensions, this file will end with *.sln*.)

   Visual Studio loads the *WorldCapitals* page, properties, and program code for the solution. Solution Explorer, a tool window on the right side of the screen, lists some of the files in the solution.

Visual Studio provides a special option named Always Show Solution to control several options related to solutions within the IDE. The option's check box is located on the Projects And Solutions | General tab of the Options dialog box, which you open by clicking the Options command on the Tools menu. If the check box is selected (the default position), a subfolder is created for each new solution, placing the project and its files in a separate folder beneath the solution. Also, if you keep the default selection for Always Show Solution, a few options related to solutions appear in the IDE, such as commands on the File menu and a solution entry in Solution Explorer. If you like the ideas of creating separate folders for solutions and seeing solution-related commands and settings, I suggest that you keep the default (selected) option for this check box. You'll learn more about these options at the end of the chapter.

Projects and Solutions

In Visual Studio, programs under development are typically called projects or solutions because they contain many individual components, not just one file. Visual Basic 2012 programs include a project file (*.vbproj*), a solution file (.sln), one or more markup files (*.xaml*), and several supporting files organized into various subfolders.

A *project* contains files and other information specific to a single programming undertaking. A *solution* contains all the information for one or more projects. Solutions are therefore useful mechanisms to manage multiple related projects. The samples included with this book typically have a single project for each solution, so opening the project file (*.vbproj*) has the same effect as opening the solution file (*.sln*). But for a multiproject solution, you will want to open the solution file.

The Visual Studio Tools

At this point, you should take a few moments to study the Visual Studio IDE and identify some of the programming tools and windows that you'll be using as you complete this book. If you've written Visual Basic programs before, you'll recognize many (but perhaps not all) of the programming tools. Collectively, these features are the components that you use to construct, organize, and test your Visual Basic programs. A few of the programming tools also help you learn more about the resources on your system, including the larger world of databases and web site connections available to you. There are also several powerful help tools.

The menu bar provides access to most of the commands that control the development environment. Menus and commands work as they do in all Windows-based programs, and you can access them by using the keyboard or the mouse. Located below the menu bar is the Standard toolbar, a collection of buttons that serve as shortcuts for executing commands and controlling the Visual Studio IDE. My assumption is that you've used Word, Excel, or some other Windows application enough to know quite a bit about toolbars, and how to use familiar toolbar commands, such as Open, Save, Cut, and Paste. But you'll probably be impressed with the number and range of toolbars provided by Visual Studio for programming tasks. In this book, you'll learn to use several toolbars; you can see the full list of toolbars at any time by right-clicking any toolbar in the IDE.

Along the bottom of the screen you may see the Windows taskbar. You can use the taskbar to switch between various Visual Studio components and to activate other Windows-based programs. You might also see taskbar icons for Windows Internet Explorer, antivirus utilities, and other programs installed on your system. In most of my screen shots, I'll hide the taskbar to show more of the IDE.

The following illustration shows some of the tools and windows in the Visual Studio IDE. Don't worry that this illustration looks different from your current development environment view. You'll learn more about these elements (and how you adjust your views) as you work through the chapter.

The main tools visible in this Visual Studio IDE are the Designer, Solution Explorer, the Properties window, and the XAML tab of the Code Editor. You should locate these tools and remember their names now, as you'll be using them often. You might also see more specialized tools such as the Toolbox, Document Outline window, Device window, Server Explorer, and Object Browser; alternatively, these tools may appear as tabs within the IDE. Because no two developers' preferences are exactly alike, it is difficult to predict what you'll see if your Visual Studio software has already been used. (What I show is essentially the fresh-download (or out-of-the-box) view, with the Designer displaying the World Capitals user interface contained in *MainPage.xaml*.)

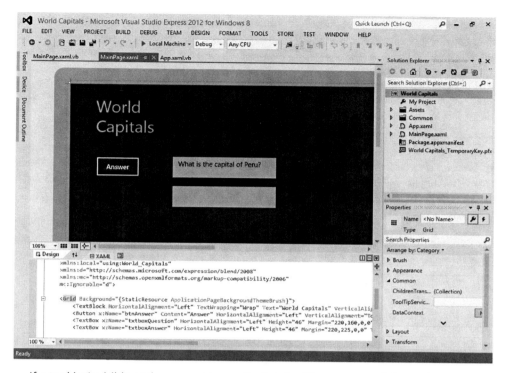

If a tool isn't visible and you want to see it, click the View menu and then select the tool. Because the View menu has expanded steadily over the years, Microsoft has moved some of the less frequently used View tools to a submenu called Other Windows. Check there if you don't see what you need.

The reason I said your IDE view probably doesn't match the preceding image is because the exact size and shape of the tools and windows in the IDE depend on how your particular development environment has been configured. With Visual Studio, you can align and attach, or *dock*, windows to make visible only the elements that you want see. You can also partially conceal tools as tabbed documents along the edge of the development environment and then switch back and forth between documents quickly. For example, if you click the Toolbox label on the left side of the screen, the Toolbox panel will fly out, ready for use. If you click another tool or window in the IDE, the Toolbox panel will return to its concealed position.

Trying to sort out which tools are important to you now and which you can learn about later is a difficult early challenge when you're learning the busy Visual Studio interface. Your development environment will probably look best if you set your monitor and Windows desktop settings so that they maximize your screen space, but even then things can get a little crowded. (In fact, some experienced Visual Studio programmers use two monitors to display different views of the software.)

The purpose of all this tool complexity is to add many new and useful features to the IDE while providing clever mechanisms for managing the clutter. These mechanisms include features such as docking, autohiding, floating, and a few other window states that I'll describe later. Visual Studio 2012 also hides rarely used IDE features until you begin to use them, which has also helped to clean up the IDE workspace.

If you're just starting out with Visual Studio, the best way to deal with feature overload is to hide the tools that you don't plan to use often to make room for the important ones. The crucial tools for beginning Visual Basic programming—the ones you'll start using right away in this book—are the Designer window, the Properties window, Solution Explorer, and the Toolbox. You won't use the Document Outline, Server Explorer, Class View, Object Browser, Device, or Debug windows until later in the book, so feel free to hide them by clicking the Close button on the title bar of any windows that you don't want to see.

In the following exercises, you'll start experimenting with the crucial tools in the Visual Studio IDE. You'll also learn how to display a web browser within Visual Studio and more about hiding the tools that you won't use for a while.

The Designer Window

If you completed the previous exercise ("Open a Visual Basic project"), the World Capitals project is loaded in the Visual Studio development environment. However, the user interface, or page, for the project might not yet be visible in Visual Studio. (More sophisticated projects might contain several pages, but this first example program needs only one.) To make the page of the World Capitals project visible in the IDE, you display it by using Solution Explorer.

> **Note** If you don't currently have the World Capitals project loaded, go back to and complete the exercise in this chapter titled "Open a Visual Basic project."

Display the Designer window

1. Locate the Solution Explorer window near the upper-right corner of the Visual Studio development environment. If you don't see Solution Explorer (if it is hidden as a tab in a location that you cannot see or isn't currently visible), click the View menu and then select Solution Explorer to display it.

> **Note** From here on in this book, you'll sometimes see a shorter method for describing menu choices. For example, "Choose View | Solution Explorer" means "Click the View menu and then select Solution Explorer."

When the World Capitals project is loaded, Solution Explorer looks like this:

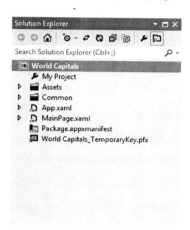

Like most basic Windows 8 applications, this Visual Basic solution contains an *App.xaml* file that holds global project settings and resources; an *Assets* folder that contains any splash screen and logo files for the project; a *Common* folder, which contains common classes and XAML styles that simplify your development tasks; a *deployment package manifest*, containing build and distribution settings for your file; and one or more user interface windows, or *pages*, which you can identify because they have the extension *.xaml*.

2. Click the expansion arrow to the left of the *MainPage.xaml* file in the Solution Explorer window.

   With the *MainPage.xaml* file expanded, Solution Explorer looks like this:

In this project, the main page of the World Capitals program is defined by the *MainPage.xaml* file. (*MainPage.xaml* is the default name for the main page when you create a new application without a specific template.)

You can open *MainPage.xaml* in Design view so that you can examine and modify the user interface with graphical design tools, or you can open the file in the Code Editor, where you can modify the user interface with XAML, a special user interface definition language designed for Windows applications and other computer programs.

Below the *MainPage.xaml* file, you will see a second file, named *MainPage.xaml.vb*. This file is also associated with the user interface of the World Capitals project. *MainPage.xaml.vb* is called a *code-behind file* because it contains a listing of the Visual Basic program code connected to the user interface defined by *MainPage.xaml*. As you learn how to program in Visual Basic, you'll become very adept at customizing this file.

Solution Explorer is the gateway to working with the various files in your project—it is an essential tool. When you double-click a file in Solution Explorer, it opens the file in an appropriate editor, if direct editing of the file is allowed.

3.   Double-click the *MainPage.xaml* file in Solution Explorer to display the project's user interface in the Designer window, if it is not already visible. Use the vertical scroll bar if necessary to adjust your view of the user interface.

The World Capitals page is displayed in the Designer, as shown here:

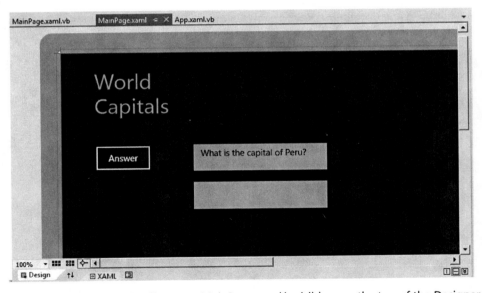

Notice that a tab with the file name *MainPage.xaml* is visible near the top of the Designer window, along with additional tab names. You can click a tab at any time to display the contents of the various files, even if the windows become covered.

As noted previously, the *MainPage.xaml* file is the visual representation of the program's user interface. However, you can readily examine the XAML markup used to define the user interface by double-clicking the XAML tab of the Code Editor at the bottom of the Designer window. Or, if the XAML tab is already open in the Code Editor, you can examine the XAML markup for the user interface and use the window's scroll bars to view any part of the markup that is not currently visible.

4. Double-click the XAML tab to display the XAML markup for the page in the Code Editor, and scroll to the top of the window to see the entire document.

You'll see the following:

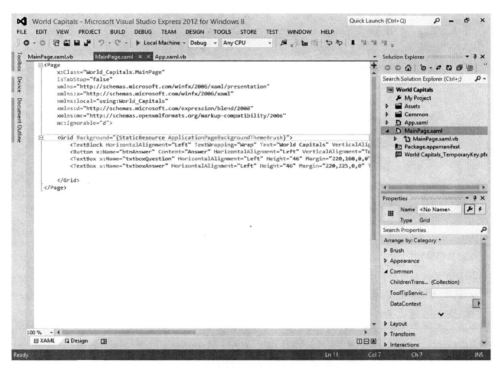

The XAML contents of *MainPage.xaml* appear in the Code Editor, and it is this structured information that controls how Visual Studio and Windows will display the application's user interface and graphics. If you know some HTML, this should look somewhat familiar. XAML contains *markup*—instructions whose primary purpose is to tell a program how to display things on the screen. The XAML markup shown here is displayed between *<Page* and *</Page>* tags, and is further indented to make the information readable. The first seven lines below *<Page* define the resources used to create the user interface. Below these lines, the section between *<Grid* and *</Grid>* defines the objects in the user interface. This XAML content defines one button, two text boxes, and one text block. If you look at the screen illustration of the Designer again, you can see how these elements appear visually. You can even see specific property settings for the objects being assigned through individual property names (like *HorizontalAlignment*) and values (like *Left*).

You'll learn a lot more about XAML markup in later chapters. For now, you should know that the Designer window allows you to see both a *preview* of the user interface and the XAML markup that defines the specific characteristics of objects that appear on the preview page.

Visual Studio programmers often want to see both panes of information side by side as they work on a program. In fact, if you've built an HTML application in the past for the web, this whole concept might seem a little familiar, as a number of web design tools also display page layout at the top of the screen, while showing HTML code at the bottom.

Tip There are some handy buttons along the bottom of the Designer window and Code Editor that allow you significant control over the split-screen behavior of these elements. At the bottom left of the Designer window are XAML and Design tabs, as well as a handy Document Outline button, which opens a separate window to display the objects within the user interface organized by type. At the bottom right of the Designer window are Vertical Split, Horizontal Split, and Expand Pane/Collapse Pane buttons, which control how the Designer window and Code Editor are arranged. Expand Pane/Collapse Pane is especially useful; it is a toggle that allows you to view the windows one at a time or side by side.

5. Click the Design tab to display the project's main page in the Designer window again.

6. Click the Expand Pane button to display the XAML markup that renders the page in a window below the Designer window.

Now you'll try running this simple program within Visual Studio.

Running a Visual Basic Program

World Capitals is a simple Visual Basic program designed to familiarize you with the programming tools in Visual Studio. The page you see now has been customized with four objects (one button, a text block, and two text boxes), and I've added one line of program code to a code-behind file to make the program ask a simple question and display the appropriate answer. You'll learn more about creating objects like these and adding Visual Basic code to a code-behind file in Chapter 2, "Creating Your First Windows 8 Application." For now, try running the program in the Visual Studio IDE.

Run the World Capitals program

1. Click the Start button (the right-facing arrow next to the words *Local Machine*) on the Standard toolbar to run the World Capitals program in Visual Studio.

Tip You can also press F5 or click the Start Debugging command on the Debug menu to run a program in the Visual Studio IDE.

Visual Studio loads and compiles the project into an *assembly*, an EXE file that contains data and code in a form that can be used by the computer. This particular assembly also contains information that is useful for testing, or *debugging*, which is a fundamental part of the software development process. If the compilation is successful, Visual Studio runs the program in the IDE. (This is known as running the program on a *local machine*, as opposed to running on a remote computer somewhere on the web or in a software simulator of some kind.)

While the program is running, an icon for the program appears on the Windows taskbar. After a moment, you will see the World Capitals user interface running as any application would under Windows 8. The program looks just like the preview version did within the Visual Studio Designer:

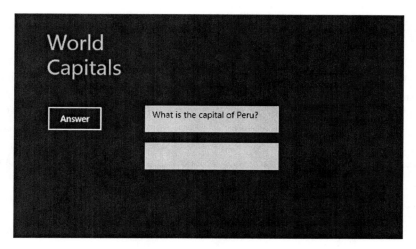

World Capitals now asks you a question: What is the capital of Peru?

2. Click the Answer button to reveal the solution to the question, and the program should display the answer (Lima) below the question.

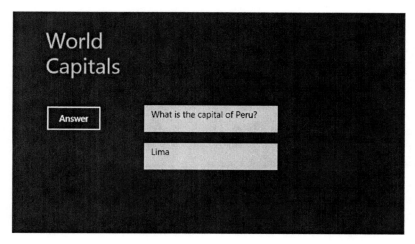

3. Close the application by dragging the title bar (or top portion of the screen) to the bottom of the screen (or however you normally terminate a Windows 8 application).

When you move the mouse cursor to the top edge of the screen, it changes to a hand, which provides some visual feedback as you drag the title bar to the bottom of the screen to terminate the program. After the application closes, you can press the Windows key or click the Visual Studio program icon on the desktop to activate the IDE again.

The World Capitals application may continue to run for a moment or two as the Visual Studio IDE catches up with the terminate-program request that you just issued. (For example, you may see the phrase *Running* in the Visual Studio title bar, which indicates that a program in the IDE is still executing.) You can force an immediate stop to any running application in the Visual Studio IDE by clicking the Stop Debugging button on the toolbar.

After the program has stopped running, you will notice a few changes in the IDE. For example, you will likely see an Output window at the bottom of the IDE with information about how the assemblies in the application were compiled and executed. This is the expected behavior within Visual Studio after a program has been compiled and run. The Output window provides a fairly detailed listing of what happened during compilation, a process that involves several stages and the loading of a number of files and resources called *libraries*. This record of the process is especially valuable when the compilation fails due to an unforeseen programming mistake or error. (Something that you will certainly experience, though not yet!)

4. After you've reviewed the content of the Output window, click its Close button to hide it.

I won't emphasize the Output window much in the early chapters of this book, but if you encounter an inadvertent error as you write your own programs, you'll find this tool useful. Most of the time, though, you'll can simply close the window to allow more room for examining your code.

It's time to learn about another useful development tool.

The Properties Window

In the IDE, you can use a tool known as the Properties window to change the characteristics, or property settings, of one or more user interface elements on a page. A *property setting* is a quality of one of the objects in your program, such as its position on the screen, its size, the text displayed on it, and so on. For example, you can modify the question about capitals that the program asks to appear in a different font or font size by adjusting property settings. (With Visual Studio, you can display text in any font installed on your system, just as you can in Excel or Word.)

The Properties window contains a list of the properties for the object that is currently selected in the Designer window. For example, if a button object is selected in the Designer, the properties for the button object will be visible in the Properties window. The first property listed at the top of the Properties window is the *Name* property, and you will use this property to name your objects if you plan to customize them using Visual Basic code. (By default, new XAML objects are unnamed.) Although there are a lot of properties for each object on a page, Visual Studio assigns default values for most of them, and you can quickly find the properties that you want to set by arranging them using the Arrange By drop-down box at the top of the Properties window.

You can change property settings from the Properties window while you are working on a page, you can change a property setting by editing the XAML markup for a page, and you can add Visual Basic code to a page's code-behind file to instruct Windows to change one or more property settings while a program is running.

As you'll learn later, you can also customize the event handlers for objects on a page by using the Event Handlers button (which looks like a lightning bolt) near the top of the Properties window. *Event handlers* are custom Visual Basic routines that run when the user interacts with the objects on a page by clicking, tapping, dragging, and other actions.

To get some practice setting properties, you'll edit the text in a button object, and you'll change the font weight and style of a text block object to bold and italic, respectively.

Change properties

1. Click the Answer button on the page that is currently loaded in the Designer window.

    To work with an object on a page, you must first select the object. When you select an object, resize handles appear around it, and the property settings for the object are displayed in the Properties window. You'll also see numbers indicating the distance (in pixels) to the top and left edges of the window.

2. Press Alt+Enter to display the Properties window, if it is not currently visible.

    The Properties window might or might not be visible in Visual Studio, depending on how it has been configured and used on your system. It usually appears below Solution Explorer on the right side of the IDE. (If it is visible but not active, you might click the Properties window to activate it.)

You'll see a window similar to this one:

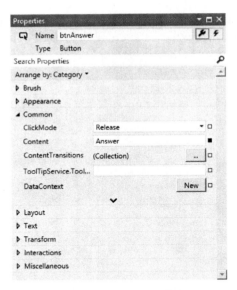

The Properties window lists all the property settings for the selected button object, named *btnAnswer*. Property names are listed in nested groups, and the default view displays the properties alphabetically by category. (*Brush* is first, *Appearance* is second, *Common* is third, and so on.) When you expand the property groups, the property names are generally listed on the left side, and the property settings are listed on the right. Some property settings, like Brush, are made by selecting color values with a design tool, so there are a variety of ways to set properties—not just entering text via the keyboard.

3. In the Common property group (containing the most typical properties for a button object), see that the *Content* property is set to "Answer."

    "Answer" is the text that currently appears on the page's main button, and you can change it to whatever you would like using the Properties window. Add an exclamation point now to the current value to add a little more emphasis to the button.

4. Click after "Answer" in the *Content* text box, type an exclamation mark (!), and then press Enter.

    The *Content* property setting is changed to "Answer!" in three places: within the Properties window, on the page in the Designer window, and within the XAML markup in the Code Editor.

    Note that instead of pressing the Enter key to change a property setting, you can simply click another location in the Properties window. (Click in another text box, for example.) Just don't inadvertently adjust another property setting by clicking around.

Now you'll change the font style of the text block object to bold and italic. The text block object currently contains the text "World Capitals."

5. Click the "World Capitals" text block object on the page. A text block object is an excellent way to display descriptive text on a page.

6. In the Properties window, click the Text property group (not the *Text* property in the Common group that is currently visible).

7. Click the Bold button to change the font weight to bold.

8. Click the Italic button to change the font style to italic.

Visual Studio records your changes and adjusts the property settings accordingly. Your screen should look like this:

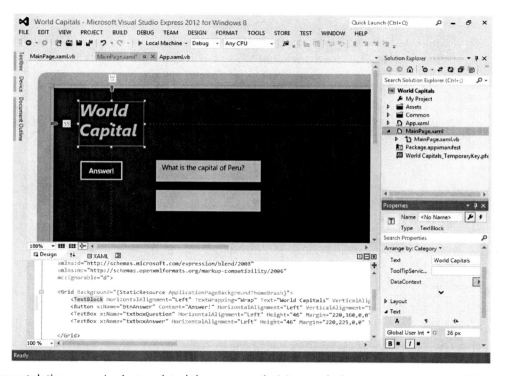

Congratulations—you've just updated three properties! As you design your programs, you'll have numerous font, color, and style options to choose from. And you've just learned how to use the Properties window—one of the important skills in becoming a Visual Basic programmer.

Thinking About Properties

In Visual Basic, each user interface element in a program (including the page itself) has a set of definable properties. You can set properties at design time by using the Properties window, or by editing properties in the XAML markup for the page that defines one part the program's user interface. Properties can also be set or referenced in Visual Basic code to make changes to program elements while the application runs. (User interface elements that receive input often use properties to receive information into the program.) At first, you might find properties a difficult concept to grasp. Viewing them in terms of something from everyday life can help.

Consider this bicycle analogy: a bicycle is an object you use to ride from one place to another. Because a bicycle is a physical object, it has several inherent characteristics. It has a brand name, a color, gears, brakes, and wheels, and it's built in a particular style. (It might be a road bike, a mountain bike, or a tandem bike.) In Visual Basic terminology, these characteristics are properties of the bicycle object. Most of the bicycle's properties were defined when the bicycle was built. But others (tires, travel speed, and options such as reflectors and mirrors) are properties that change while the bicycle is used. The bike might even have intangible (that is, invisible) properties, such as manufacture date, current owner, value, or rental status. And to add a little more complexity, a company or shop might own one bicycle or (the more likely scenario) an entire fleet of bicycles, all with different properties. As you work with Visual Basic, you'll set the properties of a variety of objects, and you'll organize them in very useful ways. Working with properties is a fundamental task in object-oriented programming.

Moving and Resizing the Programming Tools

With numerous programming tools to contend with on the screen, the Visual Studio IDE can become a pretty busy place. To give you complete control over the shape and size of the elements in the development environment, Visual Studio lets you move, resize, dock, and autohide most of the interface elements that you use to build programs.

To move one of the tool windows in Visual Studio, simply click its title bar and drag the window to a new location. If you position the window somewhere in the middle of the IDE and let go, it will *float* over the surface of Visual Studio, unattached to other tool windows. If you drag a window along the edge of another window, it attaches to that window, or *docks* itself. Dockable windows are advantageous because they always remain visible. (They don't become hidden behind other windows.) If you want to see more of a docked window, simply drag one of its borders to view more content.

If you want to completely close a window, click the Close button in the upper-right corner of the window. You can always open the window again later by clicking the appropriate command on the View menu.

If you want an option somewhere between docking and closing a window, you might try *autohiding* a tool window at the side, top, or bottom of the Visual Studio IDE by clicking the tiny Auto Hide pushpin button on the right side of the tool's title bar. This action removes the window from the docked position and places the title of the tool at the edge of the development environment on an unobtrusive tab. When you autohide a window, you'll notice that the tool window remains visible as long as you keep the mouse pointer in the area of the window. When you click another part of the IDE, the window slides out of view.

To restore a window that you have autohidden, click the tool tab at the edge of the development environment. (You can recognize a window that is autohidden because the pushpin in its title bar is pointing sideways.) By clicking the tool tab repeatedly at the edge of the IDE, you can use the tools in what I call peekaboo mode—in other words, to quickly display an autohidden window, click its tab, check or set the information you need, and then click its tab again to make it disappear. If you ever need the tool displayed permanently, click the Auto Hide pushpin button again so that the point of the pushpin faces down, and the window then remains visible.

A useful capability of Visual Studio is also the ability to dock windows as tabbed documents (windows with tab handles that partially hide behind other windows). You can also manually dock tool windows where you would like by dragging the windows and using the docking guides that appear as tiny squares on the perimeter of the IDE. A centrally located *guide diamond* will also help you manually dock tool windows by giving you a preview of where the windows will go.

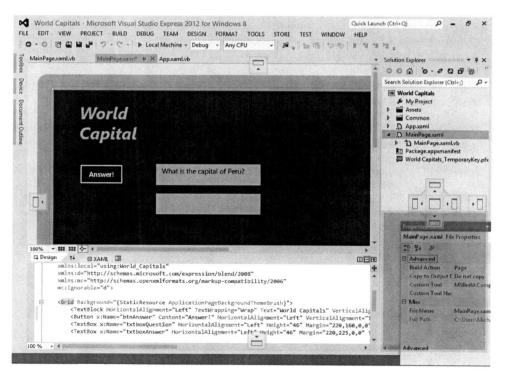

The docking guides are changeable icons that appear on the surface of the IDE when you move a window or tool from a docked position to a new location. Because the docking guides are associated with shaded, rectangular areas of the IDE, you can preview the results of your docking maneuver before you actually make it. Your window orientation changes will not stick until you release the mouse button.

Since docking and auto-hiding techniques take some practice to master, I recommend that you use the following exercises to experiment with the window-management features of the IDE. After you complete the exercises here, feel free to configure the Visual Studio tools in a way that seems comfortable for you.

Moving and Resizing Tool Windows

To move and resize one of the programming tool windows in Visual Studio, follow these steps. This exercise demonstrates how to manipulate the Properties window, but you can work with a different tool window if you want to.

Move and resize the Properties window

1. If the Properties window isn't visible in the IDE, click Properties Window on the View menu.

   This will activate the Properties window is in the IDE and highlight its title bar.

2. Click the Window Position toolbar menu button (the small arrow icon) on the Properties window title bar, and then click Float to display the window as a floating (undocked) window.

3. Using the Properties window title bar, drag the window to a new location in the development environment, but don't dock it.

   Moving windows around the Visual Studio IDE gives you some flexibility with the tools and the look of your development environment.

   Now you'll resize the Properties window to see more object property settings at once.

4. Point to the lower-right corner of the Properties window until the pointer changes to a double-headed arrow (the resizing pointer). Then drag the lower-right border of the window down and to the right to enlarge the window.

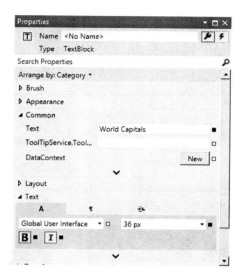

You can work more quickly and with more clarity of purpose in a bigger window. Feel free to move or resize a window when you need to see more of its contents.

Docking Tool Windows

If a tool window is floating over the development environment, you can move it to a new place by dragging the window to the handy docking guides. You can also maximize a floating tool window by double-clicking its title bar. (If you double-click the title bar again, it will return to its original shape.) Try docking the Properties window in a different location now.

Dock the Properties window

1. Verify that the Properties window (or another tool that you want to dock) is floating over the Visual Studio IDE in an undocked position.

   If you completed the previous exercise, the Properties window should be undocked now.

2. Drag the title bar of the Properties window to the top, bottom, right, or left edge of the development environment (your choice), taking care to drag the mouse pointer over one of the docking guides (small squares with arrows) on the perimeter of the Visual Studio IDE, or one of the centrally located rectangles in a tight pattern, called collectively a *guide diamond*.

As you move the mouse over a docking guide, a blue, shaded rectangle representing the Properties window snaps into place, giving you an indication of how your window will appear when you release the mouse button. Note that there are several valid docking locations for tool windows in Visual Studio, so you might want to try two or three different spots until you find one that looks right to you. (A window should be located in a place that's handy and not in the way of other needed tools.)

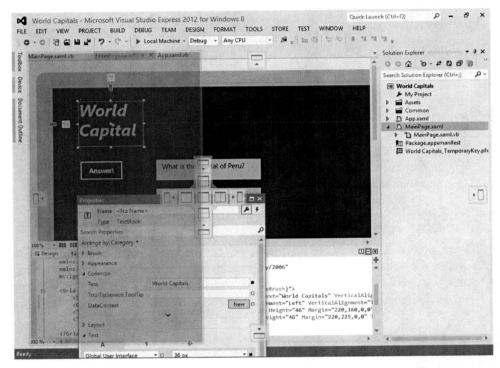

3. Release the mouse button to dock the Properties window, and the window should snap into place in its new home.

Tip To switch between dockable, tabbed document, hidden, and floating styles, right-click the window's title bar (or tab, if it is a tabbed document), and then click the option you want. Although the Properties window works very well as a dockable window, you'll probably find that larger windows work best as tabbed document windows.

4. Try docking the Properties window several more times in different places to get the feel of how docking works.

I guarantee that although a few of these window procedures may seem confusing at first, after a while they'll become routine for you. In general, you want to create window spaces that have enough room for the information you need to see and use while you work on more important tasks in the Designer window and in the Code Editor.

Hiding Tool Windows

To hide a tool window, click the Auto Hide pushpin button on the right side of the title bar to conceal the window beneath a tool tab on the edge of the IDE, and click it again to restore the window to its docked position. You can also use the Auto Hide command on the Window menu (or right-click a title bar and select Auto Hide) to autohide a tool window. Give it a try now.

Use the Auto Hide feature

1. Locate the Auto Hide pushpin button on the title bar of the Properties window.

   The pushpin is currently in the *down*, or pushed-in, position, meaning that the Properties window is "pinned" open and autohide is disabled.

2. Click the Auto Hide button on the Properties window title bar.

   The Properties window will slide off the screen and be replaced by a small tab named Properties.

   The benefit of enabling autohide, of course, is that it frees up additional work space in Visual Studio while keeping the hidden window quickly accessible.

3. Click the Properties tab.

   The Properties window should immediately reappear.

4. Click the mouse elsewhere within the IDE.

   The window disappears again.

5. Finally, display the Properties window again, and then click the pushpin button on the Properties window title bar.

   The Properties window returns to its familiar docked position, and you can use it without worrying about it sliding away.

   Spend some time moving, resizing, docking, and autohiding tool windows in Visual Studio now to create your version of the perfect work environment. As you work through this book, you'll want to adjust your window settings periodically to adapt your work area to the new tools you're using.

> **Tip** Visual Studio lets you save your window and programming environment settings and copy them to a second computer or share them with members of your programming team. To experiment with this feature, click the Import And Export Settings command on the Tools menu and follow the wizard instructions to export (save) or import (load) settings from a file.

Switching Among Open Files and Tools Using the IDE Navigator

Visual Studio has a feature that makes it even easier to switch among open files and programming tools in the development environment. This feature is called the *IDE Navigator*, and it lets you cycle through open files and tools by using key combinations, in much the same way that you cycle through open programs on the Windows taskbar. This feature is especially useful when you have a lot of files open in the IDE. Give it a try now.

Use the IDE Navigator

1. Hold down the Ctrl key and press Tab to open the IDE Navigator.

    The IDE Navigator opens and displays the active (open) files and tools in the IDE. Your screen will look similar to the following:

    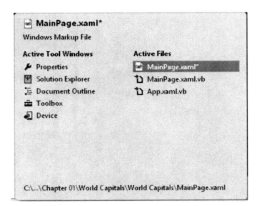

2. While holding down the Ctrl key, press Tab repeatedly to cycle through the active files until the file you want is highlighted.

    To cycle through the files in the reverse direction, hold down Ctrl+Shift and press Tab.

3. While holding down the Ctrl key, use the arrow keys to cycle through both the active files and the active tools. You can also select an active file (or tool) by clicking its name.

4. When you're finished with the IDE Navigator, release the Ctrl key.

The last selected item in the IDE Navigator will become active.

Opening a Web Browser Within Visual Studio

A handy feature in Visual Studio is the ability to open a simple web browser within the development environment. The browser appears as a tabbed document window in the IDE, so it takes up little space but can be opened immediately when needed. You could open a stand-alone web browser (such as Internet Explorer) and keep it nearby on the Windows taskbar, but running a web browser within Visual Studio makes examining web sites and copying data into Visual Studio even easier. Try using the Visual Studio web browser now.

Open the Visual Studio web browser

1. Click the Other Windows submenu on the View menu and then click the Web Browser command.

The Web Browser window appears, as shown here:

The browser is a tabbed document window by default, but you can change it to the float position by right-clicking the window title bar and then clicking the Float command.

 Tip You can change the default page that appears in the Web Browser window by changing the setting in the Options dialog box. Open the Options dialog box by clicking Options on the Tools menu. Expand Environment, and then click Web Browser. Change the Home Page setting to a URL you want for the default page.

2. Experiment with the browser and how it functions within the IDE.

   Although the browser is more basic than Internet Explorer or another full-featured browser, you may find it a useful addition to the Visual Studio tool collection. You can also open and run Internet Explorer (or another browser) directly from the Windows taskbar.

3. When you're finished, click the Close button on the right side of the web browser title bar to close the window.

Customizing IDE Settings to Match This Book's Exercises

Like the tool windows and other environment settings within the IDE, the compiler and personal settings within Visual Studio are highly customizable. It is important to review a few of these settings now so that your version of Visual Studio is configured in a way that is compatible with the step-by-step programming exercises that follow. You will also learn how to customize Visual Studio generally so that as you gain programming experience, you can set up Visual Studio in the way that is most productive for you.

Checking Project and Compiler Settings

If you just installed Visual Studio, you are ready to start this book's programming exercises. But if your installation of Visual Studio has been on your machine for a while, or if your computer is a shared resource used by other programmers who might have modified the default settings (perhaps in a college computer lab), complete the following steps to verify that your settings related to projects, solutions, and the compiler match those that I use in the book.

Check project and compiler settings

1. Click the Options command on the Tools menu to display the Options dialog box.

   The Options dialog box is your window to many of the customizable settings within Visual Studio. To assist you in finding the settings that you want to change, Visual Studio organizes the settings by category.

2. Expand the Projects And Solutions category and then click the General item within it.

This group of check boxes and options configures the Visual Studio project and solution settings.

3. So that your software matches the settings used in this book, adjust your settings to match those shown in the following dialog box:

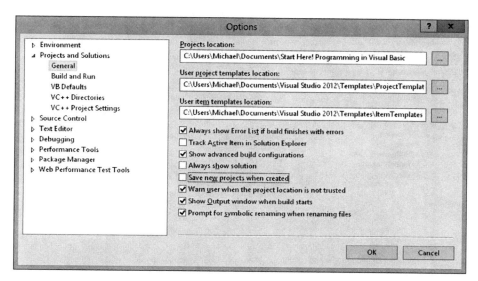

In particular, I recommend that you clear the check marks (if you see them) from the Always Show Solution and Save New Projects When Created check boxes. The first option shows additional solution commands in the IDE, which is not necessary for solutions that contain only one project (the situation for most programs in this book). The second option causes Visual Studio to postpone saving your project until you click the Save All command on the File menu and provide a location for saving the file. This delayed-save feature allows you to create a test program, compile and debug the program, and even run it without actually saving the project on disk—a useful feature when you want to create a quick test program that you might want to discard instead of saving. (An equivalent situation in word-processing terms is when you open a new Word document, enter an address for a mailing label, print the address, and then exit Word without saving the file.) With this default setting, the exercises in this book prompt you to save your projects after you create them, although you can also save your projects in advance by selecting the Save New Projects When Created check box.

You'll also notice that I have browsed to the location of the book's sample files (Start Here! Programming in Visual Basic) in the top text box on the form to indicate the default location for this book's sample files. Most of the projects that you create will be stored in this folder, and they will have a "My" prefix to distinguish them from the completed project I provide for you to examine. (Be sure to change this path to the location of the book's sample files on your computer.)

After you have adjusted these settings, you're ready to check the Visual Basic compiler settings.

4. Click the VB Defaults item in the expanded Projects And Solutions section.

Visual Studio displays a list of four compiler settings: Option Explicit, Option Strict, Option Compare, and Option Infer. Your screen looks like this:

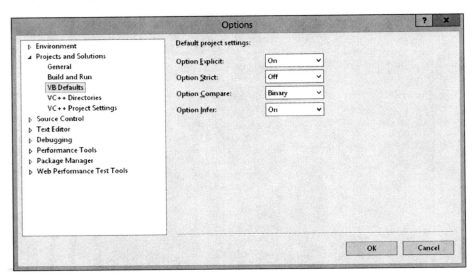

Although a detailed description of these settings is beyond the scope of this chapter, you'll want to verify that Option Explicit is set to On and Option Strict is set to Off—the default settings for Visual Basic programming within Visual Studio. Option Explicit On is a setting that requires you to declare a variable before using it in a program—a very good programming practice that I want to encourage. Option Strict Off allows variables and objects of different types to be combined under certain circumstances without generating a compiler error. (For example, a number can be assigned to a text box object without error.) Although this is a potentially worrisome programming practice, Option Strict Off is a useful setting for certain types of demonstration programs.

Option Compare determines the comparison method when different text strings are compared and sorted. For more information about comparing strings and sorting text, see Chapter 9, "Managing Data with LINQ."

Option Infer was a new setting in Visual Basic 2008. When you set Option Strict to Off and Option Infer to On, you can declare variables without explicitly stating a data type. Or rather, if you make such a declaration, the Visual Basic compiler will infer (or take an educated guess about) the data type based on the initial assignment you made for the variable. You'll learn more about the feature in Chapter 6, "Visual Basic Language Elements."

As a general rule, I recommend that you set Option Infer to Off to avoid unexpected results in how variables are used in your programs. I have set Option Infer to Off in most of the sample projects included in the sample files.

Feel free to examine additional settings in the Options dialog box related to your programming environment and Visual Studio. When you're finished, click OK to close the Options dialog box.

You're ready to exit Visual Studio and start programming.

Exiting Visual Studio

When you're finished using Visual Studio for the day, save any projects that are open and close the development environment. Give it a try.

Exit Visual Studio

1. Save any changes you've made to your program by clicking the Save All button on the Standard toolbar.

    You've made a few changes to your project, so you should save your changes now.

2. On the File menu, click the Exit command.

    The Visual Studio program closes. You are now ready to create your first program from scratch in Chapter 2.

Summary

Each chapter in this book concludes with a Summary section that offers a review of what the chapter has presented. You can use these sections to quickly recap what you have learned in each chapter before you move on to the one that follows.

This chapter introduced you to Visual Studio 2012 Express for Windows 8 and the IDE that you use to open and run Visual Basic programs. You can create Windows 8 apps by opening a new or existing solution in Visual Studio, and then adding to the solution with the assorted programming tools provided by the product. In this chapter, you learned how to display the user interface of a Visual Basic program, how to examine the objects on a page, and how to change property settings with the Properties window.

As you toured the Visual Studio IDE, you learned how to use menu commands, how to open and run a program, how to examine XAML markup for a page in the Code Editor, and how to move important tool windows around the IDE. You also learned how to customize settings in Visual Studio by using the Options command on the Tools menu.

The Visual Studio IDE is a busy place, with many more commands and features than this chapter covered. However, as you continue reading this book, you will be introduced to the most important programming tools and techniques one step at a time. Although you worked with a very simple Windows 8 application in this chapter, Visual Studio is capable of creating a variety of powerful programs for a number of different hardware environments or platforms. These platforms include Windows 8 and earlier operating systems, Windows Phone, web applications for numerous browsers, Xbox system games, and Windows Azure (cloud-computing) web servers. By learning Visual Basic 2012, you will be well positioned to benefit from many of the most exciting technologies in the marketplace.

Chapter 2

Creating Your First Windows 8 Application

After completing this chapter, you'll be able to

- Create the user interface for a Windows 8 application.

- Add XAML controls to a page.

- Move and resize objects on a page.

- Set the properties for objects in the user interface.

- Write Visual Basic program code for an event handler.

- Save, run, and test a program.

- Build an executable file and deploy the application.

CHAPTER 1, "GETTING TO KNOW VISUAL BASIC 2012," introduced you to Microsoft Visual Studio 2012 and the development tools that you can use to build Microsoft Visual Basic applications. In this chapter, you'll learn how to create your first Windows 8 application from scratch. The program will be a simple Internet-browsing tool that displays active webpage content in a window and also keeps track of the web addresses that you use as you run the program.

Although the project itself is quite basic, it will teach you essential programming techniques that you will use each time that you write a program. You will create a basic user interface with XAML controls, adjust property settings for the controls, and add Visual Basic program code to create an event handler. Along the way, you'll learn how to use the Visual Studio Toolbox, how to use the *Button*, *TextBox*, and *WebView* controls, and how to use the Code Editor to create a Visual Basic code-behind file for the user interface. You'll also learn how to run and test a program, how to save your changes, and how to deploy an application so that it is ready to use on your computer.

Web List: Your First Visual Basic Program

The Windows 8 application that you are going to create is Web List, a program that displays live webpage content and also keeps track of the web sites that you visit in a text box. The tool allows you to rapidly examine and record a list of favorite web sites, and it also shows you how to view web site information directly on the home page of an application. Here's what the Web List program will look like when it's finished:

The Web List user interface contains one button, two text boxes, and a web browser window that allows you to examine the live contents of any web site you wish. I produced these elements by creating four objects on the Web List application page and then changing several properties for each object. After I designed the user interface, I used Visual Basic program code to create an event handler for the Visit Web Site button, which executes when the user types a web address in the first text box and clicks the Visit Web Site button. To re-create Web List, you'll follow three essential programming steps in Visual Studio: creating the user interface, setting the properties, and writing the Visual Basic program code. The following list outlines the development process for Web List:

1. Create the user interface (requires four objects).

2. Set the properties (requires nine properties).

3. Write the program code (requires one object).

Creating the User Interface

In this exercise, you'll start building Web List by creating a new project and then using XAML Toolbox controls to construct the user interface.

Create a new project

1. Start Visual Studio 2012.

2. On the Visual Studio File menu, click New Project.

> **Tip** You can also start a new programming project by clicking the New Project link on the Visual Studio Start page. (The link is formatted in blue in most configurations.)

The New Project dialog box opens, as shown here:

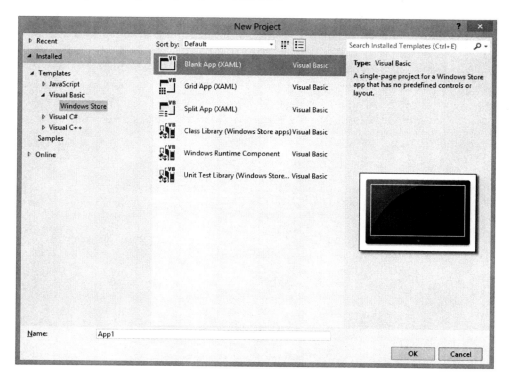

The New Project dialog box provides access to the major project types available for writing Windows 8 applications, which are also called Windows Store apps. Since the most recent selection I made in this dialog box was Visual Basic, the Visual Basic templates are currently visible, but other programming templates and resources are also available, including those for Microsoft Visual C#, Microsoft Visual C++, and JavaScript.

3. In the Visual Basic template group, click the Blank App (XAML) project.

Visual Studio prepares the development environment for a basic Windows 8 application with no predefined controls or layout.

4. In the Name text box, type **My Web List**.

Visual Studio assigns the name My Web List to your project. (You'll specify a folder location for the project later.) I'm recommending the "My" prefix here so you don't confuse your new application with the Web List project I've created for you on disk.

> **Tip** If your New Project dialog box contains Location and Solution Name text boxes, you need to specify a folder location and solution name for your new programming project now. The presence of these text boxes is controlled by a check box in the Project And Solutions category of the Options dialog box, but it may not be the default setting. (You display this dialog box by clicking the Options command on the Tools menu.) Throughout this book, you will be instructed to save your projects (or discard them) after you have completed the programming exercise. For more information about this delayed-saving feature and default settings, see the section entitled "Customizing IDE Settings to Match this Book's Exercises" in Chapter 1.

5. Click OK to create the new project in Visual Studio.

Visual Studio cleans the slate for a new programming project and displays Visual Basic code associated with the blank application template in the IDE. Your screen will look like this:

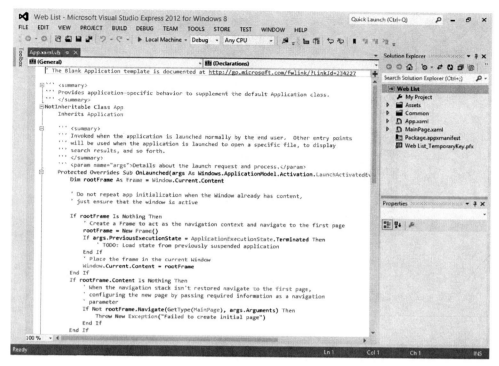

You won't spend too much time with this code right now. What you see is standard start-up code for a Windows 8 application created within Visual Studio, and it is stored in the file *App.xaml.vb* within the project. Although each project contains an *App.xaml* file, your work today will begin in the application's user interface, which is stored in the *MainPage.xaml* file. You'll display that user interface now and enhance it with Toolbox controls.

Create a user interface

1. Open Solution Explorer if it is not currently visible, and then double-click the file *MainPage.xaml*.

   Visual Studio opens *MainPage.xaml* in a Designer window and shows the upper-left corner of the application's main page. Below this page, you'll see the Code Editor with several lines of XAML markup associated with the user interface page in the Designer window. As you add controls to the application page in the Designer window, the Code Editor reflects the changes by displaying the XAML statements that will create the user interface. Your screen should look like this:

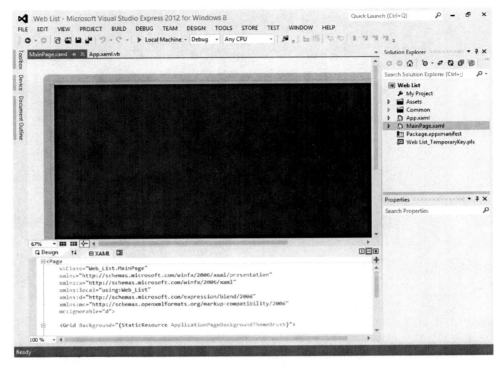

Now let's get to know the Designer window a bit better.

2. Click the scroll box in the Designer window's vertical scroll bar and drag it down.

When you drag a scroll box in the Designer window, you can see more of the user interface you are working on.

3. Click the scroll box on the Designer window's horizontal scroll bar and drag it right. (Likewise, when you drag a horizontal scroll box, you can see hidden parts of the user interface.)

Near the lower-left corner of the Designer window, you'll see a Zoom tool, which allows you to zoom in on the current application page (to see more detail) or zoom out (to see more of the page). The current value of the Zoom tool is 100%. You can select a different value by clicking the Zoom tool's drop-down button.

4. Click the Zoom drop-down button and then click Fit All.

The entire application page now fits within the Designer window. Depending on your screen resolution and the amount of screen space you have designated for the other IDE tools, you'll see a somewhat smaller version of the page.

> **Tip** If your mouse has a mouse wheel, you can move quickly from one zoom setting to the next by holding down the Ctrl key and rotating the mouse wheel. This feature works whenever the Designer window is active.

It is important to be able to quickly view different parts of the application page in different sizes while you build it. Sometimes you want to see the entire page to consider the layout of controls or other elements, and sometimes you need to view portions of the page up close. Now return to the original setting.

5. Click the Zoom drop-down button, and then click 100%.

Now you'll open the Toolbox.

6. If the Toolbox is not currently visible, click the Toolbox tab or click the Toolbox command on the View menu.

The Toolbox window contains a large collection of user interface controls that you can add to your application. Because you are building an application for Windows 8, the types of controls that are displayed in the Toolbox are so-called *XAML controls*—that is, structured elements that control the design of an application and can be successfully organized on a page by the XAML parser within Visual Studio. There are other types of Toolbox controls for other types of applications (Windows forms controls, HTML controls for web applications, and so on), but you don't have to worry about that now—Visual Studio automatically loads the proper controls into the Toolbox when you open a new solution.

Your screen should look like this:

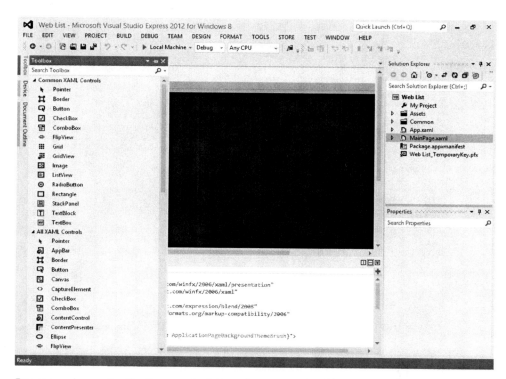

For convenience, the Toolbox controls have been organized into two groups: Common XAML Controls (those controls that appear in many applications), and All XAML Controls (a list of all the XAML controls that are currently installed on your system). Keep in mind that the Toolbox window is like any other tool window in the Visual Studio IDE. You can move it, resize it, or pin it as needed. Most programmers have the Toolbox open while adding controls to a new page, and then they pin it to the side of the IDE, as you'll do in the following step.

Next, you'll practice adding a text box object to the page.

7. Click the *TextBox* control in the Toolbox, and then click the Auto Hide button on the Toolbox title bar to pin the Toolbox to the IDE, if it is not already pinned.

   Remember that when you pin a window to the IDE, the Auto Hide pushpin points in the down direction. Putting the Toolbox in this position will stop it from obscuring any of the Designer window while you work.

8. Move the mouse pointer to the upper-left corner of the Designer window, and then drag right and down to create a rectangular-shaped text box object on the page.

   When you release the mouse button, Visual Studio creates a XAML text box object on the page, as shown here. (You may need to reposition the Designer window to see what is shown in the illustration.)

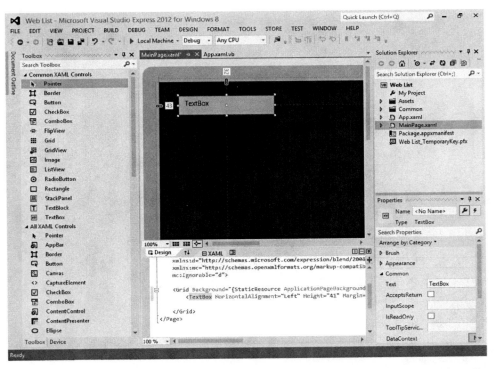

The text box is currently enclosed with selection handles, indicating that the object is selected in the IDE. The property settings of the selected object are loaded into the Properties window, and below in the Code Editor, XAML markup for the text box object appears nested within a grid object. All Windows 8 app user interfaces created with XAML markup have a grid object as their base layout element, and the controls that you add to the page appear nested within this main grid.

Move and resize a text box

1. Point to the lower-right corner of the new text box object, click the sizing handle on the corner of the text box, and drag it to a new location.

   As you drag the corner, the text box object will be resized, although the upper-left corner of the text box will remain in place.

   Whenever an object is selected in the Designer window, you can resize it by using the sizing handles. As you make sizing adjustments, grid lines reveal the dimensions of the object in pixels, and you can use the grid lines to create objects of a uniform size, or to align an object with another object on the page. Your selected text box will also have little locking icons at the top and left edges of the text box. These locks indicate that the element is *locked*, or frozen, a set distance from the edge of the window, but you can adjust this by clicking the locks, which open and close like a toggle.

2. Click the middle of the text box object and slowly drag it around the application page.

   The text box floats around the surface of the page, and the grid lines and sizing information adjust as you move the object.

   It is very simple to move objects on a page in the Designer window. As you make these adjustments, note that your changes are recorded in XAML markup in the Code Editor, as well as in the Designer window.

3. Position the text box so that it is 40 pixels from the left edge of the page and 24 pixels from the top edge of the page, and has a height of 32 pixels and a width of 420 pixels.

   These dimensions will be fine for the single-line text box that the user will use to enter the web address (URL) that they want to browse to when the program runs. Your Designer window should look like this:

Now you'll add a button object to the page. The Toolbox should currently be visible, since you pinned it to the IDE.

Add a button object

1. Click the *Button* control in the Toolbox and then move the mouse pointer over the application page.

   The mouse pointer changes to crosshairs and a button icon. The crosshairs are designed to help you draw the rectangular shape of the button on the page. You can also create a button with the default size by double-clicking the *Button* control in the Toolbox.

2. Drag the pointer down and to the right. Release the mouse button to complete the button, and watch it snap to the page.

3. Resize the button object so that it is 40 pixels high and 140 pixels wide.

 Tip At any time, you can delete an object and start over again by selecting the object on the page and then pressing Delete. Feel free to create and delete objects to practice creating your user interface.

4. Move the button object so that it is below the text box object. Snap lines will appear as you move the object, and the right edge of the button will snap to the right edge of the text box when aligned.

   Your screen should look like this:

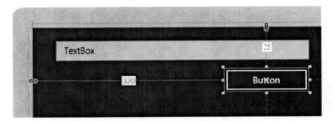

Now you'll add a second (larger) text box object to the page. This text box object will contain the list of web sites that you visited while the Web List program was running.

Add a second text box

1. Use the horizontal scroll bar in the Designer window to make the right side of the application page more visible.

   You're going to add the second text box object to the right side of the application page.

2. Click the *TextBox* control in the Toolbox, move the mouse to the Designer window, and then create a second text box object on the page. Make the text box about the same width but much taller than the first one.

Visual Studio creates a second text box object on the page. Your screen will look like this:

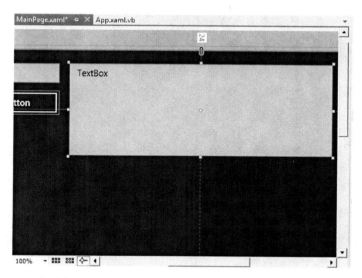

Now you'll add a large web browser window on the page to display information from the web sites that you visit. This object is created by using the *WebView* control in the Toolbox. *WebView* is not a full-featured web browser like Internet Explorer. However, it was added to the XAML Toolbox to give Visual Studio programmers a simple way to display live web information in a Windows 8 application.

Add a web view object

1. Click the *WebView* control in the Toolbox. (You'll find it in the All XAML Controls section.)

2. Using the drawing pointer for the control, create a very large rectangular box on the page below the button object and second text box object.

The goal with this object is to display as much of the web browser as possible. However, for web content that extends beyond the viewing area, the web view object will allow users to scroll up and down to see more information.

3. After you create the object, you may wish to close the Toolbox window or adjust the amount of zoom magnification in the Designer window to make as much of the page visible in the IDE as possible.

Your final page should look like this in the Designer window:

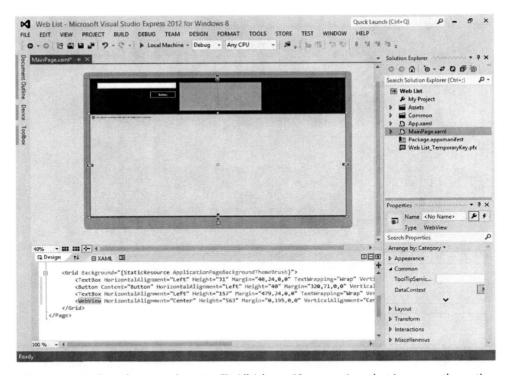

In my Designer window, the zoom is set to Fit All (about 40 percent) so that I can see the entire application page. Also note how the Code Editor now shows XAML markup for four objects: a text box, a button, a second text box, and a web browser. Now you're ready to customize your interface by setting a few properties.

Setting the Properties

As you discovered in Chapter 1, you can change properties by selecting objects on a page and changing their settings in the Properties window. You'll start by changing the property settings for the first text box.

Set the web address text box

1. Click the first text box you created on the page. The text box object is selected and is surrounded by resize handles.

2. Open the Properties window.

Tip If the Properties window isn't visible, click the Properties Window command on the View menu, or press Alt+Enter.

3. At the top of the Properties window, click the Name property text box. The *Name* property will appear selected in the Properties window. Although not all XAML controls on a page need a name, you do need to specify one if you plan to use the control in Visual Basic program code. Setting the *Name* property for this text box will give you something that you can make reference to later.

4. Type **NewURL** and press Enter.

As you name the objects on a page, it is useful to follow some basic naming conventions that make the objects easy to recognize in your code-behind file. In this case, I've specified *NewURL* because the object will hold the new web address or URL that the user of the program wants to browse to. Programmers sometimes name objects according to numeric patterns as well, such as *TextBox1*, *TextBox2*, and so on.

Now you'll put a sample URL in the text box to show users the pattern that you want them to follow.

5. In the Common category, click the *Text* property, type **http://www.msn.com**, and press Enter.

The *Text* property holds the text that is currently displayed in the text box object on the page, and if you look in the Designer window now, you'll see that the default text has changed from "TextBox" to "http://www.msn.com."

A text box object can contain one or more lines of text. You can modify the text that appears in a text box by using the Properties window, by directly editing the XAML markup associated with the text box in the Code Editor, or by modifying the *Text* property of the text box in the Visual Basic code-behind file so that the text box changes while the program is running.

The following screen shot shows what the Properties window looks like after you have set the *Name* and *Text* properties. It shows the window slightly expanded and floating over the IDE, which is probably a good way to use the tool when you first start using it. Once you get the hang of it, however, you'll find it easiest to use the Properties window in its docked position.

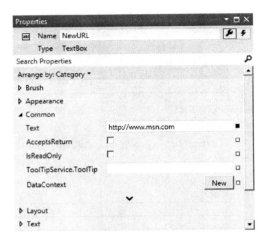

Now you'll change the *Name* property for the second text box object on the page.

6. Click the second text box object, and use the Properties window to change the *Name* property of the text box to **AllSites**.

   You'll give the larger text box this name because you'll use it to list all of the web sites that the user visits while the program runs. The text box should be big enough to list up to a dozen web sites.

7. Click the *Text* property for the *AllSites* text box, delete the text that is there, and then press Enter.

   The Properties window removes "TextBox" from the *AllSites* text box in the Designer. This is done to prevent text from being displayed in the text box when the program starts.

8. In the Common category, click the *IsReadOnly* check box.

   You'll see a check mark in the check box, indicating that the *IsReadOnly* property has been set to *True*. This setting will prevent the user from editing content in the *AllSites* text box while the program is running, although they can still copy information from the text box to the Clipboard by selecting text in the object with the mouse and pressing Ctrl+C.

Now you'll set a property for the button object in the program.

Set the Content property of the button object

1. Click the button object on the page.

   The button will be selected and surrounded by resize handles.

   The XAML *Button* control uses the *Content* property to store the text that is displayed on a button, so you'll edit that property now. The text that is currently displayed is "Button," but you'll change it to "Visit Web Site" to make the element more descriptive.

2. Use the Properties window to change the *Content* property of the button object to **Visit Web Site**.

Once you make the change, the text is updated in the Properties window, in the button object on the page, and in the XAML markup in the Code Editor.

Now you'll set a few properties for the web view object in the program.

Set the properties of the web view object

1. Click the web view object on the page.

The XAML *WebView* control is a no-frills web browser that allows you to quickly display web-page content in a Windows 8 application. It is useful because you can't easily start Internet Explorer or another web browser from within a Windows 8 program.

Adding direct access to the web from a Windows application is an exciting feature. You'll update the *Name* property of the web view object now so that you can use this interesting tool in Visual Basic code.

2. Use the Properties window to change the *Name* property to **WebView1**.

 Tip While you are working with the web view object, you might notice that in the Designer window, the object displays the following message: "This element is enabled only when the application is running." This means that the web browser will not work while you are creating your application, so you can't preview how web content will appear until you actually run the program. Not to worry—testing how your program works is part of the overall development process, which I'll discuss later in the book.

Now you'll center the horizontal and vertical alignment of the web content so that the user can see it clearly within the application window that you have designed.

3. In the Properties window, expand the Layout category and scroll down a bit so that you can see the *HorizontalAlignment* and *VerticalAlignment* properties.

These properties control how content is aligned within the web view object. The default is left for *HorizontalAlignment* and top for *VerticalAlignment*. However, you'll want to specify center alignment for both properties. You change these values in the Properties window by clicking one of the four alignment buttons, each of which contains a visual representation of the alignment.

4. Click the center-alignment button for the *HorizontalAlignment* property.

5. Click the center-alignment button for the *VerticalAlignment* property.

Your Properties window will look like this:

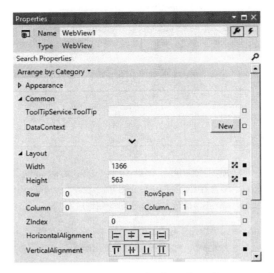

Congratulations! You are finished setting the properties for the Web List program. Now you'll write a few lines of Visual Basic program code to navigate to web sites as needed, and to keep track of the web sites that the user has visited.

Reading Properties in Tables

In this chapter, you've set the properties for the Web List program one step at a time. In future chapters, the instructions to set properties will be presented in table format unless a setting is especially tricky. Table 2-1 lists the properties you've set so far in the Web List program, as they will look later in the book. Settings you need to type in are shown in quotation marks. ("" means that you should delete the text currently in the property setting.) You shouldn't type the quotation marks.

TABLE 2-1 Web List Properties

Object	Property	Setting
Text box 1	*Name*	NewURL
	Text	"http://www.msn.com"
Text box 2	*Name*	AllSites
	Text	""
	IsReadOnly	True
Button 1	*Caption*	"Visit Web Site"
Web view	*Name*	WebView1
	HorizontalAlignment	Center
	VerticalAlignment	Center

Writing the Visual Basic Code

Now you're ready to write the code for the My Web List program. Because most of the objects you've created already "know" how to work when the program runs, they're ready to receive input from the user and process it. The inherent functionality of objects is one of the great strengths of Visual Studio and Visual Basic—after XAML objects are placed on a page and their properties are set, they're ready to run. However, the core of the My Web List program—the code that starts the web browser and copies each web site that is visited to a text box—is still missing. This computing logic can only be built into the application by using program statements—code that clearly spells out what the program should do at each step of the way. Because the Visit Web Site button drives the program, you'll create an event handler that runs, or *fires*, when the user clicks this button. The event handler will be created using Visual Basic code in a file that is connected to the page you just built.

In the following steps, you'll create an event handler for a button click event using the Code Editor.

Use the Code Editor to create an event handler

1. In the Designer window, click the button object.

2. Open the Properties window, and next to the *Name* property text box, click the Event Handlers button (a square button displaying a lightning bolt icon).

   A long list of events that the button object can detect fills the Properties window. Typical events that a button object might respond to include *Click* (a mouse click), *DoubleClick* (two mouse clicks in quick succession), *DragOver* (an object being dragged over a button), and *Drop* (an object being dragged over and dropped on a button). Since Visual Basic is at its core an event-driven programming language, much of what you do as a software developer is create user interfaces that respond to various types of input from the user, and then you write event handlers that manage the input.

   Most of the time, you will only need to write event handlers for a few events associated with the objects in your programs. (The list of events is quite comprehensive, however, to give you many options.)

   To create an event handler for a particular event, you double-click the text box next to the event in the Properties window. Since you want to load a webpage each time that the user clicks the button in your program, you'll write an event handler for the button's *Click* event.

3. Double-click the text box next to the *Click* event in the Properties window.

   Visual Studio inserts an event handler named *Button_Click_1* in the *Click* text box, and opens the *MainPage.xaml.vb* code-behind file in the Code Editor. Your screen should look like this:

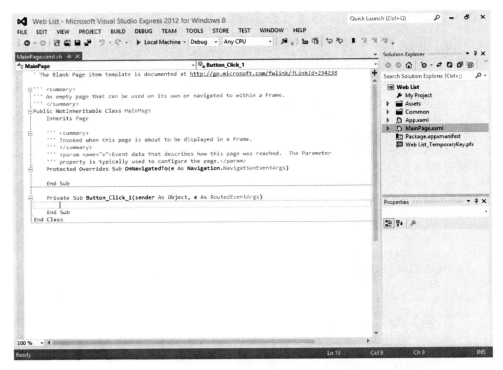

Inside the Code Editor are program statements associated with the *MainPage* template that you opened when you started this project. This is Visual Basic program code, and you may notice right away that some of the code is organized into concise units, known as *procedures*. There is a procedure called *OnNavigatedTo*, and there is a new event handler procedure that you just created called *Button_Click_1*.

The *Sub* and *End Sub* keywords designate a procedure, and the keywords *Protected* and *Private* indicate how the procedure will be used. You'll learn more about these keywords later.

When you double-clicked the *Click* text box in the Properties window, Visual Studio automatically added the first and last lines of the *Button_Click_1* event procedure, as the following code shows:

```
Private Sub Button_Click_1(sender As Object, e As RoutedEventArgs)

End Sub
```

The body of a procedure fits between these lines and is executed whenever a user activates the interface element associated with the procedure. In this case, the event is a mouse click, but as you'll see later in the book, it could also be a different type of event. Programmers refer to this sequence as "triggering an event."

Tip You may also notice lines of text highlighted with green type in the Code Editor. In the default settings, green type indicates that the text is a *comment*, or an explanatory note written by the creator of the program, so that it might be better understood or used by others. The Visual Basic compiler does not execute, or *evaluate*, program comments.

4. Type the following program code and press the Enter key after the last line:

```
WebView1.Navigate(New Uri(NewURL.Text))
AllSites.Text = AllSites.Text & NewURL.Text & vbCrLf
```

As you enter the program code, Visual Studio formats the text and displays different parts of the code in color to help you identify the various elements. When you begin to type the name of an object property, Visual Basic also displays the available properties for the object you're using in a list box, so you can double-click the property or keep typing to enter it yourself.

Your screen should now look like this:

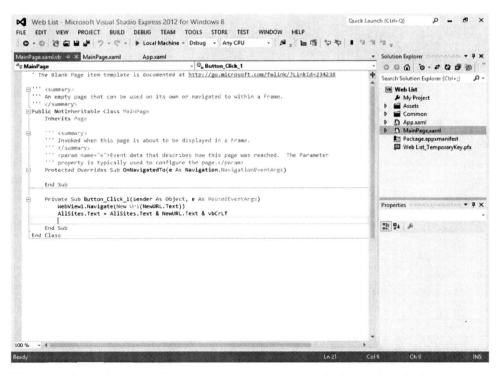

If Visual Basic displays an additional error message, you might have misspelled a program statement. Check the offending line against the text in this book, make the necessary correction, and continue typing. (You can also delete a line and type it again from scratch.)

Program statements are a little like complete sentences in a human language—statements can be of varying lengths but must follow the grammatical rules of the language. In Visual Studio, program statements can be composed of keywords, properties, object names, variables, numbers, special symbols, and other values. As you enter these items in the Code Editor, Visual Studio uses a feature known as IntelliSense to help you write the code. With IntelliSense, as Visual Studio recognizes language elements, it will automatically complete many expressions.

> **More Info** You'll learn more about Visual Basic language fundamentals in Chapter 6, "Visual Basic Language Elements."

5. Click the Save All command on the File menu to save your additions to the program.

   The Save All command saves everything in your project—the project file, the pages, the code-behind files, the assets, the package manifest, and other related components in your application. Since this is the first time that you have saved your project, the Save Project dialog box opens, prompting you for the name and location of the project. (If your copy of Visual Studio is configured to prompt you for a location when you first create your project, you won't see the Save Project dialog box now—Visual Studio just saves your changes.)

6. Browse and select a location for your files.

   I recommend that you use the *My Documents\Start Here! Programming in Visual Basic\ Chapter 02* folder (the location of the book's sample files), but the location is up to you. Since you used the "My" prefix when you originally opened your project, this version won't overwrite the practice file that I built for you on disk.

7. Clear the Create Directory For Solution check box.

   When this check box is selected, it creates a second folder for your program's solution files, which is not necessary for solutions that contain only one project (the situation for most programs in this book).

8. Click Save to save your files.

   Notice that the object names in the Code Editor (*WebView1*, *NewURL*, and *AllSites*) are now displayed in normal type.

> **Tip** If you want to save just the item you are currently working on (the page, the code module, or something else), you can use the Save command on the File menu. If you want to save the current item with a different name, you can use the Save As command.

A Look at the Visual Basic Code-Behind File

The *Button_Click_1* event handler is executed when the user clicks the Visit Web Site button on the page. The procedure uses some interesting Visual Basic code, which is worth looking at before moving on.

The first statement uses the *Navigate* method of the *WebView1* object to load a webpage into the window you created earlier in this project:

```
WebView1.Navigate(New Uri(NewURL.Text))
```

Navigate is a *method*, or a statement that performs a specific action for an object in your program. The web view object has numerous methods, but the *Navigate* method is the one that prompts web view to load a webpage. Right now, you should notice that the *Navigate* method is connected to the *WebView1* object by a period (.), which is the same syntax that is used to reference a property in program code.

In parentheses following the *Navigate* method is a reference to the text that the user has entered into the first text box on the page (New*URL*). The text is stored in the *Text* property, and the *New Uri* keywords are used to put the user input into a standard format used for web addresses—the so-called *uniform resource indicator (URI)* format. Since this is a simple demonstration program, I am assuming that the user is entering the web address in the proper way. In fact, if an incorrect or badly formatted web address is entered, the program will not load the webpage and there will be little indication that something went wrong. This is not what you would do in a commercial application, of course, and I'll show you later in the book how to be much more deliberate about handling errors introduced by the user.

The second statement builds the list of web sites that the user visits while the program runs:

```
AllSites.Text = AllSites.Text & NewURL.Text & vbCrLf
```

Each web site is entered through the *Text* property of the *NewURL* object. This *Text* property is combined with the current contents of the *AllSites* text box through the string concatenation operator (&), which appends each new web site that is entered to the bottom of the list. A line break is added to the end of each line by the *vbCrLf* constant. You'll learn more about the string concatenation operator when you learn about how Visual Basic computes mathematical and textual operations in Chapter 6.

With just two lines of Visual Basic code, your program is complete. Now you are ready to run the application.

Running Visual Basic Applications

To run a Visual Basic program from the development environment, you can do any of the following:

- Click Start Debugging on the Debug menu.

- Click the Start Debugging (Local Machine) button on the Standard toolbar.

- Press F5.

Try running the My Web List program now. If Visual Studio has difficulty compiling your program or displays an error message, you might have made a typing mistake or two in your program code. Try to fix it by comparing the printed version in this book with the one you typed, or load Web List from this book's sample files and run it.

Tip When you run the My Web List program, you will use the WebView control to display live information from the Internet in your application. By default, if Visual Studio encounters any type of error when loading web pages into the WebView control, it will display an error message in a dialog box entitled "Visual Studio Just-In-Time Debugger." If you click "Yes" in this dialog box, you will enter debugging mode (or break mode) and be able to learn more about the error message. If you click "No", you can suppress the error message and keep running the My Web List program.

Internet script errors can occur for a variety of reasons on the web. Most of these errors are simple warning messages that are not too serious. To suppress Just-In-Time script debugging for now, while you are still getting your feet wet with Visual Studio, I recommend that you click Tools | Options | Debugging | Just-In-Time, remove the check mark from the Script check box, and then click OK. After you complete this chapter, you can restore this setting.

Run the My Web List program

1. Click the Start Debugging button on the Standard toolbar (the green arrow button with the words "Local Machine" next to it).

    The My Web List program will compile and run in the IDE. After a few seconds, the user interface appears, just as you designed it. The Microsoft MSN web site (*http://www.msn.com*) appears in the first text box as a sample web site you can browse to.

2. Click the Visit Web Site button.

    The program uses the *Navigate* method of the *WebView1* object to access the site. The web site appears in the web view object, and the web site URL appears in the second text box on the page. Your screen will look like this:

3. Enter a new URL in the first text box, such as **http://www.plu.edu**, and then click Visit Web Site. (This is the university where I teach, but you can substitute your own favorite web address.)

4. Visual Basic immediately adds the web site to the list of visited sites and loads the webpage into the web browser. Keep in mind that the content in the web browser is live—you can click around within the webpages and move from link to link as you would on a normal webpage. To see webpage content that is not currently visible, simply press the Down Arrow key or rotate the mouse wheel.

5. Enter a third URL in the text box, such as **http://msdn.microsoft.com**, and then click Visit Web Site.

6. Enter a fourth URL in the text box, such as **http://www.microsoftpress.oreilly.com**, and then click Visit Web Site.

Your screen will look like this:

Now that you've entered four or five web sites, you can begin to see the value of the web site address list that is slowly accumulating in the second text box. Visual Basic offers you the power to track all types of information, including a list of the web sites that you have visited. If you would like to save the list for future use, simply select the contents of the text box with your mouse, press Ctrl+C to copy the list to the Clipboard, open an application such as Notepad or Microsoft Word, and then press Ctrl+V to paste the list into the open document.

When you're finished experimenting with the Web List program, close the application. You've just tested your first Windows application!

Sample Projects on Disk

If you didn't build the My Web List project from scratch (or if you did build the project and want to compare what you created to what I built as I wrote the chapter), take a moment to open and run the completed Web List project now, which is located in the *My Documents\Start Here! Programming in Visual Basic\Chapter 02* folder on your hard disk (the default location for the practice files for this chapter). If you need a refresher course on opening projects, see the detailed instructions in Chapter 1. If you are asked if you want to save changes to the My Web List project, be sure to click Save.

Note The *Start Here!* programming series is designed to be a hands-on learning experience, so you will benefit most from building the projects on your own as you read this book. But after you have completed the projects, it is often a good idea to compare what you have with the practice file solution that I provide, especially if you run into trouble. To make this easy, I will give you the name of the solution files on disk before you run the completed program in most of the exercises that follow.

After you have compared the My Web List project to the Web List solution files on disk, reopen My Web List and prepare to compile it as an executable file. If you didn't create My Web List, use the book's solution file to complete the exercise.

Building an Executable File and Deploying

Your last task in this chapter is to complete the development process and create an application for Windows, or an executable file. Windows applications created with Visual Studio have the file name extension .*exe* and can be run on any system that contains Windows and the necessary support files. Visual Studio installs the support files that you need when you deploy a completed project—including the .NET Framework files—automatically.

Since you are creating an application for the Windows 8 user interface, you will need to deploy this program on a computer running Windows 8, because your application is designed for that environment. Chapter 12, "Future Development Opportunities and the Windows Store" introduces you to the Windows Store, an online purchasing and distribution system that allows Visual Studio programmers to sell their Windows 8 applications to customers around the world.

Before you prepare your app for the Windows Store, however, you need to know a little more about programming, and also a little more about how applications are compiled and tested. When Visual Studio programmers complete the initial design and functionality of their application, they typically test their program systematically to verify that the code works as expected under a variety of operating conditions. Often, more than one developer, or *tester*, is involved in the process, and they typically use a variety of machines, operating systems, and computing scenarios to test the seaworthiness of the application. If you examine the Build, Debug, and Test menus in the Visual Studio IDE, you'll begin to see how elaborate this process can actually be.

To assist in the testing and compilation process, Visual Studio allows you to create two types of executable files for your Windows application project: a *debug build* and a *release build*.

Debug builds are created automatically by Visual Studio when you create and test your program. They are stored in a folder called *bin\Debug* within your project folder. The debug executable file contains debugging information that makes the program run slightly slower.

Release builds are optimized executable files stored in the *bin\Release* folder within your project. To customize the settings for your release build, you click the [*ProjectName*] Properties command on the Project menu, and then click the Compile tab, where you'll see a list of compilation options that looks like the following screen. The Solution Configurations drop-down list box on the Standard Visual Studio toolbar (circled in the following image) indicates whether the executable is a debug build or a release build. If you change the Solution Configurations setting, the path in the Build Output Path text box will also change.

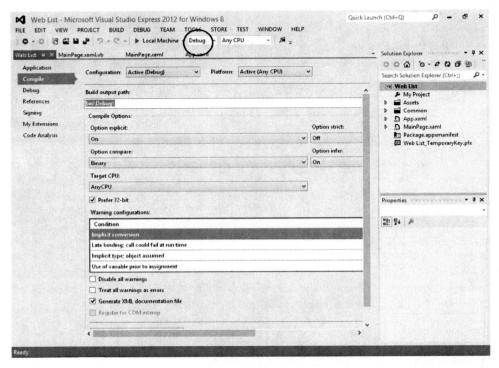

The process of preparing an executable file for a specific computer is called *deploying* the application. As noted, when you deploy an application with Visual Studio, the IDE handles the process of copying all the executable and support files that you will need to register the program with the operating system and run it. Visual Studio allows you to deploy applications *locally* (on the computer you are using) or *remotely* (on a computer attached to the network or Internet).

In the following exercise, you'll deploy a release build for the My Web List application locally and create an application icon for the program on the Windows Start page. In Chapter 12, you'll learn more about packaging applications that have been tested and prepared for the Windows Store.

Deploy a release build for a Windows 8 application

1. Click the Solution Configurations drop-down list box on the Standard toolbar, and then click the Release option.

   Visual Studio will prepare your project for a release build, with the debugging information removed. The build output path is set to *bin\Release*.

2. On the Build menu, click the Deploy My Web List command.

The Build command creates a *bin\Release* folder in which to store your project (if the folder doesn't already exist) and compiles the source code in your project. The Output window appears to show you milestones in the assembly and deployment process. The result is an executable file named *My Web List.exe*, which Visual Studio registers with the operating system on your computer.

Visual Studio deploys the application locally because Local Machine is currently selected on the toolbar next to the Start button. This is the desired behavior here, but you can also deploy applications on a remote machine (i.e., a computer attached to yours via a network or the Internet) by selecting the Remote Machine option. If you select this option, you'll be presented with a dialog box asking for more information about the remote connection. Keep in mind that remote deploying is mostly designed for testing purposes. The best way to install completed applications via the Internet is through the Windows Store.

When you deploy an application built for the Windows 8 user interface, Windows automatically creates a new program icon for the application on the Start page. You can use this icon to launch the program whenever you want to run it. Try running My Web List now from the Windows Start page on your computer.

3. Open the Windows Start page, and browse to the list of applications that are currently installed. (The most recent applications are typically located on the right side of the Start page.)

My Windows Start page currently looks like this:

4. Click the My Web List application icon.

   The My Web List program will load and run in Windows.

5. Test the application again, browsing to several web sites. When you are finished, close the application.

6. Return to Visual Studio, and close the Output window and the My Web List properties page. Note that you can view and change compilation options whenever you want—the properties page is always there.

7. On the File menu, click Exit to close Visual Studio and the My Web List project.

8. Click Save if you are prompted to, and the Visual Studio development environment will close.

Congratulations on completing your first Windows 8 application!

Tip Would you like to add to a Visual Basic program after you've finished working with it? Simply restart Visual Studio and check the Recent Projects pane on the Start page. The last few projects that were open in Visual Studio will be listed there, and you can click the project and pick up where you left off. If the project is not there (if you worked on it some time ago), click the Open Project command on the File menu and browse your computer's hard disk to find it. Most programmers edit and revise their projects over a period of days, weeks, and months. It is very simple to add to an existing Visual Basic project or to move components from one project to the next.

Summary

This chapter described how to create a Windows 8 application by using Visual Studio and the Visual Basic programming language. The process is very straightforward conceptually. First, you create a user interface on an application page by using controls from the XAML Toolbox. The XAML Toolbox offers numerous controls for user interface features that have been optimized for use in Windows 8. The Designer window allows you to place and resize the controls on the application page so that they look good and take on the design of the Windows 8 user interface. Once a Toolbox control is placed on a page, it is referred to as an object.

The next step is adjusting the property settings for one or more objects by using the Properties window. Before you can adjust the properties for an object, you must select the object in the Designer window. Once an object is selected, its property settings fill the Properties window, and you can adjust them by clicking, typing, and selecting values from list boxes. In the Web List project you created in this chapter, you adjusted property settings for the text box, button, and web view objects.

The third step is creating event handlers for the objects in your program that are manipulated in some way by the user. Event handlers are written in the Code Editor with Visual Basic program code. This Visual Basic code, sometimes referred to as a Visual Basic code-behind file, follows the syntax rules of the Visual Basic programming language and connects the developer to the power and functionality of the Windows operating system. Event handlers and other Visual Basic routines are considered the core of a Visual Studio program; they process information, calculate values, set object properties, and use object methods. In the My Web List project, you created the *Button_Click_1* event handler, which opens a webpage and adds the current web site to a text box when the user clicks the Visit Web Site button.

After the user interface and code-behind file for a project are complete, the application is ready to be tested against a variety of operating conditions. When you are finished testing your project, you can deploy it locally or remotely, which involves compiling the project into an executable file and registering it with the operating system. Finally, you can package your finished application and upload it to the Windows Store for global sales and distribution, a process that will be discussed more fully in Chapter 12.

Chapter 3

Using Controls

After completing this chapter, you'll be able to

- Use the *Ellipse* and *TextBlock* controls to customize your application's user interface.

- Use the *CheckBox* and *RadioButton* controls to receive input from the user.

- Use the *MediaElement* control to add music and video to your application.

CHAPTER 2, "CREATING YOUR FIRST WINDOWS 8 APPLICATION," introduced you to the process of writing a Microsoft Visual Basic program for the Windows 8 user interface. In this chapter, you'll continue learning how to build an attractive interface for your Windows app using XAML Toolbox controls. The techniques emphasized here involve adding controls to an application page and then manipulating those controls with Visual Basic program code. The more practice you have with XAML controls, the easier it will be for you to build your own programs.

First, you'll learn how to use the *Ellipse* and *TextBlock* controls to display shapes, titles, and other useful information on a page. As one of several shaped controls, the *Ellipse* control offers you full access to the rich color and texture palettes available to Windows 8 applications. The *TextBlock* control makes it easy to add titles, labels, and other textual information to a page and update that information while the program is running. Next, you'll use the *CheckBox* and *RadioButton* controls to receive mouse or touch pad input from the user while a program is running. *CheckBox* is useful when you want to offer users a list of check box options to choose from, and they are free to make any combination of selections that they like. Alternatively, the *RadioButton* control works best when users need to select a *single* option from a list of choices. As you learn to use these controls, you'll also learn more about Visual Basic program code and how to fix occasional programming mistakes with error-correction tools.

Finally, you'll learn how to add music and video playback support to your application with the *MediaElement* control. *MediaElement* opens and plays audio and video files in a variety of file formats. In addition to these playback features, *MediaElement* offers properties and methods that allow you to pause, rewind, change volume, and adjust other attributes, so you can control the playback just as you like.

Using the *Ellipse* and *TextBlock* Controls

The *Ellipse* and *TextBlock* controls, like several other controls in the Microsoft Visual Studio XAML Toolbox, have their roots in Windows Presentation Foundation (WPF) controls. WPF was created in the late 2000s to give Visual Studio programmers who targeted Windows and the .NET platform the ability to add cutting-edge graphics, video, and animation features to their applications. With the re-lease of Windows 8, a number of popular WPF controls (like *Ellipse* and *TextBlock*) have been updated for the Windows 8 user interface, and a few new controls just for Windows 8 (like *ProgressRing*) have been added to the XAML Toolbox. In this way, Visual Studio 2012 has carried forward earlier technol-ogies and combined them with new advancements in connectivity, security, and user interface design.

You use the *Ellipse* control to create an elliptical object on a page, and the object can be ad-justed to appear in a variety of sizes, textures, and colors. Each ellipse is drawn with a given height and width, and these values are stored in the *Height* and *Width* properties of the object. The *Fill* property fills the interior space of an ellipse with a particular color and pattern. The *Stroke* property sets the color of the outer edge of the ellipse, and the *StrokeThickness* property sets the width of the outer edge.

I often find it useful to add one or more large, elliptical shapes to an application's user inter-face when I want to highlight an important title or piece of text. For this reason, I am discussing the *TextBlock* control in the same section of this book as the *Ellipse* control. You have already worked with the *TextBox* control, which displays one or more lines of text in a rectangular box that is suitable for user input or output. The *TextBlock* control is a simpler device, useful mostly for displaying a bit of text that does not change very often in a program. However, you can modify the text that is displayed by a *TextBlock* object by using the *Text* property in Visual Basic program code.

The next two exercises describe how to use the *Ellipse* and *TextBlock* controls in a simple Windows 8 application.

Create a colorful background shape with the *Ellipse* control

1. Start Visual Studio 2012.

2. On the Visual Studio File menu, click New Project.

   The New Project dialog box opens.

3. In the Visual Basic template group, click the Blank App (XAML) project.

   Visual Studio prepares the IDE for a basic Windows 8 application with no predefined layout.

4. In the Name text box, type **My Display Banner**.

   Visual Studio assigns the name My Display Banner to your project. As I noted in Chapter 2, I'm recommending the "My" prefix here so that you don't confuse your new application with the Display Banner project I've created for you on disk.

5. Click OK to create the new project in Visual Studio.

   Visual Studio opens a new programming project and displays the Visual Basic code associated with the blank application template.

6. Open Solution Explorer if it is not currently visible, and then double-click the file *MainPage.xaml*.

   Visual Studio opens *MainPage.xaml* in the Designer window.

7. If the Toolbox is not currently visible, click the Toolbox tab or click the Toolbox command on the View menu.

8. Click the *Ellipse* control in the Toolbox, move the mouse pointer to the Designer window, and then drag right and down to create a large ellipse shape on the page.

   You'll find the Ellipse control in the All XAML Controls category. When you release the mouse button, Visual Studio creates a XAML ellipse object on the page, as shown here:

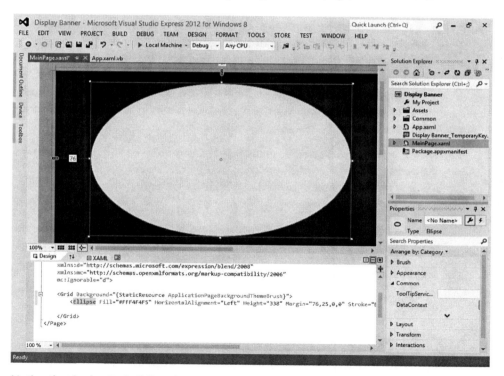

Notice that in the Code Editor, XAML markup for the ellipse object now appears, with several properties already assigned based on your work in the Designer. The Properties window also displays several of the properties of the ellipse object.

9. Enlarge the Properties window so that you have plenty of room to make additional adjustments to the properties in the Brush category.

You can configure many of the most interesting properties by using the Color Resources editor, a pane within the Brush category of the Properties window.

10. In the Brush category, click the *Fill* property, and then click near the top of the vertical hue bar in the Color Resources editor.

The hue bar contains all the colors of the visible spectrum in their purest (most saturated) form. When you click near the top of the bar, you will see bright red or orange colors. These are the colors at the top of the traditional color wheel, although for ease of use, the color wheel has been stretched out vertically in this tool. On the right side of the hue bar are red, green, and blue color values, which collectively create the hue that you have selected on the hue bar. As you click around the bar, different color values will appear.

Tip The red, green, and blue color values are stored numerically in your program so that they can be easily recalled or modified, and if you want, you can also edit these values in the XAML markup for the ellipse object. Over the past decade, leading software developers and independent standards bodies have worked to make these color values consistent, and they can be used in computer applications as well as digital photography and video. So, if you see colors that you like in another application or setting, you can use the same color values in Visual Studio programs.

11. With a high red value selected in the hue bar, fine-tune the fill color by clicking somewhere in the middle of the color saturation bar. (The color saturation bar is the large rectangle containing gray on the left and bright red or orange on the right.)

Color saturation controls the mixture of black and white that is added to the color you have selected from the hue bar. Values on the right side of the color saturation bar have the most vivid colors. Pastel colors have more white, and colors with black appear more subdued.

Your Properties window will look something like the following. (If you are reading the printed version of this book, you may not see the sunset orange color that currently fills the Fill property bar.)

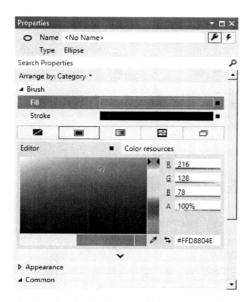

Notice that in the lower-right corner of the Color Resources editor there is a color-value text box containing a pound sign (#) and an eight-digit alphanumeric value. (In my Properties window, the number is currently #FFD8804E.) This is called a hexadecimal color value—that is, a number specified in base-16 arithmetic that represents the RGB and saturation values that you have just selected. This unique hexadecimal code will represent your fill color selection for the ellipse.

Interestingly, there are standardized names for many of the popular hue-and-saturation mixes; (in other words, familiar titles that are easier to remember than obscure hexadecimal values). These standardized names include White, Black, Purple, Salmon, Olive, Lime, LemonChiffon, and Aquamarine. You can find a complete list of these values (with corresponding color samples) in the Microsoft Developer Network (MSDN) documentation for Windows 8 apps. On the web, browse to *http://msdn.microsoft.com/* and search for the topic "Colors by Saturation." There are dozens of values, many with entertaining, stylized names.

You'll try using a few of the standardized color names in the color-value text box now.

12. In the color-value text box, type **LemonChiffon** and press Enter.

An off-white color with yellow hues and lots of white saturation appears in the ellipse in the Visual Studio IDE. Notice that the name LemonChiffon is no longer visible however; that familiar name has been replaced with the hexadecimal value #FFFFFACD.

13. In the color-value text box, type **FireBrick** and press Enter.

A deep red color (hexadecimal value #FFB22222) appears in the ellipse. You'll keep this color for the fill effect.

Now you'll change the color for the *Stroke* property in the Brush category, which controls the color of the outer edge of the ellipse object.

14. Click the color box for the *Stroke* property; the color is currently set to black (#FF000000).

15. In the color-value text box, type **White** and press Enter.

The *Stroke* property is changed to White. When you run the program, the red ellipse will have a thin white border.

16. Scroll down in the Properties window and open the Appearance category for the ellipse object.

Three properties settings are very useful here. You can adjust the *Opacity* property to make the ellipse appear transparent by reducing the *Opacity* property from 100 percent to a smaller value (such as 50 percent). A smaller value will reveal objects beneath the ellipse object if you have created them, or simply the application page if not. The *Visibility* property determines whether the ellipse object can be seen. The default value is *Visible*, but if you specify *Collapse*, perhaps to remove the shape as the program runs, the object will completely disappear. Finally, the *StrokeThickness* property lets you specify the thickness (in pixels) of the ellipse border—that is, the border you just filled with white. You'll modify this property now.

17. Type **5** in the StrokeThickness text box and press Enter.

Visual Studio increases the size of the white border to 5 pixels, which produces a much more noticeable edge. Your Properties window should look like this:

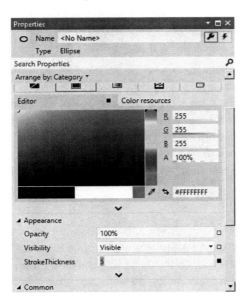

One impressive visual effect you can create with an ellipse object is a *gradient brush color pattern*—that is, a pattern that gradually transitions from one saturation value to another throughout the ellipse. This creates a shadow effect in the ellipse, and the result is an astonishing improvement over what you could create just a few years ago in Windows Forms applications. You'll try adding a gradient brush pattern as your last color effect in this section.

18. Click the color box for the *Fill* property again in the Brush category.

19. Click the *Gradient Brush* button, which is the third of five brush patterns below the color boxes for the *Fill* and *Stroke* properties.

20. Click the color saturation box to specify a color value that you would like to use.

    Visual Studio applies the color in a gradient brush pattern, moving from dark at the top of the ellipse to light at the bottom. Isn't that a beautiful sight?

    Now run the program to see what the completed ellipse shape looks like while the application is running.

21. Click the Start Debugging button on the Standard toolbar.

    The My Display Banner program runs, and the ellipse fills the screen with a colorful gradient pattern and a white border. My ellipse looks like the one in the following illustration:

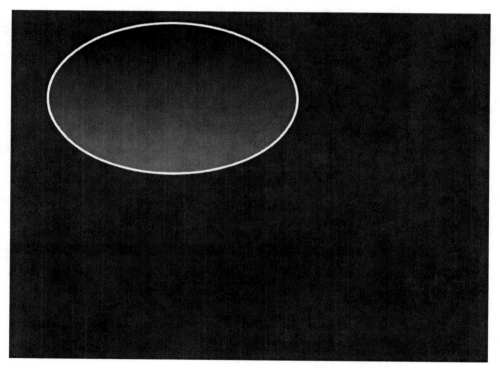

22. When you're finished looking at the colorful ellipse, close the application.

23. Click the Save All command on the File menu to save your project, and specify the *My Documents\Start Here! Programming in Visual Basic\Chapter 03* folder.

Now you'll add a *TextBlock* control to display some text in your application.

Add a *TextBlock* control to display text on the page

1. Open the Toolbox and click the *TextBlock* control.

2. Move the mouse pointer to the Designer window, and then create a large rectangle-sized text block object on top of the ellipse object.

    When you release the mouse button, Visual Studio creates a XAML text block object on the page. Resize the text block if necessary so that it looks like this:

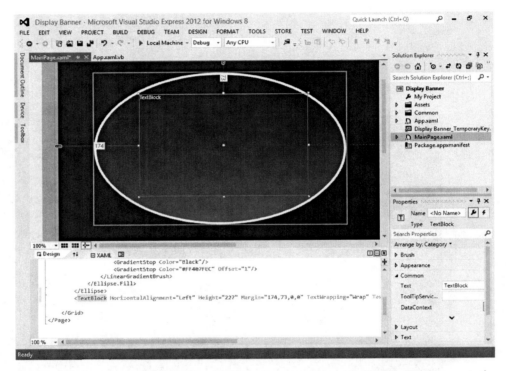

The *TextBlock* control is designed to display text on your page. Unlike the *TextBox* control, which is designed for user input and to display one or more lines of text, the *TextBlock* control is primarily used to display titles, labels, and other textual effects in your programs. You can update the text stored in the *TextBlock* control by setting the *Text* property, either with the Properties window or using program code.

3. In the Properties window, change the *Text* property of the text block object to **Imagine** and press Enter.

    Visual Studio displays "Imagine" in the Properties window and in the Designer window. Now you'll increase the point size of the title (a display banner for the page) and apply other formatting effects.

4. In the Properties window, in the Text category, click the Font Size text box, type **98**, and press Enter.

   The Font Size text box offers a variety of font sizes up to 72, but in this case you're typing a larger number to create a big impact on the screen. However, if "Imagine" now wraps in the text block object, you can specify a smaller size.

5. In the Properties window, in the Transform category, under Projection, click the Z text box, type **30**, and press Enter.

   The X, Y, and Z text boxes allow you to rotate the contents of the text block object in three dimensions (that is, along the x, y, and z axes). This allows you to create some interesting text-formatting effects. The effect you achieve in this case is making the word "Imagine" rotate upward.

6. Move and resize your new textual effect so that it is in the center of the ellipse on the page.

   Your screen should look something like this:

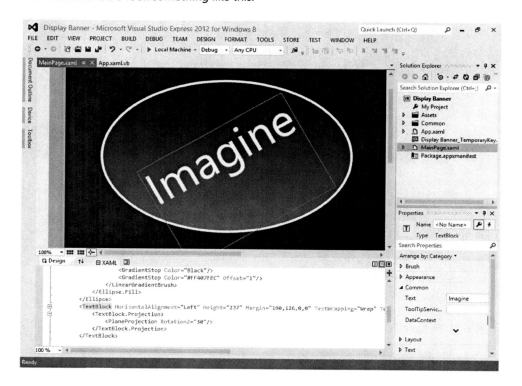

7. Click the Start Debugging button on the Standard toolbar.

The Display Banner program runs, and the ellipse fills the screen with a rotated banner title named Imagine in the middle of the shape. Your screen should look like this:

8. When you're finished examining your work, close the application.

9. Click the Save All command on the File menu to save your changes.

10. Click the Close Project command on the File menu to close the project you're working on.

You've learned how to use the *Ellipse* and *TextBlock* controls to customize your user interface. Now let's move on to some useful tools that will allow you to receive input from the user.

Using the *CheckBox* and *RadioButton* Controls

Windows 8 applications offer several useful ways to receive input from the user. As you've already learned, *TextBox* controls allow you to receive typed input, such as names, numbers, and other textual information. You can also use menus and dialog boxes to receive input from the user. As you'll learn in the following walkthroughs, two core user-input features in Windows 8 applications are the *CheckBox* and *RadioButton* controls, which are designed to receive mouse, touch pad, or keyboard input from the user. You'll learn how to add *CheckBox* and *RadioButton* controls to a page, and how to process click input with Visual Basic program code.

Add a check box to the page

1. On the Visual Studio File menu, click New Project.

   The New Project dialog box opens.

2. In the Visual Basic template group, click the Blank App (XAML) project.

3. In the Name text box, type **My Click Input**.

   Visual Studio assigns the name My Click Input to your project. I selected this name because you will be adding both a check box and radio buttons to the page.

4. Click OK to create the new project in Visual Studio.

   Visual Studio opens a new programming project with a blank application template.

5. Open Solution Explorer if it is not currently visible, and then double-click the file *MainPage .xaml*.

   Visual Studio opens *MainPage.xaml* in the Designer window.

6. Open the Toolbox, and double-click the *CheckBox* control.

   You'll find the *CheckBox* control in the Common XAML Controls category. When you double-click *CheckBox*, Visual Studio creates a XAML check box object on the page in the upper-left corner, as shown here:

   In the Code Editor below, Visual Studio also inserts the XAML markup for a new check box object into your project.

7. Drag the check box object to a more central location on the page.

8. In the Properties window, set the *Name* property for the check box object to **CheckBox1**.

   Now you'll create a text box object on the form next to the check box.

9. Open the Toolbox again and double-click the *TextBox* control.

10. Drag the text box object to the right of the check box object, adjust the width of the text box so that it is about three times longer than the check box, and then set the *Name* property of the text box to **TextBox1**.

Notice that helpful alignment indicators appear when you place one object next to another on the page.

11. In the Properties window, delete the current contents of the text box object by clearing its *Text* property and pressing Enter.

12. Click the check box object again and set its *Content* property to **Date**.

The *Content* property is like the *Text* property—it indicates what text is displayed in the object when the program runs.

Fine-tune the objects on your page so that they look like this:

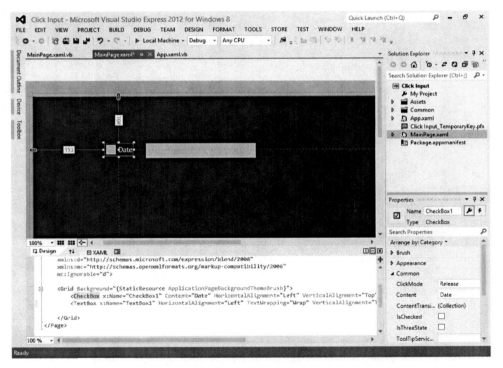

13. With the check box object selected, return to the Properties window, and click the Event Handler button (the lightning bolt) near the *Name* text box.

The Event Handler button displays the events that your check box can respond to. The Properties window offering the various options looks like this:

As you may recall from Chapter 2, an event handler is a named procedure of Visual Basic program code that exists in a code-behind file associated with your user interface. Event handlers manage user input and other transactions that take place while your program is running.

You create an event handler for a particular event by double-clicking the text box next to the event in the Properties window. Most of the time, you'll write an event handler for the *Checked* or *Click* events when using check boxes, although there are also more sophisticated (and obscure) options available to you. In this exercise, you'll write an event handler for the *Click* event of the check box.

14. Double-click the text box next to the *Click* event in the Properties window.

Visual Studio inserts an event handler named *CheckBox1_Click* in the *Click* text box, and opens the *MainPage.xaml.vb* code-behind file in the Code Editor. Since you have not yet saved or compiled the project, the *CheckBox1* object name in the event handler may appear underlined, but that will change shortly.

15. Type the following Visual Basic program statements into the Code Editor between the *Private Sub* and *End Sub* statements:

```
If CheckBox1.IsChecked Then
    TextBox1.Text = System.DateTime.Today
Else
    TextBox1.Text = ""
End If
```

Your Code Editor will look like the following when you are finished:

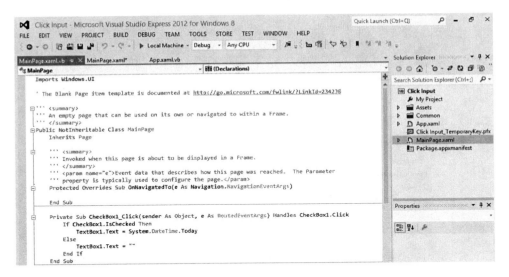

Here are a few notes about the Visual Basic statements that you have just typed. (For a complete introduction to Visual Basic code syntax, see Chapter 6, "Visual Basic Language Elements.")

First, the five lines you entered are referred to in programming circles as an *If...Then...Else* code block—a decision structure that evaluates one or more conditions and takes a course of action based on the result. This event handler is executed when the user clicks the Date check box in the program, firing the *Click* event. But you really can't know whether the user is adding a check mark or clearing a check mark unless you test to see whether the box is checked or not. You do this with the following statement:

```
If CheckBox1.IsChecked Then
```

The *IsChecked* property contains a *Boolean value* (that is, a yes or no value). When you test this value and discover that the box is checked, the event procedure will copy the current date to the text box on the page. On the other hand, if you examine *IsChecked* and discover that there is no longer a check mark there, then the event procedure copies an empty string—signified by an empty quotation (" ")—to the text box on the page.

The current date is gathered by using the *System.DateTime.Today* property. Since my computer is configured to display the date format customary in North America, the example that I show will be in *xx/xx/xxxx* format (in other words, month/day/year). You will see something different if you are running this program with different system settings.

Now you'll save and run the program to see how your new check box works.

16. Click the Save All command on the File menu to save your additions to the program.

Specify the *My Documents\Start Here! Programming in Visual Basic\Chapter 03* folder for your project. Notice that after you save the project, the underlined object names in the Code Editor are no longer flagged as errors.

17. Click the Start Debugging button on the Standard toolbar.

The My Click Input program compiles and runs. A Date check box and an empty text box appear on the page.

18. Click the Date check box.

Your program places a check mark in the check box and runs the *CheckBox1_Click* event procedure, and your Visual Basic code displays the current date in the text box. Your screen should look something like this:

19. Click the Date check box again.

Visual Studio removes the check mark and runs the *CheckBox1_Click* event procedure a second time. This time, the *Else* clause of the *If...Then...Else* decision structure is executed, and since the check box is no longer checked, an empty string is copied to the text box object.

You can follow these same programming steps to add any number of check boxes to your user interface.

20. Experiment with the check box a few more times, and then end the My Click Input program.

Now you'll add a few radio buttons to your project. Radio buttons are similar to check boxes in that they receive click input from the user; however, radio buttons are mutually exclusive—when you select one radio button in a group, the other radio buttons are cleared.

Add radio buttons to a page

1. Display the *MainPage.xaml* file again in the Designer window, if it is not currently visible.

2. Open the Toolbox, and then double-click the *TextBlock* control.

   Visual Studio adds a text block object to the upper-left corner of the page.

3. Drag the new text block below the Date check box and set its *Text* property to **Select text color:**. In the Text category, set the *FontSize* property for the text block to **16**.

4. Open the Toolbox again, and then double-click the *RadioButton* control.

   You'll find the *RadioButton* control in the Common XAML Controls category. When you double-click *RadioButton*, Visual Studio places a XAML radio button object on the page in the upper-left corner.

5. Create two more radio buttons in the same way, and then drag all three button objects to a central location on the page beneath the Date check box and the first text box.

   Your screen should look like the following. In addition to the button locations, notice the XAML code that also appears in the Code Editor for the *RadioButton* controls.

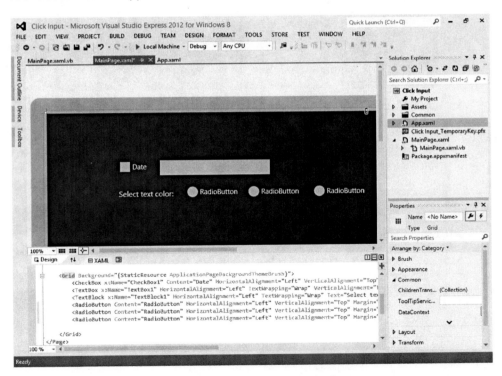

Now you'll set a few important properties for the new radio buttons.

6. Click the first radio button, set its *Name* property to **RadioButton1**, its *GroupName* property to **Color**, and its *Content* property to **Red**.

The familiar *Name* property allows you to reference the button object individually in program code. However, the *GroupName* property, used here for the first time, allows you to organize all three radio buttons into a group. This is the secret for connecting the buttons so that they work in a mutually exclusive fashion—when one is selected, the others are not, just like an old-fashioned in-dash car radio. Finally, the *Contents* property is set to *Red* because you'll use this radio button to set the text in the "Select text color:" text block to red if it is selected.

Now you'll adjust property settings for the remaining buttons.

7. Click the second radio button, set its *Name* property to **RadioButton2**, its *GroupName* property to **Color**, and its *Contents* property to **Blue**.

8. Click the third radio button, set its *Name* property to **RadioButton3**, its *GroupName* property to **Color**, and its *Contents* property to **Yellow**.

The *GroupName* property for these objects remains the same (*Color*), but the buttons have their own unique names and *Content* properties.

9. Adjust the spacing now among the radio button objects to make them a little closer together.

Your page should look like this:

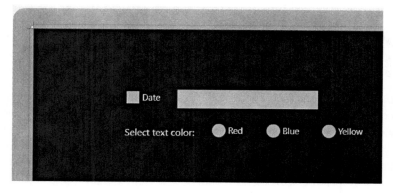

Now you'll add the Visual Basic program code to change the foreground color in the text block object based on the user's selection in the radio button group. To accomplish this task, you'll name the text block object and write three event handlers for the *Checked* events in the radio buttons.

10. Select the text block object on the page (the element containing the string "Select text color:") and return to the Properties window.

11. Set the *Name* property of the text block object to **TextBlock1**.

12. Now select the first radio button, and in the Properties window, click the Event Handler button to display the list of events for the radio button object.

13. Double-click the text box next to the *Checked* event text box in the Properties window.

Visual Studio inserts the event handler title *RadioButton1_Checked* in the *Checked* text box, and then opens the *MainPage.xaml.vb* code-behind file in the Code Editor.

14. Type the following Visual Basic code between the *Private Sub* and *End Sub* statements (press Enter after you type the line):

```
TextBlock1.Foreground = New SolidColorBrush(Colors.Red)
```

This program statement changes the color of text in the *TextBlock1* object to red. The *TextBlock1* object is the label on your application's main page. The text color is controlled by the *Foreground* property, which you can also set using the Properties window.

The color red is applied to the text block in an interesting way. Red, along with the many brush colors that you learned about when experimenting with the *Ellipse* control, is actually a hexadecimal value that is located in the *Colors* class within the Windows Runtime API. So, rather than specifying a specific numeric value for the color red, you can create a new brush color for the text box by using the *New* keyword, the *SolidColorBrush* class, the *Colors* class, and the *Red* value (or property) within the *Colors* class.

After you type in the program statement, Visual Studio underlines the *Colors* class with a jagged blue line indicating that it does not recognize the *Colors* name. You've seen this before—when Visual Studio does not recognize something that you type, the IDE highlights it and encourages you to address the problem. However, this particular syntax error arises because you have not yet included information about where to find *Colors.Red* in the .NET Framework's vast collection of features. The information is located in a special library of classes known as the *Windows.UI* namespace.

A *namespace* is a hierarchical library of classes organized under a unique name. By default, Windows 8 applications automatically include a reference to most of the common namespaces that they will need to accomplish their work. However, you can also reference individual namespaces by placing an *Imports* statement and the namespace name at the top of a Visual Basic code-behind file. This approach is necessary if there is some confusion about which class or feature you are using (sometimes there is more than one class with the same name), or if you want to define an *alias*, or shorthand notation, for a namespace reference that is lengthy and cumbersome.

> **Tip** For more information about using namespaces in the .NET Framework, see Chapter 8, "Using the .NET Framework."

15. Hold the mouse pointer over the *Colors* class until the red Error Correction Options button appears next to the bug.

Like the spelling checker in Microsoft Word, the Visual Studio IDE not only detects and highlights programming mistakes, but it helps you try to fix them.

16. Click the Error Correction Options button.

A summary of the problem and a list of potential fixes appears in the Code Editor. Your screen will look like this:

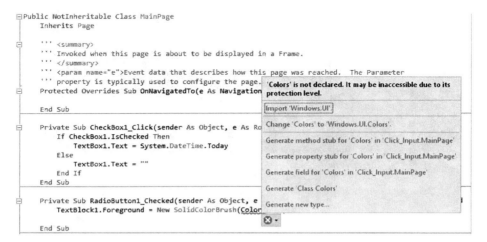

Selecting either the first or second option listed in this window will correct your problem. (Both indicate you need to reference the *Windows.UI* namespace.) However, you'll select the first option (adding an *Imports* statement to the code-behind file) because you'll be making several references to this resource.

17. Click the first option (Import 'Windows.UI') in the dialog box.

Visual Studio adds the statement *Imports Windows.UI* to the top of the code-behind file, and this fixes the problem. (The namespace needs to be defined before it can be used in the *MainPage* class, which defines the features of the user interface.)

Note that most *Imports* statements are made at the top of the code-behind file; however, you can also make project-wide imports if you specify them on the References tab of the Project Properties window.

Now the *Colors* issue has also been fixed in the code—it is no longer highlighted with that jagged blue line indicating an error. Your Code Editor will look like the following (I've scrolled up so that you can see the *Imports* statement):

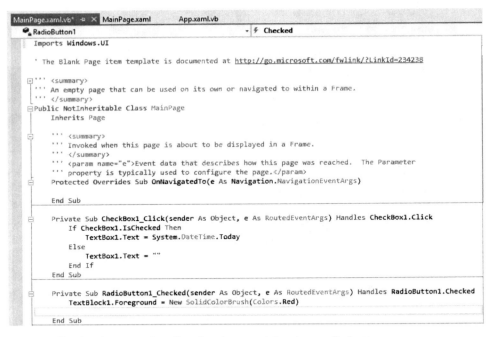

Now you'll write the event handlers for the remaining two radio buttons.

18. In Solution Explorer, double-click the *MainPage.xaml* file name to display the page in the Designer window again.

19. Click the second radio button (Blue), open the Properties window, click the Event Handler button, and double-click the *Checked* event text box.

    Visual Studio opens the *RadioButton2_Checked* event handler in the Code Editor.

20. Type the following program statement for the event handler and press Enter when finished.

```
TextBlock1.Foreground = New SolidColorBrush(Colors.Blue)
```

This statement is almost identical to the event handler for the first radio button. The only difference is the *Blue* color value. Notice also that when you enter the *Colors* class this time, Visual Studio recognizes it and does not indicate a syntax error. The IDE now knows that the *Colors* class is a member of the *Windows.UI* namespace.

 Tip When you are working with nearly identical program statements in the Code Editor (like the two previous statements), you can copy and paste code from one procedure to the next (and then make your edits) to save time.

21. Now return to the Designer window and use the Properties window to create a *Checked* event handler for the third radio button.

22. When the *RadioButton3_Checked* event handler appears in the Code Editor, enter the following statement:

```
TextBlock1.Foreground = New SolidColorBrush(Colors.Yellow)
```

Again, the only difference between this program statement and the previous two is the color value *Yellow*. Now you're finished entering program code for the My Click Input program.

23. Click the Save All command on the File menu to save your additions to the program.

24. Click the Start Debugging button to compile and run the project.

The My Click Input program starts and the user input tools appear on the application page, including your new radio buttons.

25. Click the Date check box.

Visual Studio places a check mark in the check box and displays the current date in the text box. Now you'll experiment with the three radio buttons that adjust the text color in the text block object. (What you see on the screen will look more distinctive than what I can show you in the printed book.)

26. Click the Red button.

The *RadioButton1_Checked* event handler changes the text block's foreground color to red. Your screen should look like this:

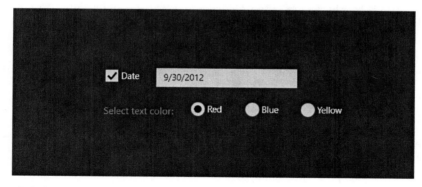

27. Click the Blue button.

The *RadioButton2_Checked* event handler changes the text to blue.

28. Click the Yellow button.

The *RadioButton3_Checked* event handler changes the text to yellow.

29. Test the program thoroughly by removing the check mark from the Date text box and selecting the three colors in different combinations.

30. When you're finished, exit the My Click Input project.

If you want to continue experimenting, you can go back into the event handlers and try setting the text block's *Foreground* property to different colors or adjusting different color characteristics in the application.

31. When you're finished working with My Click Input, click the Close Project command on the File menu to close the application.

You've learned how to process user input with check boxes and radio buttons. You've also learned to process input selections by writing program statements in event handlers, and you've fixed a few programming mistakes with the error-detection and error-correction tools in the Visual Studio IDE. Now you'll learn to add interest to your application with the *MediaElement* control.

Using the *MediaElement* Control to Add Music and Video

Windows 8 applications should be designed to be interesting and fun, as well as practical and secure. The *MediaElement* control in the XAML Toolbox allows you to create programs that are both entertaining and eminently useful. *MediaElement* opens and plays audio and video files in a program, and offers users numerous properties and methods to help you control media playback. As of this writing, Windows 8 programmers are using the *MediaElement* control to play background music, display video clips in applications, launch training videos, organize or distribute media files, play custom sounds, manage audio annotations, and much more.

Once you become familiar with *MediaElement* and playing basic audio and video files, you can expand your learning by exploring the many properties and methods that *MediaElement* has to offer. Since the majority of modern laptops, tablet devices, and desktop computers have the ability to record audio and video files through built-in hardware components, the ability to work with media files in a program has become fairly standard.

Thinking about Media Files

Before you get started, it might be useful to learn a little bit about the internal format of your audio or video files and the overall size of the files that you are working with.

Audio and video files are stored electronically in a variety of formats, and some of the proprietary ones (such as Apple iTunes) are not supported by the Visual Studio *MediaElement* control. This limitation might seem frustrating, but it is part of the business strategy for many companies and their interest in protecting media files from being distributed illegally. However, a large number of audio and video formats are supported by *MediaElement*, and in the cases where certain media files are not supported, there are often software tools on the market that will help you convert media from one file format to another.

As of this writing, the current list of audio and video formats supported in Windows 8 applications include MPEG-4 (*.3g2, .3gp2, .3gp, .3gpp, .m4a, .m4v, .mp4v, .mp4, .mov*), MPEG-2 (*.m2ts*), ASF (*.asf, .wm, .wmv*), ADTS (*.aac, .adt, .adts*), MP3 (*.mp3*), WAV (*.wav*), AVI (*.avi*), and AC-3 (*.ac3, .ec3*). For more information about the list of valid media formats, you can search for "Supported audio and video formats (Windows 8 style apps)" on MSDN (*http://msdn.microsoft.com*).

High-resolution video files present additional problems for software developers. These files can be encoded in unusual ways, and they are often very large and cumbersome to work with (a gigabyte in size and larger), making it tricky to distribute applications with large video resources. However, there are typically alternatives to packaging giant video files in a project. For example, you can edit the longer video files into smaller (concise) video clips, you can lower the resolution of video files, and you can also design your application so that it runs video resources from the network or the web, rather than embedding the files in your project. In short, thinking about media format and media size issues is an important part of the planning for applications that will use media files.

Beyond these basic considerations, however, the process for using media files in an application is quite simple. In the following exercise, you'll learn how to play an audio file in a Visual Basic program using the *MediaElement* control. Later in the chapter, you'll learn how to use the same skills to load and play a video file.

Play audio media with the *MediaElement* control

1. On the Visual Studio File menu, click New Project.

   The New Project dialog box opens.

2. Click the Blank App (XAML) project template and type **My Media Sample** in the Name text box.

3. Click OK to create the new project in Visual Studio.

   Visual Studio opens the new project with a blank application template.

4. Double-click the file *MainPage.xaml* in Solution Explorer.

   Visual Studio opens *MainPage.xaml* in the Designer window.

5. Open the Toolbox, open the All XAML Controls category, and double-click the *MediaElement* control.

   Visual Studio places a new media player object in the upper-left corner of the application page. Like other new objects in the Designer, you can now move the object to a new location and customize it with property settings. However, the *MediaElement* control is essentially a behind-the-scenes tool; it is not visible to the user unless the control is displaying a video clip (which will be covered in second example, not the first). For now, you can leave the media element object where it is.

The *Source* property of the *MediaElement* control specifies the name of the media file that will be loaded into the control for playback. However, before you can assign this property in the Properties window, you need to add one or more valid media files to the Assets folder for your application.

The Assets folder is visible in Solution Explorer. The typical contents of this folder include a logo for your application, a splash screen, and other artwork that is part of your project. A selection of default (placeholder) files were created in the Assets folder for your program when you created the new project in Visual Studio. You will add an audio file to this folder now.

6. Right-click the Assets folder in Solution Explorer to display a helpful shortcut menu of Visual Studio commands.

7. Point to the Add command, and then click Existing Item.

8. In the Add Existing Item dialog box, browse to the *My Documents\Start Here! Programming in Visual Basic\Chapter 03* folder and click Electro Sample, an MP3 file containing electronic music created by Henry Halvorson.

   You may also be able to locate valid audio files on your system in the Libraries category, in the My Music folder.

9. Click Add to add the music file to your project in the Assets folder.

   Visual Studio inserts the file, and it appears now in Solution Explorer under Assets, as shown in the following illustration:

   Now you're ready to assign this music asset to the Source property of the media element object.

10. Click the media element object in the Designer window, and then open the Properties window.

11. Change the *Name* property to **MediaElement1**.

12. Expand the Media category, scroll down to the *Source* property, and click the Source list box.

Your new media file (*Electro Sample.mp3*) appears in the list.

13. Click the media file to link it to the media element object.

In the Properties window are a few other important properties that you can adjust during the design phase of your project. *AutoPlay* is typically not necessary (most MP3 files play automatically when loaded into the media player), but you can force autoplay with this check box if necessary. The *Position* property specifies the location within the media file where playback will begin—very useful if there is a specific moment in the file you want to begin at. The *IsLooping* property is a Boolean value that allows you to run the media file over and over again if you like. Finally, *Volume* allows you to set an initial volume level for the media playback, which you can adjust with property settings in an event handler while the program is running, if you like.

Now you're ready to save and run the project.

14. Click the Save All command on the File menu to save your project, and specify the *My Documents\Start Here! Programming in Visual Basic\Chapter 03* folder.

15. Click Start Debugging on the toolbar.

The My Media Sample application runs, and immediately the selected audio file begins to play. However, since the *MediaElement* control has no user interface to interact with, you'll see nothing but a blank screen. The "Electro Sample" song simply runs until it is complete (a little less than a minute), and then the program waits for you to terminate it.

It is this easy to play music or any recorded sound sample in your application. But you can also control the playback by using a few interesting properties and methods provided by the control. Let's give them a try.

16. Close the Media Sample program.

In the following exercise, you'll add Play, Pause, Stop, and Mute buttons to the program.

Use *Button* controls to manage playback

1. Use the *Button* control in the Toolbox to add four *Button* controls to the top of the user interface page in the Designer.

2. Set the *Name* properties for the button objects to **PlayButton**, **PauseButton**, **StopButton**, and **MuteButton**, respectively.

3. Set the *Content* properties for the button objects to **Play**, **Pause**, **Stop**, and **Mute**, respectively.

Your new button objects should look like this when you're finished:

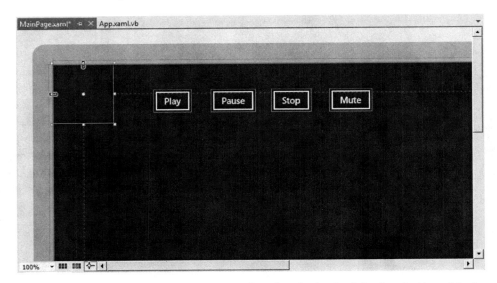

Now you'll write one-line Visual Basic event handlers for each of the four button objects.

4. Click the *PlayButton* object, open the Properties window, and then click the Event Handler (lightning bolt) button to see the list of event handlers for the *Button* control.

5. Double-click the text box next to the *Click* event to create a new event handler.

6. Enter the following line of Visual Basic program code:

```
MediaElement1.Play()
```

This line uses the *Play* method of the *MediaElement* control to play the loaded media file at the current play position. If the media file has been paused, the *Play* method will cause it to resume. If the media file has been stopped, the *Play* method will cause it to start again at the beginning.

Now you'll repeat similar steps with each of the remaining buttons, creating event handlers with appropriate methods or properties for each action.

7. Return to the Designer and click the Pause button.

8. In the Properties window, double-click the text box next to the *Click* event and type the following line of code into the *PauseButton_Click* event handler:

```
MediaElement1.Pause()
```

This line uses the *Pause* method to pause the loaded media file at the current play position. This feature can be used to give users some control as they listen to music or watch video.

9. Return to the Designer and click the Stop button.

10. In the Properties window, double-click the text box next to the *Click* event and type the following line of code into the *StopButton_Click* event handler:

```
MediaElement1.Stop()
```

This line uses the *Stop* method to end audio or video playback. Different from the *Pause* method, which temporarily stops playback but retains the current position in the track, the *Stop* method ends playback. If you execute the *Play* method after the *Stop* method, playback will begin again, but at the start of the media file.

11. Return to the Designer and click the Mute button.

12. In the Properties window, double-click the text box next to the *Click* event and type the following code:

```
MediaElement1.IsMuted = Not MediaElement1.IsMuted
```

This line uses the Boolean *IsMuted* property to mute or unmute audio playback. The statement uses the *Not* operator to switch, or toggle, the current value of *IsMuted*. If playback is currently muted, the statement will remove the muting effect. If playback is currently unmuted, the statement will mute playback.

13. Click the Save All command on the File menu to save your changes.

Now you'll run the program again to see how the four playback controls work.

14. Click Start Debugging on the toolbar.

The My Media Sample application runs, and the selected audio file begins to play. Your screen should look like this:

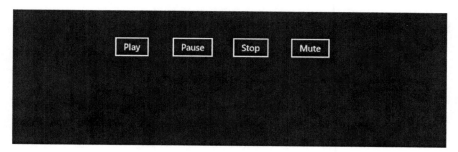

15. After a few moments of electronic music, click the Pause button.

The song pauses at the current playback position.

16. Click the Play button.

    Audio playback resumes right where you left off.

17. Click the Mute button.

    The music is muted (volume is temporarily set to 0), but playback continues.

18. After a few moments, click the Mute button again.

    The original volume setting is restored, and you'll be able to hear music again. However, you may notice that the song has advanced, and if you wait too long, the song will end. In other words, the Mute button is different from the Pause button. Although both stop the music, with Mute playback continues. (The effect is much more obvious when you are playing a video.)

19. Click the Stop button.

    Audio playback terminates.

20. Click the Play button.

    The electronic music file begins again, but at the beginning of the song.

21. Continue experimenting with the playback controls you just created. When you're finished, quit the program.

As you can see, the *MediaElement* control not only allows you to play audio files, but it provides you with interesting methods and properties to control what happens during playback. You can create buttons and other features that let the user to control what is happening, or you can control playback behind the scenes in event handlers—playing audio tracks only when you want them to be played.

In the following exercise, you'll make a few simple changes to the My Media Sample project so that it plays a video file rather than an audio file.

Play video media with the *MediaElement* control

1. Display Solution Explorer, and then right-click the Assets folder to display the shortcut menu.

2. Point to the Add command, and then click Existing Item.

3. In the Add Existing Item dialog box, browse to the *My Documents\Start Here! Programming in Visual Basic\Chapter 03* folder and click Merry-go-round, a video file in WAV format created for this book by Henry Halvorson.

    You may also be able to locate valid video files on your system in the Libraries category, in the My Videos folder.

4. Click Add to add the video file to the project's Assets folder.

   Visual Studio inserts the file, and you should be able to see it in Solution Explorer. Now you'll replace the reference to the audio file from the last exercise with the video file that you just added.

5. Click the media player element again in the Designer, and then open the Properties window.

6. In the Properties window, expand the Media category, scroll down to the *Source* property, and click the Source list box.

7. Click the new video file you just added to link it to the media element object.

   Now your video file is ready to run, but the size of your media element object on the page is not large enough to display the file. For the audio file example, you simply used the default *MediaElement* control that the Toolbox created on the page, but now the object needs to be larger.

   The screen size that you set is ultimately up to you, and you'll want to think about how the size you choose looks on a variety of device types, including desktop computers, laptops, and tablets. An additional consideration is the resolution of the video that you want to display. Typically, lower-resolution videos will look better in smaller playback windows, and they usually have smaller file sizes (a benefit for distribution). Higher-resolution videos (such as those in HD format) can provide superb video quality, but they can also be cumbersome to distribute with your projects if they are too large. (Consider the challenges of distributing a 2 GB file with your project!) For this reason, professional video-editing tools have numerous commands and features relating to video quality, format, and compression. If you plan to use a lot of video in your projects, you'll need to invest time and money in video-editing software to get the best results.

8. Display the Designer window and move the media element object below the four button objects you created in the previous exercise.

9. Increase the size of the media element object so that it takes up about one-quarter of the screen. You can fine-tune the size after you run the program.

   Now you're ready to test the application.

10. Click the Save All command on the File menu to save the changes to your project.

11. Click Start Debugging on the toolbar.

    The My Media Sample application runs, and the selected video file begins to play in the window you moved and resized. The media playback controls you created will work just as they did for the audio file, with the caveat that now you'll have both video and audio. (The *Merry-go-round* file contains an original audio track to accompany the slow movement of the merry-go-round at a local park.)

Your screen should look something like this:

12. Experiment with the Pause, Play, Stop, and Mute buttons in the project.

The *MediaElement* control is designed to work with both audio and video files, so the program's event handlers manage your playback requests with no code changes. This particular media file was edited with Windows Movie Maker.

13. When you're finished, close the project.

You can also experiment with additional audio or video files on your computer. Or you can modify the program to use additional methods or properties of the *MediaElement1* object. (Trying your own experiments is half the fun of Visual Basic programming!)

14. When you're finished working with the program, close the project.

You're finished working with the Visual Studio XAML Toolbox in this chapter.

Summary

In this chapter, you explored some of the useful controls in the Visual Studio Toolbox. Specifically, you worked with XAML controls designed for Windows 8 applications and the Windows 8 user interface. As you learned in Chapter 2, the basic steps to follow when you add controls to a Visual Basic project include moving the controls from the Toolbox to the page (where they become objects), resizing and placing the objects so that they have the proper design, adjusting property settings for the objects to control how they function, and then writing Visual Basic event handlers to handle user input and other programming tasks.

In this chapter, you learned how to use the *Ellipse* and *TextBlock* controls to explore some of the advanced graphics and display capabilities of Windows 8, and you learned how to use the *CheckBox* and *RadioButton* controls to receive input from the user. You also learned how to use *If...Then...Else* decision structures and other Visual Basic statements to handle the mouse in event handlers. As part of this process, you learned how to use the *Imports* statement to reference a namespace where common Windows programming resources are located, and you learned how to fix basic coding mistakes and use error-correction tools while working in the Code Editor.

Finally, you learned how easy it is to integrate quality audio and video media into your application with the *MediaElement* control. Visual Studio 2012 makes adding audio and video as easy as it has ever been for programmers. However, you do need to think carefully about how you will capture, edit, and distribute your audio and video files if you choose to publish your applications.

In Chapter 4, "Designing Windows 8 Applications with Blend for Visual Studio," you'll learn much more about creating effective user interfaces in Windows 8 applications. You'll get started with the powerful Blend for Visual Studio programming tool, which streamlines many of the typical tasks of designing a user interface and opens up new design possibilities for software development teams.

Designing Windows 8 Applications with Blend for Visual Studio

After completing this chapter, you'll be able to

- Open Blend and explore the Blend Artboard and design tools.

- Use Blend to add controls to a page and enhance the look of Windows 8 applications.

- Create a storyboard in Blend to add basic animation effects to a user interface.

- Write event handlers in Microsoft Visual Studio to run animation effects.

YOUR VISUAL STUDIO EXPRESS 2012 SOFTWARE installation includes an application named Blend for Microsoft Visual Studio 2012, which provides additional features and design tools for creating the user interface for a Windows 8 application. Although it is possible to create Microsoft Visual Basic programs entirely in Visual Studio (and you've learned the basic procedures for doing this), more comprehensive programming projects typically require more planning and design work before the actual coding takes place.

Often, software development teams will add a user interface design tool like Blend into the software development process, or *life cycle*, because it allows the graphics and visual effects for an application to be created by one team (using Blend) and the programming logic to be created by another team (using Visual Basic). This can be advantageous not only as a way to efficiently distribute the workload, but because different team members may have different professional skills (that is, programmers may not always be the best designers). Whether you write programs on your own or as part of a development team, Blend for Visual Studio can help you to rapidly customize the design of your applications.

This chapter provides an overview of the Blend for Visual Studio software. You'll explore using Blend to construct the user interface for a program that displays digital artwork on a page. You'll also see how to start Blend and navigate through the Blend Artboard and design tools, and how to add interesting design effects to your user interfaces, such as digital images and animation. Along the way, you'll discover that Blend is tightly integrated into the Visual Studio IDE, so you can open a project in Visual Studio, add controls and other visual effects in Blend, and then return to Visual Studio to write the code-behind files in Visual Basic—all in one programming session. Moving forward, you can construct the user interfaces for your Visual Basic programs in the Visual Studio designer, Blend, or a combination of both.

Blend for Visual Studio

Blend for Visual Studio (Blend 5.0) is a new version of the Microsoft Expression Blend software application—a design tool for creating visually distinctive user interfaces based on Windows and Microsoft Silverlight. In Blend, you design your application visually, drawing shapes and controls on the design surface, called the *Artboard*, and then you adjust their appearances using property settings. You can import images, video, and sounds into your application, and you can also create *storyboards* that animate the visual or audio elements of your design.

Why Blend Is Useful for Visual Studio Developers

As you've learned, Visual Studio 2012 is a comprehensive development tool for building Windows 8 applications from start to finish. Using the Visual Studio IDE, you can design your application's user interface, add program logic with Visual Basic code, run and test your program, and even package your project for the Windows Store—all in one place. However, in larger software development contexts—for example, when you work with a team of software developers to design and build an application—it is more common to spread out the workload, and to break the development process into discrete steps involving personnel with different skills and experiences.

Visual Studio 2012 has been built with this division of labor in mind. Product *designers* can generate ideas, produce a prototype, and build the program's user interface with tools in Visual Studio or Blend, and then experienced *programmers* can add their source code to the project and test the application to make sure that it is fully functional.

From a technical standpoint, this division of labor is made possible because both Visual Studio and Blend create the user interface for a Windows 8 application in files containing XAML markup. Since the XAML documents defining the user interface are structured in a systematic way (you'll learn more about this in Chapter 5, "Working with XAML"), you can edit them using a variety of design tools. So, while one designer is working on the user interface in Blend or Visual Studio, another developer can be busy writing the internal logic of the application in Visual Basic, including the event handlers that will run when the user interacts with various controls in the user interface. For this multiperson development process to work, of course, all team members need to be working on the same design with agreed-upon controls and user interface elements. Such a design can be discussed or written-up rather informally, or specified with precision by using a prototyping tool such as Microsoft SketchFlow. (In fact, the SketchFlow application is included in some retail versions of Visual Studio.)

With the release of Windows 8, an operating system that places a premium on user interface design and rich interaction with the user through consistent gestures and features, it is important to think carefully about how the user interface for your application will be constructed. In this chapter, you'll learn how Blend can be a helpful tool to streamline many of your design tasks. In Chapter 7, "Controlling Application Design, Layout, and Program Flow," and Chapter 10, "Managing Data with Arrays and LINQ," I'll continue the discussion about the design of Windows 8 applications and the design guidelines for programs that run in the Windows 8 user interface.

Starting Blend

Blend for Visual Studio is installed as part of the Visual Studio Express 2012 for Windows 8 installation. In the following exercise, you'll start Blend and learn how to open a new project and explore the IDE.

Open a new project in Blend

1. On the Windows Start screen, click Blend for Visual Studio.

    When Blend starts, you see the Blend user interface, or IDE, on the screen, with its menus, tools, and component windows. This workspace is similar to the IDE in Visual Studio and a variety of development products.

    You will also see an open dialog box in the center of the screen with options for creating a new project or opening an existing project. A list of recent projects is also presented if you have used Blend before.

    The following screen depicts a typical Blend for Visual Studio setup. (I captured the screen at a resolution of 1024×768, which may be smaller than what you are using on your computer.)

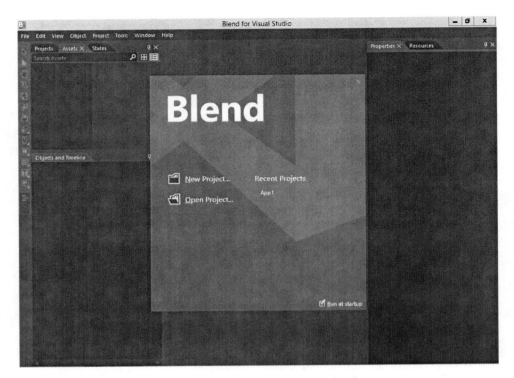

2. Click New Project to start building a new user interface in Blend.

The New Project dialog box appears, presenting options for a new HTML or XAML project, as the following screen shows:

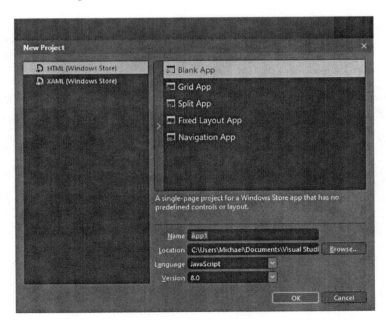

Both options are designed for building Windows 8 (or Windows Store) applications. You'll select XAML in this exercise, because you are building a Windows 8 application with XAML and Visual Basic. However, Blend also allows you to create a web-ready HTML user interface that you can customize with JavaScript code (a task that is beyond the scope of this book).

3. Click XAML (Windows Store) in the list box on the left.

   The options for XAML user interfaces appear in the dialog box.

4. Click Blank App (XAML) in the list box on the right, and then type **My Move the Chicken** in the Name text box.

   I've named this project Move the Chicken because it will display the digital photograph of a chicken on the page and then move it across the screen using animation.

5. Select the folder *My Documents\Start Here! Programming in Visual Basic\Chapter 04* in the Location text box.

6. Select Visual Basic in the Language text box.

   Your dialog box will look like this:

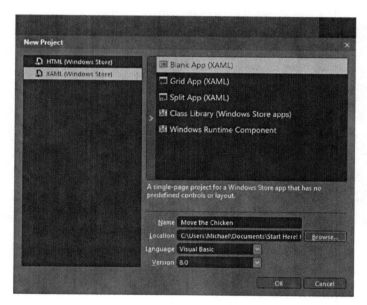

7. Click OK.

   Blend creates a new XAML/Visual Basic project in the Chapter 4 folder, complete with a solution file, various project files, several subfolders, and the other typical components of a Visual Studio programming project. The obvious difference here is that the *MainPage.xaml* page (that is, the page that defines the project's user interface) is loaded into Blend, not Visual Studio. After the new project loads, an assortment of panels and design tools also appear in the Blend IDE. In the following sections, you'll learn how these commands and features work.

Design Tools in the Blend IDE

Like Visual Studio, the Blend IDE presents a busy workspace containing numerous tools and features, as well as the user interface page that you are designing. In Blend parlance, the work surface containing the user interface page is called the Artboard, and when you have more than one page open in Blend, a Document tab at the top of the Artboard allows you to switch between the pages. The following illustration shows the Blend IDE with a new, blank page named *MainPage.xaml* on the Artboard, which is located in the middle of the screen. I selected the *Grid* object on the page before capturing this screen so that the properties of the *Grid* object would also appear in the Properties window on the right side of the screen.

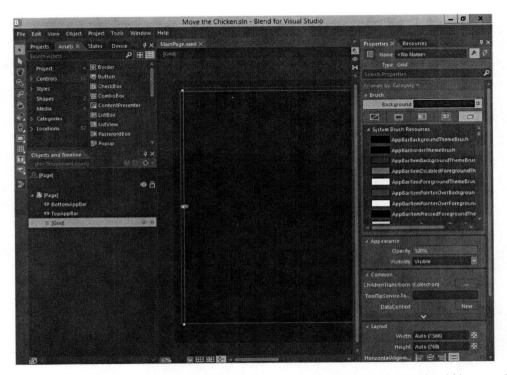

The Blend IDE shown here contains the following design tools, which you should become familiar with as you learn your way around the application. I'll be using the following tools and terms throughout the chapter:

- **Artboard**   A central design space containing the page or pages that will become the user interface of your program. The Artboard is currently in Design view now, but you can switch to XAML view or Split view by clicking the tiny icons in the upper-right corner of the Artboard.

- **Menus**   Context-sensitive menus at the top of the workspace that allow you to manage your project. Notice how the commands on the Object menu change as you select different elements in the page on the Artboard.

- **Panels** Tabbed windows containing design tools and other important commands and project settings. The panels currently visible now are Projects, Assets, States, Device, Objects And Timeline, Properties, and Resources. You can move the panels around the Blend IDE (or open and close them) just as you would in the Visual Studio IDE. (A list of the panels that are currently open appears on the Window menu.) A few panels, like Properties, are very similar to their equivalent panels in Visual Studio, while other panels offer entirely new design possibilities. For example, the Objects And Timeline panel allows you to add interesting transition effects and animations to your program's user interface.

- **Tools panel** A set of commonly used design tools that appears in a vertically oriented position on the left side of the Blend IDE. The Tools panel contains selection tools, view tools, brush and color tools, and tools for manipulating shapes, text objects, and typical controls. The final button in the Tools panel is named Assets, and it provides similar functionality to the Assets panel in the Blend IDE.

Note that the Blend IDE is fully customizable. You can move the panels and design tools around the workspace, or you can change the way that the various tools and features work by selecting the Options command on the Tools menu. You can also return the Blend IDE to its default layout by selecting the Reset Current Workspace command on the Window menu.

Now you'll practice creating an image object on the page in Blend by using the *Image* control.

Using XAML Controls in Blend

Since you have selected a new XAML application project, the controls that you can use to build your project are XAML controls. This is familiar ground, as you learned how to use several XAML controls in Chapter 2, "Creating Your First Windows 8 Application." The only real difference is that in Blend the XAML controls are located in the Assets panel, and they are organized in a slightly different way. But they are the same XAML controls that you will find in the Visual Studio 2012 Toolbox, and after the controls are placed on a page you can customize them with property settings and Visual Basic code.

In the following exercise, you'll be introduced to the *Image* control, which is used to display digital artwork, photographs, and other electronic images on a page.

Add an *Image* control to the page

1. Click the Assets panel so that it is visible in the Blend IDE (if it is not already visible).

   The Assets panel contains controls, styles, and other project resources organized by category. If you see a number next to a category in the Assets panel, it is an indication of how many items are contained within the category.

2. Click the Controls category, and then click the All subcategory.

   The names of several dozen XAML controls appear in the Assets list box.

3. Scroll down to the *Image* control and double-click it.

A new image object appears on the page in the Blend IDE. Like any new object on a page, you can move it from place to place or resize it. First, however, you'll load a piece of electronic art into the image object. The standard way to work with electronic art in a project like this is to load the art into the project's resource list first, so that it is available whenever you need it. (Often, the same piece of art is used more than once.) You'll load the electronic art now by using the Add Existing Item command on the Project menu.

4. Click Project | Add Existing Item.

You'll see the following dialog box:

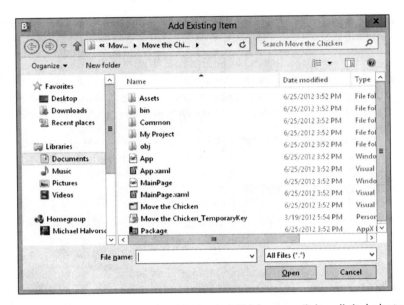

The file that I want you to load is named *Chicken.png* (it is a digital photograph of a chicken near my house), and you'll find the file in the *My Documents\Start Here! Programming in Visual Basic\Chapter 04* folder. (You are most welcome to load another file if you would like.)

5. Browse to the *Chicken.png* file, select it, and then click Open.

Visual Studio loads the file into the project, and it appears in the Projects panel below the application folder (*App.xaml*). The image artwork is now ready to be used in your project, and if you point to the *Chicken.png* file in the Projects panel, you'll see the following image:

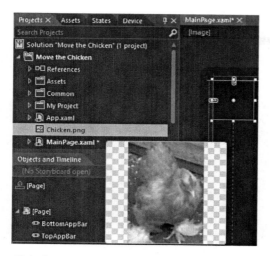

6. Click the image object on the page, and then open the Properties panel if it is not already open.

Although the Properties panel in Blend looks slightly different from the Properties window in Visual Studio, its functionality is essentially the same. You'll use the Properties panel now to set an important property for the image object—the *Source* property, which indicates what electronic image will fill the image object on the page.

7. In the Common category, click the drop-down list box arrow next to the *Source* property.

A list of electronic images appears in a list box, as shown in the following illustration. This list of items comes from the group of image resources associated with your project.

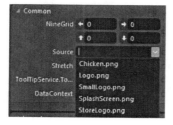

8. Click *Chicken.png*.

The chicken image appears in the image object on the page. Notice that the rectangular photo does not precisely match the square image object shape. You can either adjust the *Stretch* property of the image object to fix this or manually resize the image object on the page.

> **Tip** The *UniformToFill* setting of the *Stretch* property can be especially useful if you want to both fill the object entirely with your artwork and enlarge its size.

9. Enlarge the image object slightly and move it down toward the center of the page (but still on the left side), as shown in the following illustration.

You want to move the object down some because you are going to animate the object so that it moves up and to the right by using a storyboard a little later.

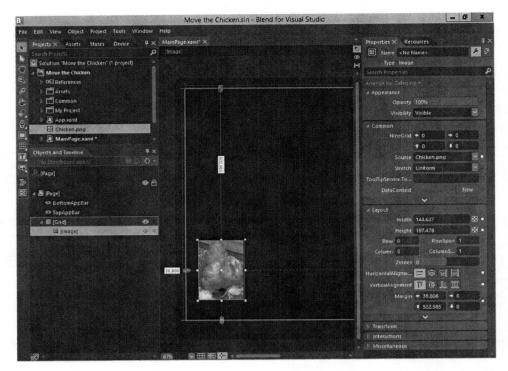

Now you'll change the *Name* property of the image object so that you can refer to the object in Visual Basic code.

10. Click the *Name* property in the Properties panel, change the property to **imageChicken**, and then press Enter.

11. Save your changes by clicking the Save All command on the File menu.

Now you'll add a *Button* control to the page so that you can run the chicken animation you'll create a little later.

Add a *Button* control to the page

1. Click the Assets panel again, open the Controls category, and then double-click the *Button* control.

   A button object appears in the upper-left corner of the page. The *Button* control works the same way in Blend as it does in the Visual Studio Designer. You'll use the *Button* control here to run the animation that you will be creating, so take a moment now to move and resize the button object, and set its *Content* and *Name* properties.

2. Change the *Content* property of the button object to **Move the Chicken**.

3. Move the object down and to the right slightly, so that it is not on the edge of the screen.

4. Set the *Name* property of the object to **btnMove**.

   Your button should now look like this:

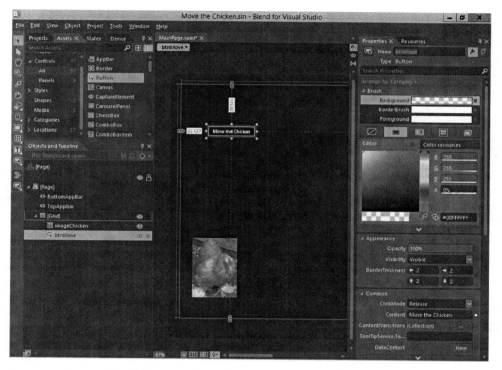

5. Save your changes by clicking the Save All command on the File menu.

   Now you'll create a storyboard to animate the image object.

Creating a Storyboard to Add Basic Animation Effects

The power of Blend for Visual Studio becomes apparent when you begin to add special effects to your user interface. In the following section, you'll learn how to put objects in motion in your user interface by using the storyboard feature. A storyboard in Blend is a special container that holds an animation timeline and various formatting effects for your project's user interface. In a storyboard, you specify *keyframes* on a timeline to indicate property changes for the objects on the form, such as where they are located or what shape or color they are. You can also adjust styles and other comprehensive settings in a project, such as the application's background color or texture.

Although it might sound complicated, animation effects are simply the rapid display of a series of images that collectively create the illusion of movement on a page. You create these visual transitions by using the storyboard feature in Blend, and then you return to Visual Studio to create event handlers that run the effects that you have created.

The Objects And Timeline panel in the Blend IDE allows you to create and edit storyboards. Blend also provides a special animation-editing mode called the *Animation workspace*, which gives you a little more space for your work with storyboards. You can switch from the Design workspace (the default view) to the Animation workspace by clicking the Window menu, pointing to the Workspaces submenu, and then clicking the Animation command. In the following exercise, you'll switch to Animation workspace mode and use the storyboard feature to create an animation that moves the image object across the screen when you click the button object.

Create a storyboard

1. Switch to the Animation workspace by selecting Window | Workspaces | Animation.

    The Blend IDE design tools and panes are reorganized slightly to give you more space on the Artboard for creating your animation.

2. Open the Objects And Timeline panel by selecting Window | Objects And Timeline.

    The active objects in your user interface appear in the Objects And Timeline panel, along with several buttons and tools that are useful for editing storyboards. The message "No Storyboard open" also appears near the top of the Objects And Timeline panel. (Two of the buttons that you will be using in this exercise, New and Close Storyboard, are located directly across from this message, and the drop-down menu indicator for the New button is visible.) Your screen should look like this:

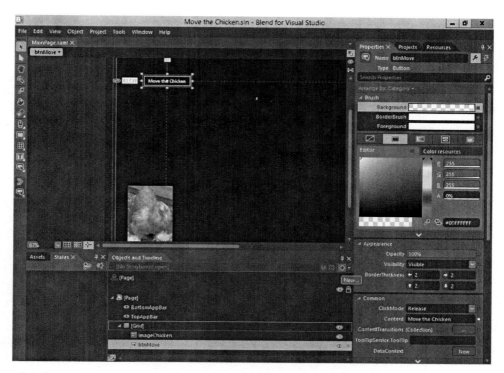

3. Click the New button in the Objects And Timeline panel.

Blend displays the Create Storyboard Resource dialog box, giving you an opportunity to name your storyboard. It is useful to type something related to the content of your animation here, so that you can use the name later in Visual Basic program code. Note that you can create more than one storyboard in an application if you want.

4. Type **DiagonalMovement** in the dialog box.

Your screen should look like this:

5. Click OK.

   Blend opens a new storyboard in the IDE. The message "DiagonalMovement timeline record-ing is on" appears at the top of the Artboard, and the Artboard is outlined in red. A timeline also appears in the Objects And Timeline panel, with vertical lines indicating seconds. A stopwatch feature is also visible above the timeline to give you an indication of where you are in the recording session. (The numbers 0:00.000 are currently visible.) Standard video playback buttons, including Go To First Frame, Go To Previous Frame, Playhead Position, Go To Next Frame, and Go To Last Frame, are also visible.

6. Click the image object on the page that currently contains the *Chicken.png* photo.

   Your screen should look like this:

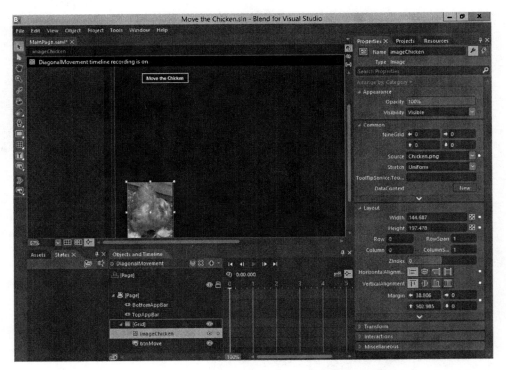

   The goal of this simple animation effect is to move the image object up and to the right, so that it appears to move diagonally when the user clicks the Move The Chicken button. Using the timeline in the Objects And Timeline panel, you can indicate how long you would like this diagonal movement to take by dragging the *play head* (the vertical yellow line) to one of the time points on the timeline. (Each vertical line indicates one second.)

7. Drag the play head to the 2-second point in the timeline. (To drag the play head, you need to click and drag the top of the play head.)

Your Objects And Timeline panel will now look like this:

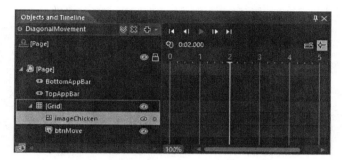

Notice that the time 0:02.000, indicating 2 seconds, now appears on the stopwatch. You can also specify times by highlighting the stopwatch and typing in the time values that you would like to use. (This feature is useful if you have very specific times that you need to hit in your animation sequences.)

Now you'll indicate the diagonal movement for the image object by adjusting the X and Y *Transform* properties in the Properties panel. You create the animation effect by specifying a beginning and ending point for the object, and specifying how long you want the transition to take (in this case, 2 seconds).

8. In the Properties panel, click the Transform category.

A number of very useful rendering effects appear in the Transform category panel. In this step, you'll adjust a *RenderTransform* effect by setting the *Translate* property. After you complete this exercise, you may want to come back to this area and experiment with the *Rotate*, *Scale*, *Skew*, and *Flip* properties, which allow you to move the selected object in two-dimensional and three-dimensional space. Although one type of storyboard animation involves movement, which we are experimenting with in this exercise, other types of storyboard animation allow you to transform or bend objects in ways that are quite compelling, especially if you combine the changes with color or brush effects.

9. In the Transform category, under *RenderTransform*, verify that the *Translate* tab is selected. Now type **300** in the X text box and **-300** in the Y text box, and then press Enter.

Your screen will look like this:

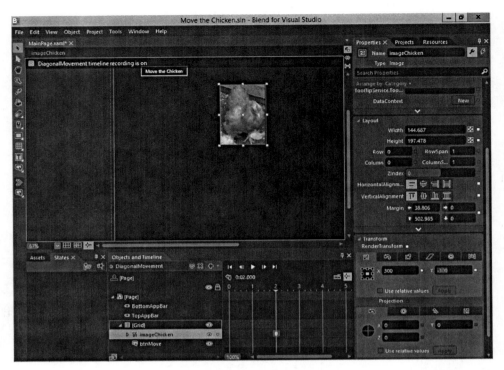

Notice that as you enter the x-coordinate and y-coordinate (which represent the distance in pixels from the original location of the image object), the image object also moves across the Artboard to the new location. The origin of this design surface is in the bottom-left corner of the page. This is why negative y-coordinate values move the object up.

In addition to the object moving on the Artboard, a subtle change also takes place on the timeline. At the 2-second mark, a keyframe icon appears on the *imageChicken* row, indicating that at that time in the storyboard, a property has changed for the selected object. A keyframe is a visual marker that a change has occurred; you add additional keyframes to a timeline by making property setting changes and clicking the Record Keyframe button to the left of the stopwatch in the Objects And Timelines panel.

Your storyboard is fairly simple now, but you might imagine a situation in which you have a number of objects on the page, and each is changing properties one or more times during an animation sequence. Keyframes allow you to manage and edit complex storyboards efficiently.

Your animation is now complete. You'll turn off recording mode now and test the animation that you have created.

10. Click the red dot to the left of the *DiagonalMovement* storyboard title, near the top of the Objects And Timeline panel.

Blend stops recording the storyboard, and the chicken image object returns to its original position on the page on the Artboard. At the top of the Artboard, the text "DiagonalMovement timeline recording is off" appears, indicating that the recording session is now over.

Now you'll run the animation effect.

Run and test a storyboard

1. Click the Play button in the Objects And Timeline panel to run the animation storyboard that you just created.

The tooltip for the Play button is visible in the following screen shot:

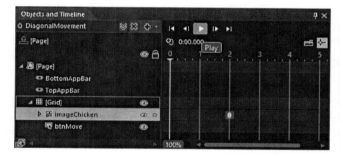

When you click Play, Blend shows the object movement as it will appear when you run the program. Over the course of 2 seconds, the chicken image drifts diagonally across the screen from left to right. When the effect is complete, your screen will look like this:

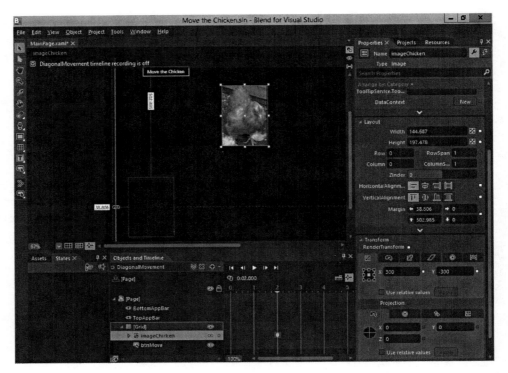

Notice that the original location of the image object is outlined on the page. You can now modify your storyboard if you like, changing the amount of time allowed for the transition, or perhaps the final location for the image object. If you drag the play head to the left, you can watch the image object slowly drift as it does during the animation. (The Go To Previous Frame and Go To Next Frame buttons also allow you to examine the transition frame by frame.)

If this were a more substantial development project, you might now continue recording additional effects, either for this particular image object or a few of the other objects on the page. Creating and testing storyboards is an iterative process that can take some time and may involve feedback from others.

2. Close the *DiagonalMovement* storyboard now by clicking the Close Storyboard button near the top of the Objects And Timeline panel.

The Close Storyboard button is to the left of the New button you used earlier in this exercise.

The storyboard closes and is removed from the Objects And Timeline panel. The image object returns to its original position on the page on the Artboard.

3. Save your changes by clicking the Save All command on the File menu.

The storyboard you created is complete, but it will not run in your application until you find some way to start, or *trigger*, the animation. In the following section, you'll return to Visual Studio and write an event handler to start the storyboard when you click the button object on your page. Writing an event handler in Visual Studio is required because Blend is primarily a design tool used for creating the user interface of an application. The actual logic required to control program execution still needs to be written in Visual Studio by using Visual Basic, C#, or another programming language.

Missing in Action: Blend Behaviors

Readers who have used Microsoft Expression Blend 4 (the previous version of Blend) to create Silverlight or Windows Presentation Foundation (WPF) applications might recall that it is possible to control storyboards from within Blend by using something called *behaviors*. These interactive actions allow you to trigger storyboards by connecting certain user actions, such as mouse clicks or mouse movements, to storyboard animations. (In Expression Blend 4, a list of useful behaviors such as *ControlStoryboardAction* are available in the Assets panel.)

However, behaviors are not currently supported in Blend for Visual Studio 2012 if you are creating XAML or HTML applications for Windows 8 and the Windows Store. Instead, you need to write event handlers in Visual Studio to launch storyboards—a straightforward technique that I will discuss next. It may be that Microsoft will add behaviors back into Blend for later releases; behaviors are useful features, especially for designers who want to control animations, and many in the Visual Studio development community (including this author) are hopeful they will return.

Writing Event Handlers in Visual Studio

As I noted at the beginning of this chapter, Blend creates new XAML projects for Windows 8 (Windows Store) applications in the same format as Visual Studio. This means that you can create a new project in Blend, and then open the project later in Visual Studio to edit or complete it. You can also switch back and forth between Blend and Visual Studio in one development session.

To prepare Blend for switching back and forth to Visual Studio, I recommend that you make a few adjustments to the Blend IDE settings before you start. These settings are especially useful for XAML projects that will be using event handler code, such as the routines that you will be writing in Visual Basic.

Complete the following steps to get ready.

Adjust Blend settings for XAML projects

1. Open the Options dialog box by selecting Tools | Options.

2. In the Options dialog box, select Project.

You will see a list of settings related to how your project is stored and how files are loaded or modified outside of Blend. The list of options may be slightly confusing, as it applies to XAML projects, HTML projects, and WPF and Silverlight files. (Only XAML projects for Windows 8 are discussed in this book.)

3. Make sure that there is a check mark in each of the first four check boxes. (By default, only the second option is selected.)

Your screen should look like this:

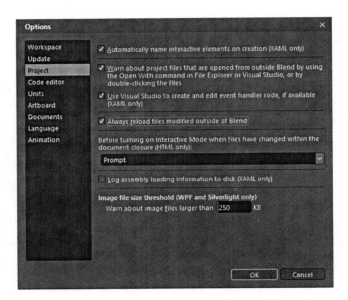

The first option forces Blend to give each new object that you create on a page a unique name so that it can be used later in Visual Basic event handlers. You may recall that you have typically adjusted the *Name* property for each new object that you planned to use later after creating it, and this check box helps with that task.

The second option forces Blend to warn you if it detects that any file in your project has been opened by a program other than Blend. This is not typically a security concern (for example, you may be editing some of the *.xaml* files or other resources from within Visual Studio), but it is a helpful precaution.

The third option requires Blend to open Visual Studio and use it to edit the event handlers for objects that are edited in Blend. (This happens, for example, if you open an event handler for an object in the Blend Properties panel.) I like this option because the Code Editor in Visual Studio has more features and functionality than the editor that you can open in Blend.

The fourth option forces Blend to reload files that have been modified outside of Blend. This is very helpful, because you may have used Visual Studio to edit the files since you last saw them in Blend, and you may want the most recent edits.

4.   Click OK, and you're ready to create your event handler in Visual Studio.

Although you could close Blend now and then start Visual Studio from the Start menu to add an event handler to the Move the Chicken solution, you'll open the Code Editor in the Blend IDE and see how Blend automatically starts Visual Studio.

Open and run the event handler

1.   Click the *btnMove* object on the page, and then open the Blend Properties panel.

2.   Click the Event Handlers button (the lightning bolt icon) near the top of the Properties panel to display the events available for the button object.

Your screen will look like this:

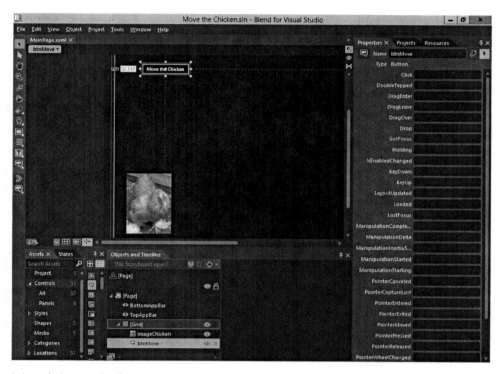

It is truly impressive how many events there are for developers to use as triggers for event handlers. In this case, you will be using the familiar *Click* event, but you could also use *DragOver*, *Drop*, *PointerEntered*, or any of a wide assortment of creative movements or gestures to begin your animation.

3. Double-click the *Click* event handler text box in the Properties panel.

   Blend places the event handler name *btnMove_Click* in the *Click* event handler text box, and then launches Visual Studio to create the event handler. A program icon for Visual Studio appears on the Windows taskbar.

4. Click the Visual Studio icon on the taskbar.

   Visual Studio opens and displays the Code Editor. The *btnMove_Click* event handler is loaded, and on the right side of the screen you'll see Solution Explorer, with the various files and folder for your active project. Welcome back to Visual Studio!

   The routine will run when the Move The Chicken button is clicked in the program. Accordingly, the event handler needs the name of the storyboard you created in Blend (*DiagonalMovement*) and an indication of what action you want to perform with the story-board. Essentially, you refer to the new storyboard container as an *object* in your program, and then you indicate what *method* (or programmatic action) you want to perform on the object. Fortunately, the Code Editor's IntelliSense feature makes it really easy to write this code in Visual Studio.

5. Type **DiagonalMovement.Begin()** between the *Private Sub* and *End Sub* statements in the event handler, and then press Enter.

   Your screen should look like this:

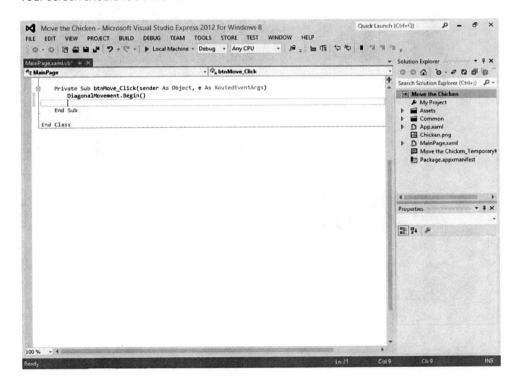

DiagonalMovement is the name of the storyboard object that you created in Blend, and *Begin* is the method you use to run the animation associated with the storyboard. This simple line of Visual Basic code will run your animation effect, but note that there are several other interesting properties and methods that you can experiment with once you learn the animation basics.

Now you'll run the event handler to see what it looks like.

6. Click Start Debugging on the Debug menu to run the program.

    The user interface appears with the photo of a chicken in the lower-left corner of the screen and a Move The Chicken button in the upper-left corner.

7. Click Move The Chicken.

    The chicken gradually moves diagonally across the screen. Notice that the effect is much smoother now that you are actually running the program and not just viewing a preview in Blend.

    Your screen should look like this:

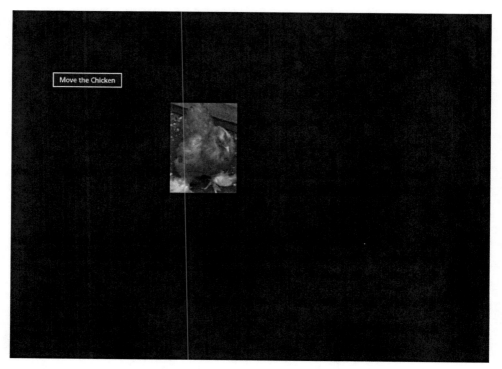

Notice that if you click the Move The Chicken button again, nothing happens. That's because the chicken is already in the final location for the animation. The effect only works one time, because the image object is already at location 300, −300 relative to the starting place of the image.

There are a variety of adjustments you could make at this point to expand the project, but let's try adding an effect that returns the chicken to its original location, so that the button moves the chicken in two directions. You'll accomplish this task by using the storyboard's *AutoReverse* property.

Edit the event handler to reverse the animation

1. Stop the program, and then return to the Code Editor in Visual Studio.

2. Create a blank line in the *btnMove_Click* event handler above the *DiagonalMovement.Begin()* statement.

3. Type the following Visual Basic program statement, so that it is now the first line under the *Private Sub* statement:

   ```
   DiagonalMovement.AutoReverse = True
   ```

   This piece of Visual Basic code references the *DiagonalMovement* storyboard again. It directs Visual Studio to reverse the animation effect after it is complete, so that the image object returns back to its original location. The timing for the reverse effect is also the same, so that (in this case) it will take 2 seconds for the chicken to move up diagonally, and 2 seconds for the chicken to move diagonally back home.

   Now you'll run the event handler again.

4. Click Start Debugging on the Debug menu.

   The user interface appears as expected with button and chicken elements.

5. Click the Move The Chicken button.

   The chicken moves diagonally across the screen, but this time it returns to its original location after the first animation sequence is complete.

6. Click Move The Chicken again.

   The entire animation sequence runs one more time. Since the autoreverse feature has returned the chicken picture to its starting place, the button is able to work over and over again. It is now a much more interesting effect.

7. Stop the program, and then return to the Code Editor in Visual Studio.

8. Save your changes by clicking the Save All command on the Visual Studio File menu.

Well done! With just this simple example, you can see that the Blend storyboard feature allows you to create effects that are much more dramatic than what you can do in the Visual Studio Designer. In reality, though, both tools create the same XAML markup, and understanding how this markup works is another way to explore the hidden power of Visual Studio and XAML-based applications for

Windows 8. Chapter 5 will dig deeper into XAML markup and structure, but before leaving Visual Studio and the Move the Chicken project, let's try one more task to explore how Visual Studio works with event handlers.

Using the *OnNavigatedTo* Event

Each time that you start a Visual Studio application, Visual Studio begins the program by triggering the *OnNavigatedTo* event for the main page in your program. Although this event is designed fundamentally to set basic characteristics and settings for your application and its design, you can also put your own code in the *OnNavigatedTo* event handler to welcome users and provide other appropriate transitions. For example, a programmer might add a so-called *splash screen* to this event handler to display application title and copyright information. You can also launch your own custom storyboards, so that users see something interesting when they load the main page of your application.

In the next exercise, you'll try launching the *DiagonalMovement* storyboard in the *OnNavigatedTo* event handler for *MainPage.xaml,* which is available to you in the Visual Studio Code Editor.

Create a startup event handler for the main page

1. In the Code Editor, click the Event Handler drop-down list box, located at the upper right of the Code Editor.

   While the *btnMove_Click* event handler is active, the Event Handler drop-down list box contains the procedure name *btnMove_Click*, but you can access other event handlers for the main page by using this list box.

   Your Code Editor looks like this:

   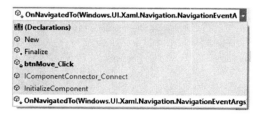

2. Click the event handler *OnNavigatedTo.*

   Visual Studio displays the event handler that runs when the main page is activated, or *navigated to.* There is not currently any code here, but you can add some simply by copying the two lines of code from the *btnMove_Click* event handler to the *OnNavigatedTo* event handler.

3. Select the following lines:

```
DiagonalMovement.AutoReverse = True
DiagonalMovement.Begin()
```

4. Click the Copy command on the Edit menu.

5. Move the mouse pointer to the *OnNavigatedTo* event handler (it should be directly above the *btnMove_Click* event handler).

6. Click the Paste command on the Edit menu.

   Visual Studio pastes the code into the event handler. Your screen should look like this:

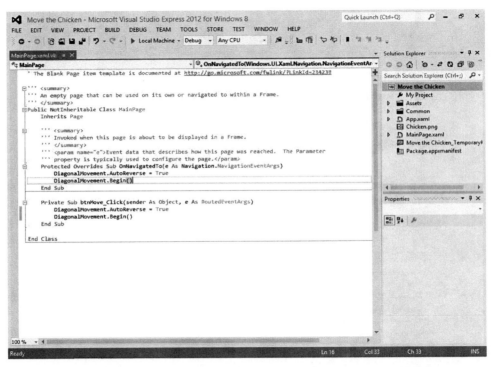

7. Now remove the statement *DiagonalMovement.AutoReverse = True* from the *btnMove_Click* event handler.

   Since you have the same statement twice in the program, you should remove the second one, as it is redundant. (Property settings like *AutoReverse* remain in effect until they are modified by something.) Note that it would not hurt anything to have the same line twice, but it is not necessary (and therefore not as elegant or efficient) to include it.

   Now you'll run the program again and see how the animation looks when you start the application.

8. Click Start Debugging on the Debug menu.

   The user interface loads, and as part of the process, the *OnNavigatedTo* event fires. The familiar chicken moves across the screen and back again, thanks to your new event handler.

9. Click Move The Chicken again.

   The animation sequence repeats, this time via the *btnMove_Click* event handler.

   You have learned how to create an opening animation effect for your programs, and also that Visual Basic code can be used in more than one place in a program. Now you'll save your changes and return to Blend, where you originally began your design work.

10. Stop the program, and then return to the Code Editor in Visual Studio.

11. Save your changes by clicking the Save All command on the Visual Studio File menu.

12. Now close Visual Studio, and then click the Blend for Visual Studio icon on the taskbar.

    Blend displays a message indicating that some of the original Blend files you were using for the project have been modified. This is to be expected, as you just added some Visual Basic code to the project using the Visual Studio Code Editor.

13. Click Yes to close the dialog box.

    Now run the project again in Blend to verify that you are indeed using the updated files.

14. Click the Run Project command on the Project menu.

    The Run Project command allows you to launch a Visual Studio project from within Blend. This is a handy feature to use whenever you are designing a Visual Studio application in Blend.

    The Move the Chicken project should run exactly as it did from within Visual Studio. Most importantly, this exercise has demonstrated how easy it is to begin a project in Blend, add to it in Visual Studio, and return to Blend for editing and testing.

15. Stop the program, and then return to Blend.

16. Now that you're done with animation, switch back to the Blend Design workspace by selecting Window | Workspaces | Design.

17. When you're finished experimenting with Blend, close the application.

You're finished working with Blend for Visual Studio for now. However, keep in mind that it is always available to you as you write your Visual Basic programs. This chapter has just tapped the essentials, but you should now know enough of the Blend IDE to begin your own explorations.

Summary

This chapter explored using Blend for Visual Studio 2012 to create visually interesting user interfaces for Windows 8 applications. Blend is a new version of the Microsoft Expression Blend software, a design tool for creating distinctive user interfaces in Windows and Silverlight-based applications. Blend allows you to design your application visually, drawing shapes, controls, and textures on the Artboard. You can then add video, sound, and animation effects to the user interface using Blend features such as storyboards and the Objects And Timeline panel.

One of the most impressive features of Blend is how tightly integrated it is with Visual Studio. You can create a new project in Blend, add controls and special effects with the Blend design tools, and then switch to the Visual Studio Code Editor to write event handlers in Visual Basic. In addition, if you are working in a team development environment, one group of designers can create the user interface for a project in Blend, and another group of developers can create event handlers in Visual Studio that manage objects behind the scenes. If you become a professional Visual Basic developer, you may spend a considerable amount of time in Blend, designing your application's user interface and adding special effects.

In Chapter 5, you'll continue learning about user interfaces in Visual Basic programs by examining the XAML markup language more closely. Whether you work in Blend or Visual Studio, all the controls that you place on a Visual Studio page are stored in one or more files as XAML markup code. These structured files provide precise rendering instructions to Windows for all the graphics in your application, so that the run-time engine can create the user interface unambiguously each time the application runs. As you'll see, you can edit your project's XAML markup directly in the Code Editor to save editing time, and you can also create new user interface elements on a page with XAML markup—all without leaving the Code Editor.

Chapter 5

Working with XAML

After completing this chapter, you'll be able to

- Understand the layout and content of XAML documents.

- Use the XAML tab of the Code Editor to modify your program's user interface.

- Adjust property settings and modify the appearance of XAML objects.

- Create new objects using XAML markup features.

IN THIS CHAPTER, YOU'LL LEARN HOW to use Extensible Application Markup Language (XAML) to control the design of your Microsoft Visual Studio program's user interface. As you've already learned, XAML (pronounced *zammel*) is a type of structured text that controls how Visual Studio and Windows will display your application's user interface and graphics when the program runs. This structured text, or *markup*, is organized in a hierarchy of named objects and *tags* (elements between the characters < and >). If you know something about the appearance of HTML, the layout of XAML documents will look somewhat familiar.

XAML is important for Microsoft Visual Basic programmers to understand because there are times when editing a XAML document is faster and more efficient than using the Visual Studio designer. There are also several user interface features and capabilities that can only be added by typing in XAML elements directly.

This chapter provides a concise overview of XAML documents and what you need to know about XAML to create Visual Basic applications. You'll learn about the structure of XAML elements and tags, how to work with XAML markup in the Visual Studio Code Editor, and how to adjust XAML property settings. You'll also learn how to add new objects to your application's user interface by entering XAML markup directly.

Understanding XAML Basics

"I bought this book to learn about Visual Basic programming. So why am I reading about XAML now?"

If you're asking this question, you're not alone.

Yet what the computer industry describes as "Visual Basic programming" actually entails a variety of software development tasks, from designing a program's user interface to writing event handlers; from using namespaces in the .NET Framework to managing database information with LINQ. With this perspective in mind, learning about XAML is just another task related to the construction of a Visual Basic application and its user interface. And in fact, you've been generating XAML each time that you have added a control to a page in this book.

What Is XAML?

When you create the user interface for a Windows 8 application in the Visual Studio designer or in Blend, you are building a XAML document behind the scenes that describes the objects, styles, and layout for your user interface. If you are using Visual Studio or Blend in Split view (with both Design and XAML views visible), you'll be able to see this XAML markup at the bottom of the screen, as shown in the following illustration:

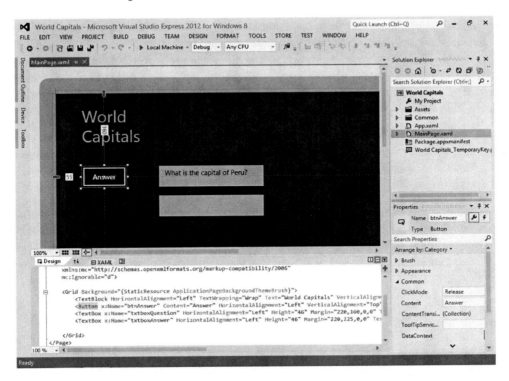

As the screen indicates, XAML documents are basically tagged text files that define the arrangement of panels, buttons, and objects on the page for a Windows or Microsoft Silverlight application. These documents appear in Visual Studio projects as *.xaml* files, and to help you identify the various elements, the Code Editor displays the objects, properties, and strings in different colors.

XAML Is Related to XML and HTML

XAML is an open Microsoft specification related to Extensible Markup Language (XML) and HyperText Markup Language (HTML). Over the past several years, Microsoft has used XAML as an alternative way to create dynamic user interfaces that run under Windows and on the web. XAML is an abstracted user interface *layer* that defines objects for different computing platforms. In the world of Windows programming, it is also an alternative to using Windows Forms for user interface development.

In Visual Studio 2010, Visual Basic programmers interested in the Windows platform were able to build their user interfaces with XAML that rendered the user interface and graphics using a technology called Windows Presentation Foundation (WPF). Likewise, Visual Basic programmers interested in web or phone development were able to build their applications with XAML and a web browser–based technology known as Silverlight. Although there are some differences between the XAML used for applications based on WPF and Silverlight applications (not all the controls are the same), the similarities between the two systems outweigh the differences. For Visual Basic programmers who want to design for Windows, web browsers, *and* Windows Phone, XAML is an emerging standard that allows for considerable interoperability among different platforms and devices.

In Visual Studio 2012, XAML is the required user interface technology for Visual Basic programmers who are creating applications for Windows 8. (Windows Forms is still allowed if you are creating Visual Basic applications for Windows 7, or desktop applications that run under Windows 8 but do not conform to the Windows 8 user interface.) However, whether you generate XAML by using the Visual Studio designer, by using a graphic design tool such as Blend, or by typing directly into the Code Editor, you are using the same core XAML technology.

XAML Elements

As I noted previously, a XAML document is simply a structured text file with formatting tags and a *.xaml* file extension. Here is what a typical XAML definition looks like for a text box object named *txtboxAnswer* from the project shown in the preceding illustration:

```
<TextBox x:Name="txtboxAnswer" HorizontalAlignment="Left" Height="46"
Margin="220,225,0,0" TextWrapping="Wrap" VerticalAlignment="Top" Width="223"/>
```

This XAML creates a text box that is left-aligned, has a height of 46 pixels, has a location on the page 220 pixels from the left margin and 225 pixels from the top margin, is formatted for text wrapping and top vertical alignment, and has a width of 223 pixels. When this XAML markup is run, it produces the empty text box shown in the in the following illustration:

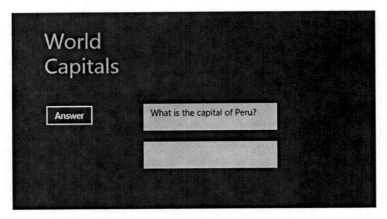

Although this text box definition actually appears on one line in the Visual Studio Code Editor, I've broken it into two lines in the book because it is so long. And in fact, to allow for easier reading in books and on the screen, XAML definitions like this are sometimes broken over several lines, as shown here:

```
<TextBox x:Name="txtboxAnswer"
         HorizontalAlignment="Left"
         Height="46"
         Margin="220,225,0,0"
         TextWrapping="Wrap"
         VerticalAlignment="Top"
         Width="223"/>
```

The preceding two text box definitions are exactly the same, save the extra carriage returns and the indentation at the start of each line in the second example. Notice that in both cases, the markup begins with the < tag and ends with the /> tag. This is an important syntax rule for XAML documents—all XAML object definitions that do not contain child elements begin with an opening angle bracket (<), indicate the class of the object (in this case, *TextBox*), and end with a forward slash and a closing bracket (/>). (You'll learn more about child elements in the "Edit XAML Markup in MainPage.xaml" exercise later in the chapter.)

You may also have noticed that each line in the XAML definition sets a *property* for the text box object. The first such setting assigns a value to the *Name* property, and the process continues until the final property, *Width*, is assigned a value of 223 pixels. Note that each property assignment contains an equal sign (=) and a value in quotation marks. You've already been making property assignments like this with the Properties windows in the Visual Studio IDE, and you should know that you can also make them directly via the XAML tab of the Code Editor. In fact, many Visual Basic programmers find the process to be a lot faster in the Code Editor.

Note In some books about XML and XAML, you will see the property names for objects being referred to as *attributes* instead of properties. This is also a correct way to describe them. Do not be confused by the different terminologies; the disparate terms simply have their roots in separate programming languages and traditions. I use the term *properties* in this book because of my roots as a Visual Basic programmer, where the term has long been current.

Namespaces in XAML Markup

The *Name* property is a bit of a special case in XAML object definitions. In the XAML for the preceding text box, the *Name* definition is prefaced by the characters *x:*, as in the following markup:

```
<TextBox x:Name="txtboxAnswer"
```

In this case, *x:Name* indicates that a *namespace* is being assigned to the text box object, and the text box will be referred to as *txtboxAnswer* in the program. This syntax is based on XML, because all namespaces in XAML conform to the rules for XML namespaces. An XML namespaces allows you to have one set of tagged elements that serve multiple purposes, each purpose represented by a different namespace, including the default namespace (where no namespace is specified). You'll learn more about the difference between XAML namespaces and .NET Framework namespaces in the next section.

Examining XAML Project Files

A useful way to begin working with XAML is to open a new Visual Basic application for Windows 8 and examine the default XAML files that Visual Studio generates. If you select the Visual Basic Blank App (XAML) template, you'll receive two XAML files, *App.xaml* and *MainPage.xaml*. Each file contains default XAML definitions for your application and user interface, and as you add to the project, the XAML files will expand. You'll also see two Visual Basic files in the project, *App.xaml.vb* and *MainPage .xaml.vb*. These files are the Visual Basic code-behind files, and although the XAML files and the Visual Basic files are related and linked together, they are written in separate languages. As you've already seen, *.xaml* files contain XAML markup, and *.vb* files contain Visual Basic code.

The following exercises step through these files and show you more about them. You'll also learn how to edit XAML files directly to change the design of your application.

Open a new Windows 8 XAML project and examine *App.xaml*

1. Start Visual Studio Express and click New Project to open a new Visual Studio application.

2. Choose Visual Basic | Windows Store under Templates, and then verify that the Blank App (XAML) template is selected.

3. Type **My XAML Editing Practice** in the Name text box, and then specify the *My Documents\ Start Here! Programming in Visual Basic\Chapter 5* folder for the location.

4. Click OK to open and configure the new project.

Visual Studio opens and a new project is created with the appropriate files. After a moment, you'll see the *App.xaml.vb* code-behind file for the Blank App template in the Code Editor, as shown in the following screen shot:

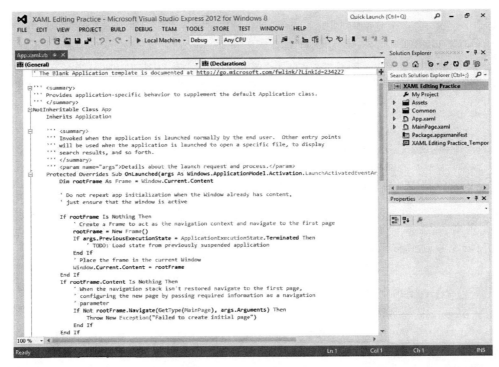

The *App.xaml.vb* file contains boilerplate code that defines the *Application* class and indicates what actions should take place when the program launches, as well as what to do when it is suspended. This is not XAML markup, but Visual Basic code, and in most cases you do not need to modify this default code listing. However, it is useful to examine the instructions in all new template files, and when you open other, more substantial Visual Basic templates, you'll see that there is more code to examine and more areas for you to complete.

Note From time to time, Microsoft changes the content of this boilerplate code, so don't be surprised if you see little differences in the default code when you compare your *App.xaml.vb* file to what I have in the sample code or to what the template provides for new projects.

Now you'll open the *App.xaml* file in the Code Editor.

5. In Solution Explorer, right-click the file *App.xaml*, and then click the View Designer command.

6. A new tab opens in the Code Editor, and the file *App.xaml* is loaded into it. (Notice that the code-behind file, *App.xaml.vb*, is still open and represented by a tab.) Your screen should look like this:

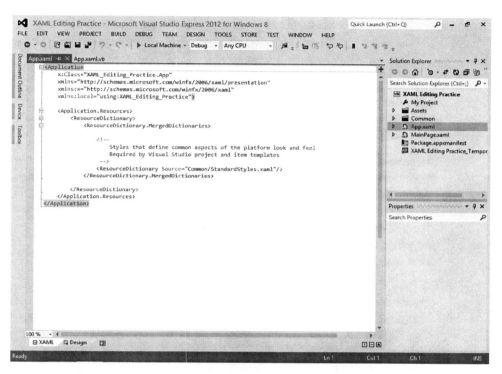

Now you'll see a few more items that you'll want to become familiar with.

First, in every XAML document, there is a core definition, or *root element*, that acts like a master container for the file. In *App.xaml*, the root element is *Application* (the core definition for this programming project), so the *App.xaml* file begins with the tag *<Application*, and near the bottom, ends with the tag *</Application>*.

Within this core definition are the various classes and namespaces that collectively mold and shape the project. These lines are typically included at the top of a XAML file. In *App.xaml*, they include the following:

```
x:Class="XAML_Editing_Practice.App"
xmlns="http://schemas.microsoft.com/winfx/2006/xaml/presentation"
xmlns:x="http://schemas.microsoft.com/winfx/2006/xaml"
xmlns:local="using:XAML_Editing_Practice">
```

The first line defines a new *partial class* associated with the application name you've selected—in this case, *My_XAML_Editing_Practice.App*. A partial class is a class whose definition may be split into multiple pieces, either across multiple files or within a single source file. The pieces of a partial class are merged when your Visual Basic project is compiled so that the resulting class is equivalent to a class specified in one location.

Note If you specified a different application name when you created the project, that name will appear here instead.

In this case, the statement connects the code-behind file, *App.xaml.vb*, to the XAML file, *App.xaml*, when the project is compiled. Each of these files holds a partial class definition, but when the project is compiled, the files form a complete class.

The second, third, and fourth lines declare XAML namespaces in the project that define default elements in the user interface. It is necessary to reference the definitions in specific documents because there are many XAML elements that have the same name, and Visual Studio needs to know which definition to use when there is a conflict. The second and third lines are standard XAML features: core namespaces that will appear in each XAML document that you create in Visual Studio or Blend. The *x* prefix, which is used here in the third line after the colon, is an *alias*, or shorthand way to refer to the classes in the namespace.

Note In this book, you will see the term *namespace* being used in two ways. In Visual Basic code, a namespace is a hierarchical library of classes in the .NET Framework organized under a unique name, such as *Windows.UI*. You can reference individual namespaces by placing an *Imports* statement at the top of a Visual Basic code-behind file. However, a XAML namespace is used in XAML markup to differentiate between multiple vocabularies that may appear together in one XML document, or to indicate portions of an XML document that serve a specific purpose. The files *App.xaml* and *MainPage.xaml* both have default XAML namespace definitions of this type.

In the body of the XAML document, the remaining lines of markup declare resources that will be used throughout the application. These resources include a dictionary that makes use of the standard styles for Windows 8 applications contained in the file *StandardStyles.xaml*. This default file is located in the application's Common folder, and it can be modified by the programmer.

Now you'll examine the markup in *MainPage.xaml*, the file where the features of your user interface are defined. You'll also make some changes to the file.

Edit XAML markup in *MainPage.xaml*

1. Right-click the *MainPage.xaml* file in Solution Explorer, and then select View Designer.

Visual Studio loads *MainPage.xaml* into the Designer. If your IDE is set for Split view (the XAML designer's default orientation), you'll see a blank page near the top of the screen, and the XAML code associated with the Blank App template near the bottom of the screen.

 Tip If the Designer is not in Split view now, switch to Split view by clicking the Horizontal Split button near the lower-right corner of the Designer.

Your screen will look like this:

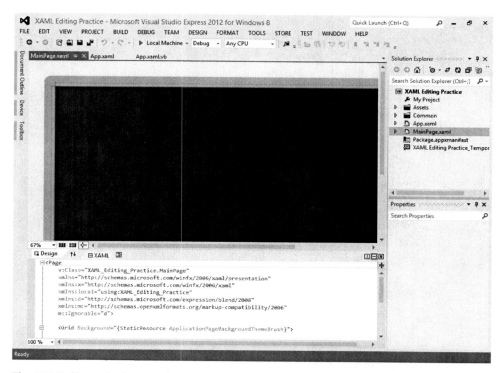

The XAML file at the bottom begins with the root element *Page*, rather than *Application*, the core container discussed in the last example. In XAML, a *Page* element organizes a selection of user interface content that you want Visual Studio to display or navigate to; in other words, it is a container for part or all of your application's user interface. Note that you may have more than one user interface page in a program, as long as each page is given a unique name.

New pages like this also require the core namespace definitions that you learned about in the *App.xaml* file previously. In addition to these namespaces, the file also includes a namespace associated with Expression Blend, as well as one related to the Microsoft Office Open XML format, as indicated by "openxmlformats.org."

2. Scroll down the XAML tab of the Code Editor to display the lines beginning with "Grid" in the *MainPage.xaml* file. You'll see the following markup:

```
<Grid Background="{StaticResource ApplicationPageBackgroundThemeBrush}">

</Grid>
```

The *Grid* element is the default user interface element that appears within the root element of *MainPage.xaml*. It is also the fundamental layout control that will hold the other controls that appear on a page. Note that each XAML file contains only one top-level *Grid* control, but it may contain other, nested controls, called *child elements*. The way that controls on a page are nested within a structured hierarchy defines their relationship to one another, and ultimately, how they are displayed in the user interface.

 Tip It may be useful for you to think of this *Grid* element as a direct reference to a .NET Framework class named *Grid* in the *Windows.UI.Xaml.Controls* namespace. In other words, elements in XAML markup are directly related to objects that you can use in Visual Basic program code. In a Windows 8 application created in Visual Studio 2012, XAML elements and Visual Basic objects are two sides of the same coin.

Currently, the grid on this blank page contains no other objects, and it is not even *visible* on the screen. (A grid is more of a layout and design feature than a visible element of your user interface.) However, the grid's background color and texture are now being set via the *Background* property for the grid and the system resource setting *ApplicationPageBackgroundThemeBrush*.

One way to adjust the *Background* property of the grid is to use the Properties window in the IDE. If you select the page itself in the Designer (not a specific object on the page), then you can open the Properties window, click the Brush category, adjust the *Background* property, and see the XAML markup updated automatically to match your selection.

However, you've already had plenty of experience adjusting properties with the Properties window. Instead, you'll now try adjusting the *Background* property by editing XAML markup in the Code Editor.

3. Click after the equal sign in the phrase "<Grid Background=" and then delete the characters in the line following the equal sign.

4. Now change the background color to blue by typing **"Blue">** after the equal sign.

Your grid definition should look like this in the Code Editor:

```
<Grid Background="Blue">

</Grid>
```

Notice that as soon as you type the closing bracket (>), the page's background color changes to blue. In addition, the IntelliSense feature offers you different color options in a drop-down list box while you type in the color name. You've now seen a major reason why it is useful to edit XAML documents from within Visual Studio—the IDE actually helps you compose your XAML by supplying useful keywords, elements, and resources.

 Tip To learn more about selecting interesting color and brush patterns, see the "Create a colorful background shape with the Ellipse control" exercise in Chapter 3, "Using Controls"; also see this chapter's final exercise, "Add a Canvas control and fill it with shapes."

5. Select File | Save All to save your changes.

You're off to a very good start with XAML documents and definitions. Now you'll add a few more controls to the grid and experiment with more useful XAML-editing techniques in the Code Editor.

Creating XAML Objects

Each of the XAML controls in the Visual Studio Toolbox can be created on a page by using the XAML tab of the Code Editor. You have the freedom to type in the markup for the controls directly, or you can add the controls using Blend or the Visual Studio Designer, and then modify the controls using XAML markup.

As you work with various objects and elements in XAML markup, you need to be mindful of the hierarchy of objects on the page that you are constructing. So far in this book, you've only added a few controls to pages as you've experimented with Visual Studio tools and features. But as you write more complex programs, the way that different objects are organized becomes central. You can group items together by placing child elements within parent elements. You can also use special container controls, such as *Canvas* and *StackPanel*, that are designed to organize child elements and display them as a group. Within XAML markup, such relationships are visible through the careful nesting of tags and optional indentation patterns.

In the following exercises, you'll get some additional practice adding XAML Toolbox controls to a grid and editing the resulting objects on the XAML tab of the Code Editor. You'll also create an event handler for a *ToggleButton* control, and you'll use the *Canvas* control to organize a group of child elements on the page to display a simple drawing.

Add *ToggleButton* and *Image* controls to the grid

1. Open the Toolbox and double-click the *ToggleButton* control.

   Visual Studio creates a toggle button object at the top of the page. The *ToggleButton* control is a useful user interface feature for gathering input from the user when the input desired is Boolean in nature—in other words, either yes or no (or more precisely, either *true* or *false*). An example of this type of control in human life is a light switch that has only on or off (yes or no) positions. In a computer program, you can use such a feature to indicate different states, such as whether an image should be displayed or not. In this way, the *ToggleButton* control has a lot in common with the *CheckBox* control, which you first encountered in Chapter 3.

   Your screen should now look like this:

   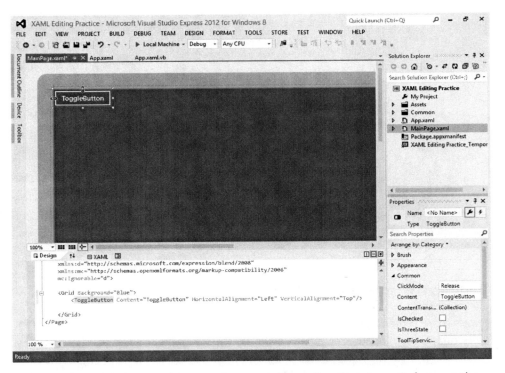

   Although the toggle button object on the page is interesting, I want you to focus on the XAML markup for the object that has now appeared on the XAML tab of the Code Editor. Notice that the following definition has appeared:

```
<ToggleButton Content="ToggleButton" HorizontalAlignment="Left"
VerticalAlignment="Top"/>
```

The *ToggleButton* object derives its core definition from the *ToggleButton* class and is delimited by start and end tags. It currently has three property settings: *Content*, *HorizontalAlignment*, and *VerticalAlignment*. (I've wrapped the line in the book because the margins are not wide enough to display the entire line as seen in the Code Editor.)

You'll adjust the *Content* property now and add two new property settings.

2. In the Code Editor, change the *Content* property from "ToggleButton" to "Display Picture."

    This property sets the text that is displayed in the button on the screen. After you finish typing the new value, it is also updated in the Designer.

3. Move the insertion point before the *Content* property name, and then type **x:Name="tbuttonDisplay"**.

    Note that at the moment you type the equal sign, the quotation marks that follow will be inserted by Visual Studio, so you don't need to type them.

    The toggle button will now have a new name (*tbuttonDisplay*), which can be used to identify the button when you create an event handler.

4. Between the *Name* and *Content* properties, type **IsChecked="True"**.

    The *IsChecked* property is a Boolean value that will determine whether the toggle button is checked (true) or not checked (false). (You need to type this property with the exact combination of uppercase and lowercase letters shown here.) You'll start the program with a value of *True* so that it displays an image in your program, which you'll specify in a moment.

5. Move the mouse pointer to the right edge of the Code Editor until the mouse pointer becomes a resizing pointer, and then enlarge the Code Editor window (if necessary) so that you can see as much of the markup as possible.

    Your Code Editor will look like this:

Now you'll create an *Image* control on the form to display the photo of a relaxing beach setting as your program starts. Before you create the control, however, add a file containing the photograph to your project in the Assets folder.

6. Resize the Code Editor window so that it is in its original (smaller) shape.

7. In Solution Explorer, display the Assets folder, which contains the default images for your project.

8. Right-click the Assets folder, point to the Add submenu, and then click Existing Item.

9. In the Add Existing Item dialog box, browse to the *My Documents\Start Here! Programming in Visual Basic\Chapter 05* folder, click the *On-the-Beach.png* file, and then click Add.

   Visual Studio adds the *On-the-Beach.png* file to the Assets folder in your project. Now it is ready to be used anywhere in your program, and it will automatically be included with your project's files when the application is compiled and packaged for distribution.

   Now you'll add an *Image* control to your page using XAML markup to display the photo.

10. Return to the XAML tab of the Code Editor, and place the insertion point on the blank line beneath the definition of the toggle button object.

11. Type the following line of markup:

```
<Image x:Name="imageBeach" Height="450" HorizontalAlignment="Left"
Source="Assets/On-the-Beach.png" VerticalAlignment="Center" Width="600" />
```

You may type the markup all on one line, or you may break the definition into multiple lines, as long as you do not attempt to break a line in the middle of a property assignment.

When you finish entering the image object definition, a new object appears on the page, containing a beach scene along the Pacific Ocean. To see more of the image, you can use the vertical scroll bar in the Designer. Your screen will look like this:

The object is named *imageBeach* so that it can be used in an event handler. The *Source* property of the image is also interesting. Notice that it contains a reference to the Assets folder, which contains a copy of the *On-the-Beach.png* file. The convenient thing about the Assets folder is that it can contain any resource for your project—music files, video files, images, text files, and so on—and when you use the Assets folder, you no longer need to know the exact location on your hard disk where the actual file is located.

12. Select File | Save All to save your changes.

Congratulations—you've learned how to modify the properties of an object in the Code Editor, and also how to type in a new control definition from scratch. Now you'll add some code to a Visual Basic event handler to *show* or *hide* the image (toggle the beach photo on or off) when the program runs.

Create an event handler for the toggle button object

1. Load the Properties windows with the settings for the toggle button object by clicking the line containing the toggle button markup in the Code Editor.

When the insertion point is in a line of markup in the Code Editor, the Properties window will contain the properties of that object. You want to display the properties now, because you are going to use the Properties window to create a new event handler.

2. In the Properties window, click the Event Handler button (the lightning bolt) near the *Name* text box.

The Event Handler button displays the events that the toggle button can respond to. The list of events in the Properties window looks like this:

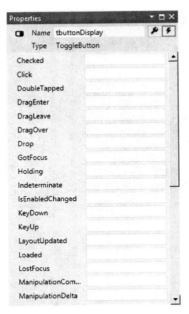

Recall that you can create an event handler for a particular event by double-clicking the text box next to the event in the Properties window. In this case, you'll write an event handler for the *Click* event, because you want to examine the state of the toggle button object each time the user clicks the button. If the button is checked after a click, you want to display the photograph on the page, or make it *visible*. If the button is not checked after a click (indicating that the toggle has been unselected or set to *false*), you want to collapse the image on the page, or make it *invisible*.

3. Double-click next to the *Click* event in the Properties window.

   Visual Studio inserts an event handler named *tbuttonDisplay_Click* in the *Click* text box, and opens the *MainPage.xaml.vb* code-behind file in the Code Editor.

4. Type the following Visual Basic statements in the Code Editor, between the *Private Sub* and *End Sub* statements:

```
If tbuttonDisplay.IsChecked Then
    imageBeach.Visibility = Windows.UI.Xaml.Visibility.Visible
Else
    imageBeach.Visibility = Windows.UI.Xaml.Visibility.Collapsed
End If
```

Your Code Editor will look like this:

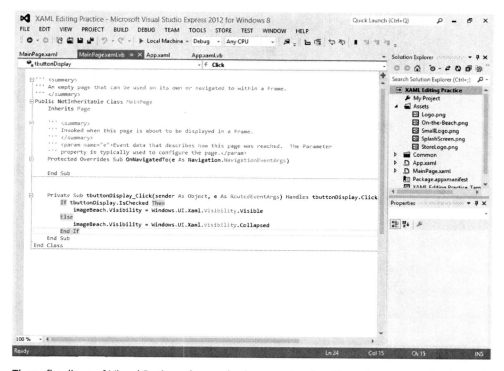

These five lines of Visual Basic code may look somewhat familiar—they use an *If...Then...Else* decision structure, similar to what you used in Chapter 3 to manipulate a *CheckBox* control. The event handler runs each time the user clicks the Display Picture button on the page. If the toggle button is checked (that is, if it appears selected or highlighted in the manner of apps in the Windows 8 user interface), then the image will be made visible by a call to *Windows.UI .Xaml.Visibility*. This particular feature is made available as part of the XAML namespace and the basic functionality of *Image* controls in the .NET Framework.

However, if the toggle button moves from a checked state to a nonchecked state, then the *Else* clause of the decision structure is executed and the image is collapsed or made invisible. The photo is not totally gone, of course, but it is temporarily hidden until the next time the user clicks the toggle button.

Now you'll save and run the program to see how your new toggle button feature works.

5. Select File | Save All to save your changes.

6. Click the Start Debugging button on the Standard toolbar.

The program compiles and runs in the IDE. The image of the Pacific Ocean beach setting appears on the page along with the toggle button, which is in displayed in a selected, or checked, state. Your screen should look like this:

7. Click the Display Picture button.

   Visual Studio toggles the button (removing the selection effect), and then fires the *tbuttonDisplay_Click* event procedure. The photo is then made invisible.

8. Click the Display Picture button again.

   The button is selected again, and the beach photo reappears.

   The XAML markup should display the user interface correctly, and the Visual Basic event procedure should function as you designed it. You can use this strategy to make a wide range of objects on your page visible or invisible, depending on various program conditions, including user input.

9. Experiment with the toggle button a few more times, and then close the program.

10. Select File | Close Solution to close the project.

Nice work with XAML and Visual Basic! Now you'll create a second Windows Store application project, and you'll practice using the *Canvas* control to create some more-sophisticated images on the page.

Add a *Canvas* control and fill it with shapes

1. Select File | New Project to open a new Visual Studio project.

2. Choose Visual Basic | Windows Store under Templates, and verify that Blank App (XAML) template is selected.

3. Type **My XAML Drawing** in the Name text box, and verify that the *My Documents\Start Here! Programming in Visual Basic\Chapter 5* folder is still selected for the location.

4. Click OK to open the new project.

   Visual Studio opens and loads the default template files.

5. In Solution Explorer, right-click the file *MainPage.xaml*, and then click View Designer.

   The Designer appears with the blank page and grid of the Blank App template. XAML markup for the page is also visible in the Code Editor.

   Now practice the new skill you learned in changing the *Background* color for page. This time, you'll specify the custom color *ForestGreen*.

6. Move the insertion pointer to the Code Editor and scroll down to the line that defines the grid background color.

7. Click after the equal sign in the phrase "<Grid Background=" and then delete the characters in the line following the equal sign.

8. Change the background color to green by typing **"ForestGreen">** after the equal sign.

   Your grid definition should look like this in the Code Editor:

   ```
   <Grid Background="ForestGreen" >

   </Grid>
   ```

   In the Designer, the page turns green, as you specified.

   Now you'll add a XAML container called a *Canvas* to the page and fill it with shape controls that collectively create a smiling face. Although you've had some experience using one *Ellipse* control to create a visual effect on the page (see Chapter 3), you have not yet used several shape controls at once to create a comprehensive drawing. The following XAML markup shows how you can accomplish this task.

9. Move the insertion point to the line below the *Grid Background* definition, and then type the following lines in the Code Editor. Feel free to use the Visual Studio IntelliSense feature as you type, and indent using the pattern shown here for clarity and readability. (In XAML markup listings, each level of indentation typically indicates that one or more child elements are being nested within a parent element.)

```xml
<Canvas>
    <Canvas.RenderTransform>
        <RotateTransform Angle="-50"
                    CenterX="425"
                    CenterY="50" />
    </Canvas.RenderTransform>
    <Ellipse Width="220"
            Height="220"
            Stroke="Black"
            Fill="PowderBlue"
            StrokeThickness="2" />
    <Ellipse Fill="Black"
            Width="120"
            Height="120"
            Canvas.Left="-50"
            Canvas.Top="-30" />
    <Ellipse Fill="Black"
            Width="120"
            Height="120"
            Canvas.Left="160"
            Canvas.Top="-20" />
    <Ellipse Fill="Chocolate"
            Width="20"
            Height="20"
            Canvas.Left="130"
            Canvas.Top="60" />
    <Ellipse Fill="Chocolate"
            Width="20"
            Height="20"
            Canvas.Left="70"
            Canvas.Top="60" />
    <Path Stroke="Black"
            StrokeThickness="5"
            Data="M 30,120 S 80,230 180,140" />
</Canvas>
```

10. If you notice a syntax error, you may need to retype one or more lines of markup.

    Typically, you'll find that it is pretty easy to forget to add closing tags at the end of each object definition. It is also a little tricky at first to avoid typing the quotation marks, as the Visual Studio IntelliSense feature tries to enter them for you.

    If you place the insertion point on the last line ("</Canvas>") when you are finished typing, the entire selection of objects on the canvas will be selected. Your screen should look like the following:

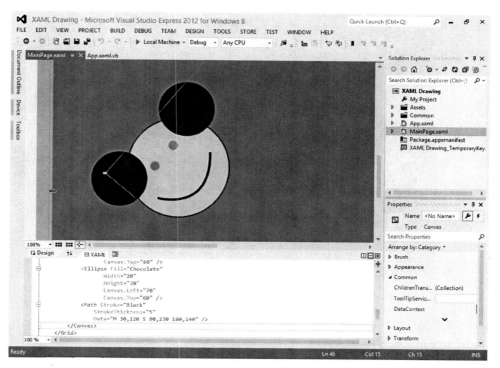

The XAML you entered creates a smiling face made up of five shaded circles and one pen drawing. The five circles comprise the face, eyes, and ears of the drawing, and they were created using five *Ellipse* elements, with property settings for fill color, height, width, and location on the canvas. The smile was created by a *Path* element, with property settings for stroke (color), pen thickness (in pixels), and various points on this line specified in pixels.

The smiling face is displayed at an angle on the canvas due to the *RenderTransform* property, which specified a –50 degree angle of rotation. Notice that this property as well as the various ellipses are all nested within the *Canvas*, *Grid*, and *Page* elements.

Now you'll save and run the program to see how your drawing looks.

11. Select File | Save All to save your changes.

12. Click the Start Debugging button on the Standard toolbar.

The program compiles and runs in the IDE. The image of the smiling face with big ears appears on the page, brushed with vibrant colors. Your screen should look like this:

Congratulations on creating several interesting effects with XAML and Visual Studio! The *Canvas* control, in particular, offers an excellent way to group elements together and apply one effect (like transformation) to all of the elements at once. You can try similar approaches with *StackPanel* and other group container controls.

13. Exit the My XAML Drawing program, and then select File | Exit to close the project and exit Visual Studio.

You now have the essential skills necessary to work with XAML markup in your projects, and to fine-tune settings in the user interface. As you continue to develop rich Windows 8 applications for the Windows Store, you can use any combination of user interface design tools that make sense for your project, including the XAML tab of the Code Editor, the Visual Studio Designer, and Blend.

Summary

This chapter explored using XAML to design the user interface for Visual Basic applications. XAML is essentially structured text organized into files with *.xaml* extensions. These files define an application's user interface by using a hierarchy of named objects and tags. Based on XML and HTML, XAML gives you access to a rich collection of Windows controls and resources that you can use to display graphics and user interface elements.

Within Visual Studio, XAML project files are visible in Solution Explorer, and you can edit them by using the XAML tab of the Code Editor. When you make changes to XAML files, the changes are immediately reflected on the page in the Visual Studio Designer. As you add Toolbox controls to the page and modify property settings with the Properties window, your revisions are added to the XAML file and you can fine-tune them with markup to create impressive effects.

In this chapter, you also learned how to use the *Image* control, the *ToggleButton* control, and the *Canvas* control. In the XAML Drawing project, you used the *Canvas* control to create a piece of custom artwork on the page, and the exercise demonstrated how you can nest parent and child elements on a grid in a XAML document. You can learn more about XAML controls and development skills in a book such as *XAML Developer Reference*, by Mamta Dalal and Ashish Ghoda (Microsoft Press, 2011).

In the next three chapters, you'll focus more intensively on using Visual Basic program code in the code-behind files of your project. Although you saw some Visual Basic code in Chapters 1 through 5, you are now ready to move deeper into the Visual Basic language, and to learn about important topics such as variables and operators, data management, code flow, mathematical functions, LINQ, and error handling. With these new skills and what you have already learned about developing Windows 8 user interfaces, you'll be ready to write your own programs and to pursue more advanced topics.

Chapter 6

Visual Basic Language Elements

After completing this chapter, you'll be able to

- Understand the syntax and format of Visual Basic program statements.

- Create variables in your programs and use them to store data.

- Work with *Integer, Decimal, String*, and other fundamental data types.

- Declare and use constants to store values that do not change.

- Work with formulas and Visual Basic operators in a program.

- Use parentheses in a formula to clarify the order of precedence in calculations.

MICROSOFT VISUAL BASIC IS AN ADVANCED programming language that allows you to control the internal logic and *program flow* of a Windows application, or how the program operates and performs useful work. In this chapter, you'll learn more about the Visual Basic programming language, and how to use fundamental program elements and syntax to create the core of a Windows 8 application. The skills that you learn will help you write better event handlers and code-behind files; additionally, you'll learn a number of useful programming conventions and best practices along the way.

First, you'll get an introduction to the anatomy of Visual Basic program statements, including how they are formatted and why Visual Basic syntax rules are so important. Next, you'll learn how to create variables in your program to store data temporarily, and you'll learn how to work with a variety of fundamental data types, including *Short, Double*, and *String*. Using variables and different data types, you'll learn how to manage input received from the user, and how to display well-formatted information on the page in appropriate user interface controls.

You'll also learn how to declare and use constants in your Visual Basic code to store values that do not change over time, such as π, a fixed mathematical entity. You'll discover how to use formulas and Visual Basic operators to compute mathematical calculations, how to debug type-mismatch problems, and also how to use parentheses in a formula to clarify what is known as the *order of precedence* in calculations. In short, you'll start creating event handlers with more calculating power in them; something that will be useful for you as you complete the remaining chapters in this book.

Understanding Visual Basic Program Statements

As you learned in Chapter 2, "Creating Your First Windows 8 Application," a line of code in a Visual Basic program is called a *program statement*. A program statement is any combination of Visual Basic keywords, properties, methods, object names, variables, numbers, special symbols, and other values that collectively create a valid instruction recognized by the Visual Basic compiler. A complete program statement can be the following line of code:

```
DiagonalMovement.Begin()
```

which uses the *Begin* method to run an animation storyboard named *DiagonalMovement*; or it can be a combination of elements, such as the following statement, which uses the *Today* property to assign the current date to the *Text* property of the *TextBox1* object:

```
TextBox1.Text = System.DateTime.Today
```

The rules of construction that must be used when you build a programming statement are called statement *syntax*. Visual Basic shares many of its syntax rules with the other development products in Microsoft Visual Studio, as well as earlier versions of the BASIC programming language. The trick to writing good program statements is learning the syntax of the most useful elements in a programming language and then using those elements correctly to process the data in your program. Fortunately, Visual Basic does a lot of the toughest work for you, so the time you spend writing program code is relatively short, and you can reuse what you've created in future programs. The Visual Studio IDE also points out potential syntax errors and suggests corrections, much as the AutoCorrect feature of Microsoft Word does.

In this chapter and the following chapters, you'll learn the most important Visual Basic keywords and program statements, as well as many of the objects, properties, and methods provided by XAML Toolbox controls and the .NET Framework. You'll find that these keywords and objects complement nicely the programming skills you've already learned and will help you write powerful programs in the future. The first topics—variables and data types—are critical features of nearly every program.

Using Variables to Store Information

A variable is a temporary storage location for data in your program. You can use one or many variables in your code, and they can contain words, numbers, dates, properties, or other values. By using variables, you can assign a short and easy-to-remember name to each piece of data you plan to work with. Variables can hold information entered by the user at run time, the result of a specific calculation, or a piece of data you want to display on a page. In short, variables are handy containers that you can use to store and track almost any type of information.

Using variables in a Visual Basic program requires some planning. Before you can use a variable, you must set aside memory in the computer for the variable's use. This process is a little like reserving a seat at a theater or a baseball game. I'll cover the process of making reservations for, or *declaring*, a variable in the next section.

Setting Aside Space for Variables: The *Dim* Statement

Explicitly declaring variables before using them is an important programming practice. To declare a variable in Visual Basic 2012, you type the variable name after the *Dim* statement. (*Dim* stands for *dimension*.) This declaration reserves room in memory for the variable when the program runs and lets Visual Basic know what type of data it should expect to store in the variable. Although this declaration can be done at any place in an event handler or procedure (as long as the declaration happens before the variable is used), most programmers declare variables in one place at the top of the event handler or procedure they are working on.

For example, the following statement creates space for a variable named *CompanyName* that will hold a textual, or *string*, value:

```
Dim CompanyName As String
```

Note that in addition to identifying the variable by name, I've used the *As* keyword to give the variable a particular type, and I've identified the type by using the keyword *String*. (You'll learn about other data types later in this chapter.) A string variable contains textual information: words, letters, symbols—even numbers. I find myself using string variables a lot; they hold names, places, lines from a poem, the contents of a file, and various other kinds of word-related data.

Why do you need to declare variables? Visual Basic wants you to identify the name and the type of your variables in advance so that the compiler can set aside the memory the program will need to store and process the information held in the variables. Memory management might not seem like a big deal to you (after all, modern desktop computers and tablets have lots of RAM and gigabytes of free disk space), but in some programs, memory can be consumed quickly, and it's a good practice to take memory allocation seriously even as you take your first steps as a programmer. As you'll soon see, different types of variables have different space requirements and size limitations.

After you declare a variable, you're free to assign information to it in your code by using the assignment operator (=). For example, the following program statement assigns the company name Blue Yonder Airlines to the *CompanyName* variable:

```
CompanyName = "Blue Yonder Airlines"
```

Note that I was careful to assign a textual value to the *CompanyName* variable because its data type is *String*. You can also assign values with numbers or symbols to the variable, such as the following:

```
CompanyName = "13 Fabrikam, Inc."
```

However, the variable is still considered a string value. The number portion could be used in a mathematical formula only if it were first converted to an integer or a floating-point value.

After the *CompanyName* variable is assigned a value, it can be used in place of the name Blue Yonder Airlines in your code. For example, the assignment statement

```
TextBox1.Text = CompanyName
```

displays "Blue Yonder Airlines" in the text box named *TextBox1* on a page.

Using Variables in an Event Handler

Variables can maintain the same value throughout a program, or they can change values several times, depending on your needs. The following exercise demonstrates how a variable named *CompanyName* can contain different text values and how the variable can be assigned to object properties.

Change the value of a variable

1. Start Visual Studio.

2. On the Start page or File menu, click Open Project.

   The Open Project dialog box opens.

3. Open the Fun with Variables project in the *My Documents\Start Here!\Programming with Visual Basic\Chapter 6\Fun with Variables* folder.

4. If the project's main page isn't visible, right click *MainPage.xaml* in Solution Explorer, and then click View Designer.

   The Fun with Variables page opens in the Designer. Fun with Variables is a *skeleton* program— it contains a page with text boxes and a button for displaying output, but little program code. (I create these skeleton programs now and then to save you time, although you can also create the project from scratch if you like.) You'll edit the code-behind file in this exercise.

The Fun with Variables page looks like this:

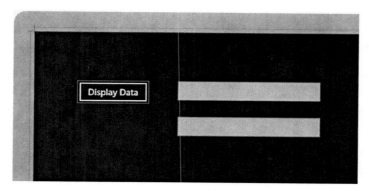

The page contains two text boxes and one button. You'll use variables to display information in each of the text boxes.

5. Double-click the Display Data button.

The *Button_Click_1* event handler appears near the bottom of the Code Editor.

6. Type the following program statements to declare and use the *CompanyName* variable:

```
Dim CompanyName As String

CompanyName = "Coho Vineyard"
TextBox1.Text = CompanyName

CompanyName = "Lucerne Publishing"
TextBox2.Text = CompanyName
```

The program statements are arranged in three groups. The first statement declares the *CompanyName* variable by using the *Dim* statement and the *String* type. After you type this line, Visual Studio places a jagged green line under the *CompanyName* variable, because it has been declared but not used in the program. There is nothing wrong here—Visual Studio is just reminding you that a new variable has been created and is waiting to be used.

 Tip If the variable name still has a jagged underline when you finish writing your program, you may have misspelled a variable name somewhere within your code.

The second and third lines assign the name "Coho Vineyard" to the *CompanyName* variable, and then display this name in the first text box on the page. This example demonstrates one of the most common uses of variables in a program—transferring information to a property. As you have seen before, all string values assigned to variables are displayed in red type.

The fourth line assigns the name Lucerne Publishing to the *CompanyName* variable (in other words, it changes the contents of the variable). Notice that the second string is longer than the first and also contains a blank space. When you assign text strings to variables or use them in other places, you need to enclose the text within quotation marks. (You don't need to do this with numbers.)

Finally, keep in mind another important characteristic of the variables being declared in this event handler—they maintain their *scope*, or hold their value, only within the event handler you're using them in. Later in this chapter, you'll learn how to declare variables and constants so that they will have scope throughout the entire page, including each event handler and procedure in the code-behind file.

Your Code Editor should look like this:

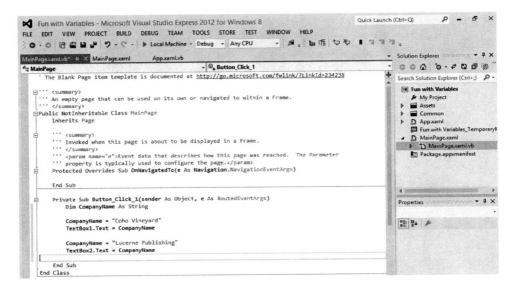

7. Select File | Save All to save your changes.

8. Click the Start Debugging button on the Standard toolbar to run the program.

   The project compiles and runs in the IDE.

9. Click Display Data.

   The program declares the *CompanyName* variable, assigns two values to it, and copies each value to the appropriate label on the page. The program produces the output shown in the following image:

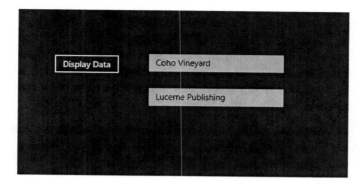

10. When you're finished working with the test application, exit the program.

The program stops, and the IDE returns.

Variable Naming Conventions

Naming variables can be a little tricky because you need to use names that are short but intuitive and easy to remember. To avoid confusion, use the following conventions when naming variables:

- Begin each variable name with a letter or underscore. This is a Visual Basic requirement. Variable names can contain only letters, underscores, and numbers.

- Although variable names can be virtually any length, try to keep them under 33 characters to make them easier to read.

- Make your variable names descriptive by combining one or more words when it makes sense to do so. For example, the variable name *SalesTaxRate* is much clearer than *Tax* or *Rate*.

- Use a combination of uppercase and lowercase characters and numbers. An accepted convention is to capitalize the first letter of each word in a variable; for example, *DateOfBirth*. (This style is sometimes called *Pascal casing*.) However, some programmers prefer to use so-called *camel casing* (making the first letter of a variable name lowercase) to distinguish variable names from functions and module names, which usually begin with uppercase letters. Examples of camel casing include *dateOfBirth*, *employeeName*, and *counter*.

- Don't use Visual Basic keywords, objects, or properties as variable names. If you do, you'll get an error when you try to run your program.

- Optionally, you can begin each variable name with a two-character or three-character abbreviation corresponding to the type of data that's stored in the variable. For example, use *strName* to show that the *Name* variable contains string data. This convention is falling out of favor, but was common in earlier versions of Visual Basic, and you should learn to recognize the pattern.

Using a Variable to Store and Process Input

One practical use for a variable is to temporarily hold information that was entered by the user. In a Windows 8 application, it is typical to gather this information by using a *TextBox* control, a *PasswordBox* control, or a *ListBox* control. The information that is entered is stored in one or more control properties, and it can also be assigned to one or more variables.

In the following example, you'll use a *TextBox* control and a variable of type *String*, and you'll learn how to format information in a string variable before you display it. Rather than create a new application, you'll simply modify the Fun with Variables program.

Process input using a *TextBox* control

1. Display the *MainPage.xaml.vb* code-behind file in the Code Editor.

   This is the location of the *Button_Click_1* event handler that you just entered. You'll delete the contents of the event handler now, and replace them with a new Visual Basic routine.

2. Select the five lines of Visual Basic program code that you just entered in the Code Editor and press the Delete key.

> **Warning** Delete only the five lines of code that you entered, not the lines beginning with *Private Sub* and *End Sub*. If you do inadvertently delete these important declarations, simply click the Undo command from the Edit menu to restore them.

   After the deletion, the *Button_Click_1* event handler contains no content. Now you'll enter some new code to declare a string variable named *FullName* and assign it the contents of the first text box. (The blank line following is simply a matter of coding style.)

3. Type the following program statements between the *Private Sub* and *End Sub* statements:

```
Dim FullName As String

FullName = TextBox1.Text
FullName = FullName.TrimStart()
TextBox2.Foreground = New SolidColorBrush(Windows.UI.Colors.Red)
TextBox2.Text = FullName
```

   Just like before, you've declared a variable of type *String* to store information. This time, you've named the variable *FullName*, because it will be holding a person's complete name. In the second program statement, you assign the contents of the first text box to the *FullName* variable. This demonstrates how you receive text input from the user by using the *TextBox* control.

Now the routine adds a few special effects to the user input you just received. The third statement uses the *TrimStart* method to remove any white space (space characters) from the first characters of the user input, something that inadvertently happens sometimes when data is entered. The result of the trimming process is then assigned to a revised version of the *FullName* variable.

TrimStart is one of many helpful string-processing methods that you can use to edit or format string input received from the user. In fact, you can trim other characters from a string by using *TrimStart* and placing the character that you want to remove in quotes between parentheses. For example, the statement

```
FullName = FullName.TrimStart("-")
```

removes any dash (-) characters that are present at the beginning of the *FullName* string variable. (The default trim character is space, so you don't have to specify that one.)

The fourth line of the event handler changes the text color of the second text box to red using the *New* keyword and the *SolidColorBrush* class. You may recall that you used this class to change the foreground color of text in Chapter 3, "Using Controls." However, note that in this case the string variable does not contain any actual brush formatting. You're just modifying the text box object that will display the string.

The fifth statement in the event handler places the contents of the *FullName* variable into the *Text* property of the second text box object, which displays the name on the page in its formatted form. Your Code Editor should look like this:

Now you'll save the program and test the new program code.

4. Select File | Save All to save your changes.

5. Click the Start Debugging button to run the program.

   The revised program runs in the IDE. You'll see a Display Data button and two empty text boxes.

6. Type **Erin M. Hagens** in the first text box.

   Your screen should look like this:

7. Click Display Data.

   The *Button_Click_1* event handler takes the name you entered and stores it in the *FullName* variable. The routine checks to see if there are any blank spaces to trim in front of the name (in this case, there are none), and then it displays the name in the second text box. The *SolidColorBrush* class changes the presentation of the text to red. Your screen should look like this (but only e-book readers will see the name displayed in red here):

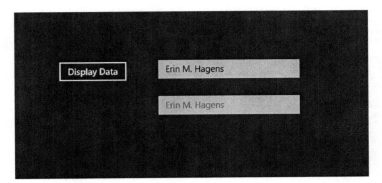

   Now you'll see how the trim feature works.

8. Remove the name from the first text box.

9. Press the Spacebar seven times, and then type **Tom Higginbotham**.

Your screen should look like this:

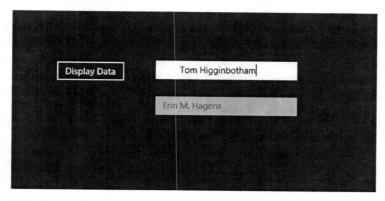

10. Click Display Data.

The *Button_Click_1* event handler stores the new name in the *FullName* variable, trims the blank spaces from the beginning of the string, and displays the revised string variable in the second text box in red type. Your screen should look like this:

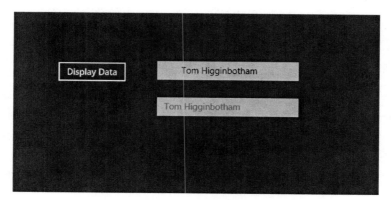

11. Continue to experiment with different string variable assignments (for example, test what happens when you enter nothing in the first text box), and when you are finished, close the application.

The program stops and the Windows Start page appears. Press the Windows key to display the Visual Studio IDE again.

12. Select File | Close Solution to close the Fun with Variables project.

You've successfully managed program input and output with a string variable, and you've also learned how to apply several interesting formatting effects to strings. Now let's move on to learn about other useful variable types.

Working with Data Types

The *String* data type is useful for managing text in your programs, but what about numbers, dates, and other types of information? To allow for the efficient memory management of all types of data, Visual Basic provides several additional data types that you can use for your variables. Many of these are familiar data types from earlier versions of BASIC or Visual Basic, and some of the data types were introduced more recently to allow for the efficient processing of data on newer 64-bit computers.

Table 6-1 lists the fundamental (or elementary) data types in Visual Basic. Types preceded by an *S* are designed for signed numbers, meaning that they can hold both positive and negative values. Types preceded by a *U* are unsigned data types, meaning that they cannot hold negative values. If your program needs to perform a lot of calculations, you might gain a performance advantage in your programs if you choose the right data type for your variables—one with a size that's neither too big nor too small.

In the following exercise, you'll see how several of these data types work. You'll also learn a little more about debugging a program that generates an exception when data types don't match.

 Note Variable storage size is measured in bits. The amount of space required to store one standard (ASCII) keyboard character in memory is 8 bits, which equals 1 byte.

TABLE 6-1 Fundamental Data Types in Visual Basic

Data Type	Size	Range	Sample Usage
Short	16-bit	-32,768 through 32,767	`Dim Artists As Short` `Artists = 2500`
UShort	16-bit	0 through 65,535	`Dim Hours As UShort` `Hours = 5000`
Integer	32-bit	-2,147,483,648 through 2,147,483,647	`Dim Population As Integer` `Population = 375000`
UInteger	32-bit	0 through 4,294,967,295	`Dim Seconds As UInteger` `Seconds = 3000000`
Long	64-bit	-9,223,372,036,854,775,808 through 9,223,372,036,854,775,807	`Dim Bugs As Long` `Bugs = 7800000016`

ULong	64-bit	0 through 18,446,744,073,709,551,615	`Dim SandGrains As ULong`
			`SandGrains =`
			`    1800000000000000000`

Single	32-bit floating point	-3.4028235E38 through 3.4028235E38	`Dim UnitCost As Single` `UnitCost = 899.99`
Double	64-bit floating point	-1.79769313486231E308 through 1.79769313486231E308	`Dim Pi As Double` `Pi = 3.1415926535`

Data Type	Size	Range	Sample Usage
Decimal	128-bit	0 through +/-79,228,162,514,264, 337,593,543,950,335 (+/-7.9...E+28) with no decimal point; 0 through +/-7.9228162514264337593543950335 with 28 places to the right of the decimal. Append "D" to the number if you want to force Visual Basic to initialize a *Decimal*	`Dim Debt As Decimal` `Debt = 7600300.5D`
Byte	8-bit	0 through 255 (no negative numbers)	`Dim RetKey As Byte` `RetKey = 13`
SByte	8-bit	-128 through 127	`Dim NegNum As SByte` `NegNum = -20`
Char	16-bit	Any Unicode symbol in the range 0–65,535. Append "c" when initializing a *Char*.	`Dim UnicodeChar As Char` `UnicodeChar = "Ä"c`
String	Usually 16-bits per character	0 to approximately 2 billion 16-bit Unicode characters	`Dim Greeting As String` `Greeting = "hello world"`
Boolean	16-bit	*True* or *False*. (During conversions, 0 is converted to *False*, other values to *True*.)	`Dim Flag as Boolean` `Flag = True`
Date	64-bit	January 1, 0001, through December 31, 9999	`Dim Birthday as Date` `Birthday = #3/17/1900#`
Object	32-bit	Any type can be stored in a variable of type *Object*. In addition, object variables can contain defined objects in your project, like a text box object named *TextBox1*.	`Dim MyControl As Object` `MyControl = TextBox1`

Use fundamental data types in code

1. Select File | Open Project to open an existing Visual Studio project.

    The Open Project dialog box appears.

2. Open the Fun with Data project in the *My Documents\Start Here!\Programming with Visual Basic\Chapter 6\Fun with Data* folder.

3. If the project's main page isn't visible, right click *MainPage.xaml* in Solution Explorer, and then click View Designer.

    The Fun with Data page opens in the Designer. Fun with Data is another skeleton program—it contains a page with two text boxes and a button for displaying the results of variable assignments and calculations. You'll add the event handler code in this exercise.

The Fun with Data page looks like this:

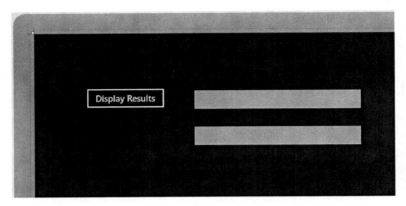

4. Double-click the Display Results button.

   The *Button_Click_1* event handler appears near the bottom of the Code Editor.

5. Type the following program statements to declare and use several variables and data types:

```
Dim Artists As Short 'Artists is a short integer variable
Artists = 2500
TextBox1.Text = Artists

Dim Pi As Double      'Pi is a double-precision floating-point variable
Pi = 3.1415926535
TextBox2.Text = Pi
```

This simple routine demonstrates how to declare and use a variable of type *Short* (called *Artists*) and a variable of type *Double* (called *Pi*). The *Artists* variable is large enough to contain integer values (whole numbers) in the range –32,768 through 32,767. This type of variable is useful when you expect to count incrementally or store other relatively small integer values (thus the name *Short*). If you plan to store larger whole numbers, you should use an *Integer* or *Long* type, which contains more space and therefore allows for bigger numbers. (See Table 6-1 for the valid ranges of these types.)

The *Pi* variable of type *Double* declared here will be able to contain double-precision floating-point values (that is, numbers with decimal places that can be extremely large or precise). This is the type of variable to use if you want to allow for numbers with many decimal places.

The event handler does not compute any values, however; it simply declares the *Artists* and *Pi* variables, assigns numbers to them, and displays the numbers in text boxes on the page. You'll learn how to compute calculations and formulas in the next section.

Your Code Editor should look like this:

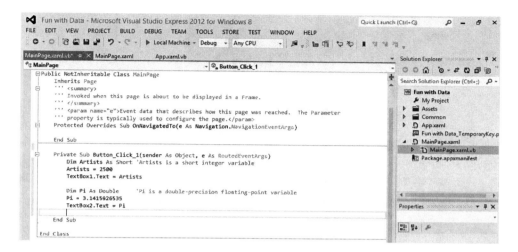

Notice that no quotation marks are used when the numeric values are assigned. Also, the comments that you added are displayed in green type. These are simply explanatory remarks for your own use, so that you can remember something about the variables. (As you learned in Chapter 2, you can add comments to a Visual Basic code listing whenever you want.)

6. Select File | Save All to save your changes.

7. Click the Start Debugging button to run the program.

   The project compiles and runs in the IDE.

8. Click Display Results.

   The program declares the *Artist* and *Pi* variables, assigns numbers to them, and copies each value to text boxes on the page. The program output looks like this:

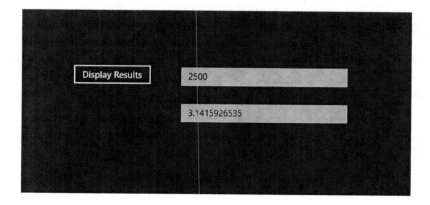

9. Close the program, and return to the Visual Studio Code Editor.

Now you'll see what happens if you modify the values assigned to the variables in unusual ways.

10. Edit the line of code that assigns a value to the *Artists* variable so that it looks like this:

```
Artists = 7300.5
```

This is actually an intentional error that you are adding to the program—just to see what happens. Since the *Artists* variable is of type *Short*, it can only be used to hold integers (that is, whole numbers). Assigning a decimal value to such a variable is a mistake. But what will Visual Studio do when you attempt to run the program?

11. Click the Start Debugging button.

The project compiles and runs in the IDE. Interestingly, the compilation succeeds—Visual Studio does not notice anything wrong with the assignment that you are making.

12. When the page appears, click Display Results.

The program declares the *Artists* and *Pi* variables again, assigns numbers to them, and copies each value to text boxes on the page. The user interface should look like this:

But did you notice what happened? The number displayed in the first text box is 7300, not 7300.5! The program simply ignored the decimal portion of the number assignment and stored the integer portion of the value. The result is a little surprising, to say the least. In programming terms, the compiler attempted to correct a *data type mismatch* by simply truncating the number.

The result is a reminder that you need to understand just what data type you are using for your variables to work properly, and that you must avoid assigning the wrong type of information to a variable or you will get unexpected results.

13. Close the program and return to the Visual Studio Code Editor.

Let's continue investigating this issue about data types and assigning proper values to a variable.

14. Edit the line of code again that assigns a value to the *Artists* variable. Change the line so that it looks like this:

```
Artists = "Leonardo da Vinci"
```

Now you've introduced another error, and this time one that seems truly unworkable. You're directing that a string value be assigned to a short integer variable. But again, what will happen when you attempt to compile and run the program?

15. Click the Start Debugging button.

The project compiles successfully again and runs as a Windows 8 application.

> **Note** For the exercises in this book, I have asked you to set the Option Strict setting to Off for the Visual Basic compiler. (The "Customizing IDE Settings to Match This Book's Exercises" section in Chapter 1, "Getting to Know Visual Basic 2012," contains more information about this and other default settings that I recommend.) If you receive a compilation error when you try to compile and run the Fun with Data project in this step, it may be because you have not changed the Option Strict setting. If so, choose Tools | Options | Projects And Solutions | VB Defaults, and then set Option Strict to Off.

16. Click Display Results.

Visual Basic launches the *Button_Click_1* event handler, declares the *Artists* variable, and attempts to assign the string value "Leonardo da Vinci" to the short integer variable named *Artists*. However, at this point the program fails and Visual Studio displays the following run-time error message:

Visual Studio has thrown an *exception*, or a run-time error that prevents the project from continuing. Although Visual Studio generally tries to manage improper variable assignments by converting from one type to another (the truncation shown in the last exercise), in this case the conversion did not work.

Your options are to stop program execution and fix the error (in this case, fix the improper variable assignment) or stop program execution and create a section of code known as an *exception handler* to account for the error. You can also click the Break button and enter break mode to learn more about what is going on in the program.

17. Click the Break button.

Visual Studio enters *break mode*, a special IDE state that allows you to watch your code being executed line by line in the Code Editor. The statement that produced the exception is high-lighted in the Code Editor, and there is an arrow in the left margin of the Code Editor indicating where the problem is. Notice that the word "Debugging" also appears in the Visual Studio title bar, as shown in the following illustration:

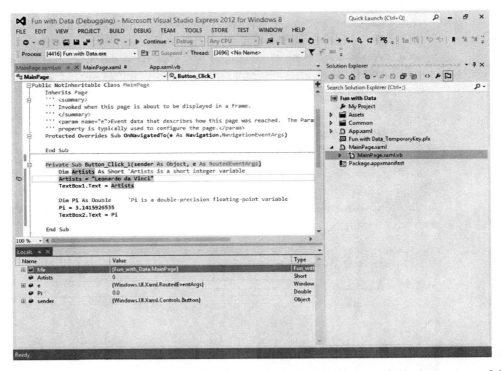

Something else that you may see in break mode is the Locals window, which shows many of the objects and variables in the project and their current values. (If you don't see the Locals window now, click the Debug menu, point to Windows, and click Locals.) Take a moment to move or resize the Locals window if you can't see its contents clearly.

In the Locals window, you'll see the *Artists* and *Pi* variables. Each currently has a "0" value. *Artists* has a "0" value because the string assignment did not work properly. *Pi* has a "0.0" value because the lines of code declaring and assigning a value to *Pi* have not been executed yet, and zero is the default value for numeric variables not otherwise assigned a value.

18. Click the Stop Debugging button on the Debugging toolbar.

Visual Studio stops program execution, closes break mode, and displays the Code Editor again. You've learned the importance of appropriate variable assignments and also a little about how programs can be debugged in break mode.

In Chapter 7, "Controlling Application Design, Layout, and Program Flow," you'll learn more about exception handlers and how to manage common run-time errors. In Chapter 9, "Debugging Applications," you'll learn more about break mode and other useful tools in the IDE for correcting mistakes in Visual Basic applications.

19. Return now to the Code Editor, and correct this data type mismatch problem by editing the incorrect program statement to its original value:

```
Artists = 2500
```

20. Compile and run the program again to verify that your debugging correction worked.

21. When you are satisfied with the fix, close the program and save your changes.

You're ready to learn about a special type of variable called a *constant*.

Constants: Variables That Don't Change

If a variable in your program contains a value that never changes (such as π, a fixed mathematical entity), you might consider storing the value as a constant instead of as a variable. A constant is a meaningful name that takes the place of a number or a text string that doesn't change. Constants are useful because they increase the readability of program code, they can reduce programming mistakes, and they make global changes easier to accomplish later. Constants operate a lot like variables, but you can't modify their values at run time. (Trying to do so results in a compilation error.)

Constants are declared with the *Const* keyword, as shown in the following example:

```
Const Pi As Double = 3.1415926535
```

This statement creates a constant named *Pi* that can be used in place of the value of π in the program code. To make a constant available to all the objects and event handlers for a page, place the statement near the top of the code-behind file (see the following exercise for the exact placement), and then all of the event handlers in the code-behind file will have access to the new constant. Or, you can place a constant declaration at the top of single event handler, and it will only have scope, or validity, in that procedure.

Note In addition to constants, variable declarations can be placed at the top of a page's class definition to make them available to all the event handlers and procedures in a code-behind file.

The following exercise demonstrates how you can place a constant declaration in a class definition for a page, so that it is available to all procedures in a code-behind file. For convenience, you'll use the same Fun with Data project you've been experimenting with.

Use a constant in a code-behind file

1. Display the contents of the *MainPage.xaml.vb* code-behind file in the Code Editor, if it is not already visible.

2. Delete the majority of the program code in the *Button_Click_1* event handler, so that only the following program statement is visible:

```
TextBox2.Text = Pi
```

This is the code that will assign the contents of the *Pi* constant to the second text box object on the page.

3. Now scroll to the top of the code-behind file and add a new, blank line beneath the following two lines:

```
Public NotInheritable Class MainPage
    Inherits Page
```

These statements begin the *MainPage* class, which defines the objects and other elements of the code-behind file for your program's user interface page. If you declare a variable or a constant here, at the top of the class definition, your variable or constant will have scope throughout the entire page, including each event handler and procedure in the code-behind file.

4. Type the following declaration:

```
Const Pi As Double = 3.1415926535
```

This declares a constant of type *Double*, much like the variable you created with the same name in the last exercise. However, since π is a value that does not change, it makes more sense to declare a constant here to hold it, rather than a variable.

Tip The location you choose for your declarations should be based on how you plan to use the constants or variables. Programmers typically keep the scope for declarations as small as possible while still making them available for code that needs to use them. For example, if a constant is needed only in a single event handler, you should put the constant declaration within that event handler. However, you could also place the declaration at the top of the page's code, which would give all the event handlers on your page access to it.

Your Code Editor should look like this:

5. Click Start Debugging to run the program.

6. Click Display Results.

The value stored in the *Pi* constant appears in the second text box, as shown here:

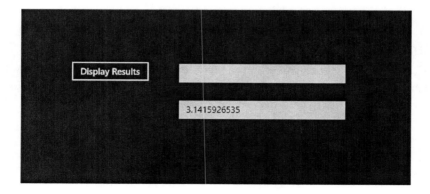

You've learned how to use a constant, and also how to declare a constant so that it has scope throughout a page. Constants are useful in program code, especially in mathematical formulas, such as Area = πr^2. The next section describes how you can use operators and constants to write this and other formulas.

7. Exit the program, and when Visual Studio returns, display the Code Editor again.

You'll use the Fun with Data program again in the next exercise.

Working with Visual Basic Operators

A *formula* is a statement that combines numbers, variables, operators, and keywords to create a new value. Visual Basic contains several language elements designed for use in formulas. In this section, you'll practice working with arithmetic (or mathematical) operators, the symbols used to tie together the parts of a formula. With a few exceptions, the arithmetic symbols you'll use are the ones you use in everyday life, and their operations are fairly intuitive. You'll see many of the operators demonstrated in the following exercises.

Visual Basic includes the arithmetic operators listed in Table 6-2.

TABLE 6-2 Arithmetic Operators

Operator	Description
+	Addition
–	Subtraction
*	Multiplication
/	Division
\	Integer (whole-number) division
Mod	Remainder division
^	Exponentiation (raising to a power)
&	String concatenation (combination)

Basic Math: The +, –, *, and / Operators

The operators for addition, subtraction, multiplication, and division are pretty straightforward and can be used in any formula where numbers or numeric variables are used. The following exercise demonstrates how you can use them in a program.

Work with basic operators

1. With the Fun with Data program loaded into Visual Studio, display the *MainPage.xaml.vb* code-behind file in the Code Editor.

    The edits from your last experiments with declaring a constant should be visible. You'll keep the *Pi* constant declaration for use in the next exercise. To begin this exercise, however, you need to clear some room.

2. Delete the program statements in the *Button_Click_1* event handler, retaining just the *Private Sub* and *End Sub* statements.

3. In the empty *Button_Click_1* event handler, type in the following code:

```
Dim Result As Single
TextBox1.Text = "5 * 4 / 3 + 2 - 1"
Result = 5 * 4 / 3 + 2 - 1
TextBox2.Text = Result
```

    This code block declares a variable named *Result* of type *Single*, which should be suitable for basic calculations that involve numbers with fractional values. To let the user know that a formula is being calculated, I place the contents of the formula in the first text box, and then assign the results of the same formula to the *Result* variable. The last line of the event procedure assigns the *Result* variable to the *Text* property of the *TextBox2* object, which displays the result of the calculation on the page.

    Now you'll run the program and see how Visual Basic calculates the formula using basic operators.

4. Click Start Debugging to run the program.

5. Click Display Results.

    The result of the calculation, 7.666667, appears in the second text box, as shown here:

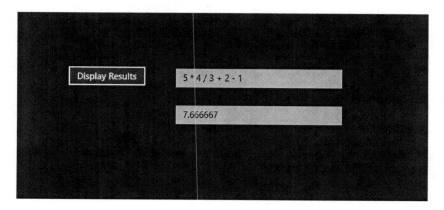

When Visual Basic computed the results of this formula, it worked from left to right, using the four basic math operators to multiply, divide, add, and subtract. You might notice that the result is actually an infinitely repeating number. Since you used a single-precision floating-point variable capable of storing seven digits, the variable rounded the seventh digit to 7 and stopped there. However, if you replace the *Single* type declaration with *Double* in the event handler, you'll see 15 significant digits in the answer (that is, 7.66666666666667). The choice simply depends on how accurate you want to be and what you would like to display.

6. Exit the program, and when Visual Studio returns, display the Code Editor again.

You'll use the Fun with Data program in the next exercise too.

Advanced Operators: \, Mod, ^, and &

In addition to the four basic arithmetic operators, Visual Basic includes four advanced operators, which perform integer division (\), remainder division (*Mod*), exponentiation (^), and string concatenation (&). These operators are useful in special-purpose mathematical formulas and text-processing applications.

Integer division (\) is a calculation that returns the quotient as a result; in other words, the number of times the divisor can divide into the dividend without remainder. (If there is a remainder in the integer division calculation, that remainder is rounded down, or *truncated*.) Remainder division (*Mod*) is similar to integer division, but rather than producing the quotient (the integer result), remainder division returns the remainder, if any, of the calculation. You'll sometimes hear this described as *modulo arithmetic* or a *modulo operation*.

Exponentiation (^) involves raising one number to the power of another number. If this process is written as b^n, the base number is b and the exponent (or power) is n.

String concatenation (&) is not a mathematical but a textual operation. It creates one string that is a combination of two strings. This is very useful for string processing and working with the content of string variables.

The following exercise modifies the Fun with Data project to show how you can calculate the area of a circle with a radius of 5 feet, which demonstrates the exponentiation operator and the *Pi* constant you declared earlier. You will also experiment with the string concatenation operator, which provides a handy way to join words or names together.

Work with advanced operators

1. Display the *MainPage.xaml.vb* file in the Code Editor.

2. Delete the code in the *Button_Click_1* event handler, retaining just the *Private Sub* and *End Sub* statements.

3. In the empty *Button_Click_1* event handler, type in the following code:

```
Dim Radius As Short = 5
Dim Area As Single = Pi * Radius ^ 2
TextBox1.Text = Area

Dim FullName As String
FullName = "Luis " & "Alverca"
TextBox2.Text = FullName
```

This code block declares two variables, named *Radius* and *Area*, and uses them to calculate the area of a circle with radius 5. The formula used is Area = πr^2, so the exponentiation operator is present, as well as the *Pi* constant declared near the top of the *MainPage* class in an earlier exercise. The result is assigned to the first text box object on the page and displayed there for the user to see.

The code block also declares a variable named *FullName* of type *String* and uses it to hold the results of a string concatenation procedure. Notice how the first string to be combined has an extra blank space near the end of it. You will often need to add or remove blank spaces in strings as you work with them. This is only one example of how the process might work.

Now you'll run the program and see how Visual Basic computes the area formula and the string concatenation.

4. Click Start Debugging to run the program.

5. Click Display Results.

The results of the calculations—78.53982 and "Luis Alverca"—appear in the text boxes on the page, as shown here:

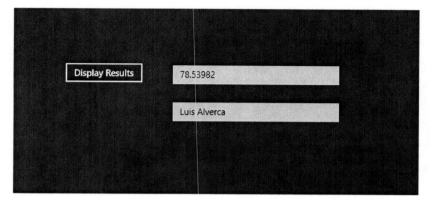

The results appear as expected. Visual Basic works with calculations of this sort extremely quickly, and you'll be impressed with the speed even as you add more variables and operators to your formulas. (But after all, isn't this what computers are *supposed* to do?)

6. Exit the program, and when Visual Studio returns, select File | Save All to save your changes.

7. You're finished working with Visual Studio and the Fun with Data program, so select File | Exit to close the project and the Visual Studio IDE.

Establishing Order of Precedence

In the previous exercises, you experimented with several arithmetic operators and one string operator. Visual Basic lets you mix as many arithmetic operators as you like in a formula, so long as each numeric variable and expression is separated from another by one operator. For example, this is an acceptable Visual Basic formula:

```
Total = 10 + 15 * 2 / 4 ^ 2
```

The formula processes several values and assigns the result to a variable named *Total*. But how is such an expression evaluated by Visual Basic? In other words, what sequence does Visual Basic follow when solving the formula? You might not have noticed, but the order of evaluation matters a great deal in this example.

Visual Basic solves this problem by establishing a specific *order of precedence* for mathematical operations. This list of rules tells Visual Basic which operator to use first, second, and so on when evaluating an expression that contains more than one operator.

Table 6-3 lists the operators from first to last in the order in which they are evaluated. (Operators on the same level in this table are evaluated from left to right as they appear in an expression.)

TABLE 6-3 Order of Precedence of Operators

Operator	Order of Precedence
()	Values within parentheses are always evaluated first.
^	Exponentiation (raising a number to a power) is second.
–	Negation (creating a negative number) is third.
* /	Multiplication and division (in no particular order) are fourth.
\	Integer division is fifth.
Mod	Remainder division is sixth.
+ -	Addition and subtraction are last.

Given the order of precedence in this table, the expression

```
Total = 10 + 15 * 2 / 4 ^ 2
```

is evaluated by Visual Basic in the following steps (shading is used to show each step in the order of evaluation):

```
Total = 10 + 15 * 2 / 4 ^ 2
Total = 10 + 15 * 2 / 16
Total = 10 + 30 / 16
Total = 10 + 1.875
Total = 11.875
```

Using Parentheses in a Formula

You can use one or more pairs of parentheses in a formula to clarify the order of precedence or impose your own order of precedence over the standard one. For example, Visual Basic calculates the formula

```
Number = (8 - 5 * 3) ^ 2
```

by determining the value within the parentheses (–7) before doing the exponentiation—even though exponentiation is higher in order of precedence than subtraction and multiplication, according to the preceding table. You can further refine the calculation by placing nested parentheses in the formula. For example

```
Number = ((8 - 5) * 3) ^ 2
```

directs Visual Basic to calculate the difference in the inner set of parentheses first, perform the operation in the outer parentheses next, and then determine the exponentiation. The result produced by the two formulas is different: the first formula evaluates to 49 and the second to 81. Parentheses can change the result of a mathematical operation, as well as make it easier to read.

Summary

This chapter explored using Visual Basic program code to write more sophisticated event handlers that leverage some of the power and capabilities of the Visual Basic language. You learned how to write program statements that have the proper formatting and syntax, how to declare variables in your programs to store data, and how to use fundamental data types to store integers, floating-point values, strings, and other types of information. You also learned how to use constants, special variables that do not change during the course of a program, to store fixed mathematical or textual values.

Variables and constants can be declared so that they have scope, or validity, throughout the event handlers and procedures in a code-behind file if the variables and constants are declared just below the class definition for a page. This optional step allows you to create variables and constants that are extremely powerful and will save you development time. However, as this chapter has shown, you can run into problems as you assign values to variables. Programmers need to use suitable caution and planning when they make variable assignments, or else type mismatches can occur. Fortunately, Visual Studio provides excellent debugging tools that you can use if this happens, including break mode.

With variables, constants, and raw numerical data in your programs, you can build mathematical formulas that create new values. Visual Basic's basic operators and advanced operators will help you write formulas that are clear and efficient. As you learn more about Visual Basic programming techniques, you will also find unary operators and bitwise operators to be useful. To clarify the order of precedence in formulas, you can add parentheses to control how a formula is evaluated by the compiler.

In Chapter 7, you'll continue working with user interface design and the Visual Basic programming language. In particular, you'll learn how to control program flow in event handlers by using decision structures, loops, and exception handlers, and how to create an information-rich, tile-based layout in a Windows 8 application.

Controlling Application Design, Layout, and Program Flow

After completing this chapter, you'll be able to

- Create a tile-based app for the Windows 8 user interface with interesting controls and typography.

- Use a *ListBox* control to present stylized menu choices to the user.

- Use a *Select Case* decision structure to process *ListBox* input.

- Use an *If...Then...Else* statement to evaluate conditions and branch conditionally.

- Use *For...Next* and *For Each...Next* loops to control program flow.

- Write an exception handler to manage error conditions.

IN THIS CHAPTER, YOU'LL LEARN MORE about the design and layout of Windows 8 applications. You'll learn to create vibrant and informative tiles on the page using the *Image* control, and you'll learn how to associate information with the tiles and process user input using the *ListBox* control. The Windows 8 design principles you'll learn will help you build visually striking user interfaces and put graphical content and typography at the center of the user's computing experience.

To help you interact with the user and manage program execution in code-behind files, this chapter will go into more detail on decision structures, loops, and exception handlers. These three multiline code blocks collectively control what is known as *program flow* in your applications—in other words, how your program executes and which statements are run under which conditions.

You'll learn how to write *Select Case* decision structures to manage *ListBox* control input, and to use *If...Then...Else* statements to test object properties and branch conditionally based on the result. You'll also learn how to write *For...Next* and *For Each...Next* loops to execute statements a set number of times and to work with collections of objects. Finally, you'll learn how to write an *exception handler* to detect run-time errors and manage program conditions so that an application encountering problems can continue working.

Creating a Tile-Based Layout for Windows Store Apps

When Microsoft released the Windows 8 operating system, it also released guidelines for how Windows 8 should be designed and constructed to take advantage of the unique features of the new operating system and platform. One of the company's primary concerns was the user experience (UX) of customers as they interacted with the Windows 8 user interface; in other words, the perceptions and emotions of users as they navigated various Windows 8 products and collaborated meaningfully with others. You can find some of these guidelines in the article "Designing UX for apps" on MSDN (*http://msdn.microsoft.com/en-us/library/windows/apps/hh779072.aspx*).

One of the main principles of these guidelines is that the user interfaces for Windows 8 applications should focus on rich user content and information, rather than the "chrome" of the operating system, such as title bars, menu bars, toolbars, scroll bars, or complex dialog boxes. Information should be presented graphically when possible, preferably in tiles or panels containing striking photographs and original art. The main application tile on the Windows Start page should be interesting and contain "live" content when possible. When the application starts, it should begin by displaying an interesting splash screen.

Careful attention should be given to the typography in Windows 8 applications. Microsoft recommends that the Segoe user interface font be used for headings and textual elements because of its clarity and because it has been optimized for ClearType, which is on by default in Windows. The background for each page in the application should be kept plain, usually to a solid color, such as black, blue, yellow, or white. The transitions between the different pages of an application are also important. Microsoft recommends that motion effects, such as transitions provided by storyboards in Blend, be used when the user moves from page to page.

Traditional desktop computers are naturally a key platform for Windows 8 applications, but so are emerging touch-based devices, such as Microsoft Surface tablets and Windows Phone. For this reason, support for touch and input gestures are important for Windows 8 applications. In fact, to be fully certified by the Windows Store for distribution, a Windows 8 application needs to offer support for mouse, keyboard, and touch input—something that will take a little planning if developers are to create programs that are ergonomic, fast, and fluid. A challenge in this vein is that developers may not have access to all types of Windows platforms and devices while they are planning and building applications.

In this chapter, you'll create the controls and Visual Basic code to assemble the Windows 8 application shown in the following illustration. You'll build the application using text formatting effects, six images, a list box, two text boxes, several event handlers and decision structures, and an exception handler to manage errors.

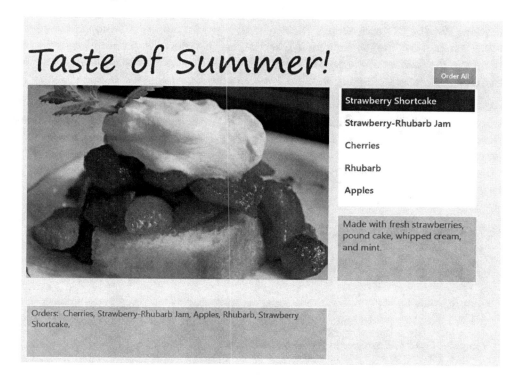

Designing Pages for User Input

In Windows Store apps, the goal is to place information on the page so that the user can manipulate it directly. In the preceding application user interface, for example, information about summer food choices is presented in a list box, and the user is encouraged to click the items that they would like to learn more about. When the user makes a selection, a compelling photo is immediately displayed in an oversized image box on the left, and additional information about the item is displayed in a text box. Although this is currently just a demonstration program (an application that you'll build step by step in this chapter), it could also be expanded to allow for online ordering, recipe and file sharing, social media connectivity, automatic news feeds, printing, and so on.

To manage the user input for such an application, care needs to be taken to write event handlers consistent with user expectations. In this case, the program waits for the *SelectionChanged* event, which takes place when the user selects an item in the *ListBox* control with the mouse or the arrow keys on the keyboard. (Touch input is not specifically demonstrated in this program, but you'll learn more about design guidelines for touch input and gestures in Chapter 11, "Design Focus: Five Great Features for a Windows 8 Application.") The five items in the list box are all assigned numbers from 0 to 4 (the first item is 0, the second item is 1, and so on). The *SelectedIndex* property of the *ListBox* control returns the number of the item selected, so that the text box can be updated and a new photo loaded.

As you'll see in the following exercise, designing pages for user input means creating attractive elements, but also learning how to manage program flow in your application. You'll do this by creating event handlers, and then within the event handlers you'll use Visual Basic statements such as *Select Case* and *If...Then...Else* to execute just the program statements that you need to run based on the input. Start the process now by adding images to a new project, creating *TextBlock*, *Image*, *ListBox*, and *TextBox* controls, and building an event handler to process input selections.

Build a tile-based layout with XAML markup

1. Start Microsoft Visual Studio Express 2012 for Windows 8 and click New Project to open a new Visual Studio application.

2. Choose Visual Basic | Windows Store under Templates, and then verify that the Blank App (XAML) template is selected.

3. Type **My Taste of Summer** in the Name text box.

4. Click OK to open and configure the new project.

   Visual Studio opens and the new project is created with the appropriate files. Now you'll add six JPG files to the Assets folder in your project to supply interesting images as the program runs. The images are digital photos of summertime fruits and activities. (The program that you are creating displays food items and information related to each selection.)

5. In Solution Explorer, right-click the Assets folder, select Add | Existing Item, and browse to the *My Documents\Start Here! Programming in Visual Basic\Chapter 7* folder.

   You'll see the following Add Existing Item dialog box:

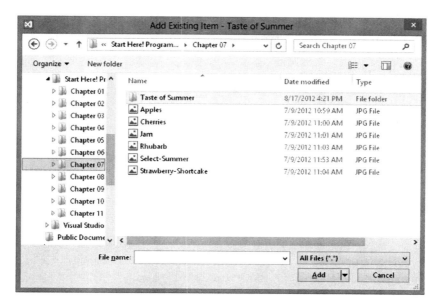

As you have already learned, the Assets folder in Solution Explorer allows you to include resources in a project so that they can be referenced easily in code and packaged with the project when it is distributed. The six JPG files in the screen shot will all be added to the project, and you'll select them all at once during the following step.

6. Hold down the Ctrl key, and then click each of the six JPG files in the Add Existing Item dialog box.

The six files (not including the Taste of Summer folder) will be selected.

Tip You can select individual or noncontiguous files in the Add Existing Item dialog box by holding down the Ctrl key and clicking each file name that you want to select. You can select a contiguous range of files by clicking the first file, holding down the Shift key, and clicking the last file in the range. (Either approach will work in this example.)

7. Click Add.

Visual Studio adds the files to the Assets folder in Solution Explorer.

Now you'll create several objects on the page by entering XAML markup. Although you could also create the objects using the Visual Studio Designer, I'll give you the XAML directly to give you more practice with the syntax of XAML formatting. (For more information about entering and editing XAML markup, see Chapter 5, "Working with XAML.")

8. Right-click the *MainPage.xaml* file in Solution Explorer, and then select View Designer.

Visual Studio loads *MainPage.xaml* into the Designer. If your IDE is set for Split view, you'll see a blank page near the top of the screen, and the XAML code associated with the Blank App template near the bottom of the screen.

Scroll to the bottom of the XAML tab in the Code Editor, until you see the following markup, which defines the basic blank grid object on the page, along with its default (black) background color:

```
<Grid Background="{StaticResource ApplicationPageBackgroundThemeBrush}">

</Grid>
```

9. Replace these lines with the following XAML markup.

The statements will create a new *ListBox* control containing five names, an *Image* control displaying an opening photograph, a *TextBlock* control containing a title for the application, and a *TextBox* control displaying information about various summer foods (currently empty). Take your time entering the text and use the Visual Studio IntelliSense feature to help you enter the markup accurately.

```
<Grid Background="Yellow">
        <ListBox Name="listboxPhotos"
                HorizontalAlignment="Left"
                Height="267"
                Margin="674,151,0,0"
                VerticalAlignment="Top"
                Width="299"
                Background="LightGreen">
            <ListBoxItem Name="List1"
                    Content="Strawberry Shortcake"
                    FontFamily="Segoe UI"
                    FontSize="20"
                    FontWeight="SemiBold"
                    Foreground="Teal"
                    Height="50"
                    Width="285"/>
            <ListBoxItem Name="List2"
                    Content="Strawberry-Rhubarb Jam"
                    FontFamily="Segoe UI"
                    FontSize="20"
                    FontWeight="SemiBold"
                    Foreground="Teal"
                    Height="50"
                    Width="285"/>
```

```
        <ListBoxItem Name="List3"
                    Content="Cherries"
                    FontFamily="Segoe UI"
                    FontSize="20"
                    FontWeight="SemiBold"
                    Foreground="Teal"
                    Height="50"
                    Width="285"/>
        <ListBoxItem Name="List4"
                    Content="Rhubarb"
                    FontFamily="Segoe UI"
                    FontSize="20"
                    FontWeight="SemiBold"
                    Foreground="Teal"
                    Height="50"
                    Width="285"/>
        <ListBoxItem Name="List5"
                    Content="Apples"
                    FontFamily="Segoe UI"
                    FontSize="20"
                    FontWeight="SemiBold"
                    Foreground="Teal"
                    Height="50"
                    Width="285"/>
</ListBox>
<Image x:Name="imageViewer"
       HorizontalAlignment="Left"
       Height="486" Margin="10,151,0,0"
       VerticalAlignment="Top"
       Width="645"
       Source="Assets/Select-Summer.jpg"/>
<TextBlock HorizontalAlignment="Left"
           Height="115"
           Margin="10,31,0,0"
           TextWrapping="Wrap"
           Text="Taste of Summer!"
           VerticalAlignment="Top"
           Width="671"
           FontFamily="Segoe Print"
           FontSize="72"
           Foreground="MediumBlue"/>
<TextBox x:Name="textboxInfo"
         HorizontalAlignment="Left"
         Height="151"
         Margin="674,434,0,0"
         TextWrapping="Wrap"
```

```
            VerticalAlignment="Top"
            Width="299"
            Background="LightGreen"
            Foreground="Teal"
            FontFamily="Segoe UI"
            FontSize="20"/>
    </Grid>
```

The *Grid*, *Image*, *TextBlock*, and *TextBox* controls should be somewhat familiar to you now, but the *ListBox* control is being introduced here for the first time. *ListBox* provides an excellent mechanism for displaying information and receiving input from the user, and it works automatically in many respects. In this XAML markup, I have assigned new items to the list box by using the *Name* and *Content* properties. Each list box item requires a unique name, so that it can be referred to in the code-behind files. Each list box item can also maintain its own unique dimensions and color settings, including unique foreground and background colors. (In this case, however, I've given the items similar settings.)

When you complete your XAML input, the Visual Studio IDE will look like this:

10. Select File | Save All to save your changes. Specify the *My Documents\Start Here! Programming in Visual Basic\Chapter 7* folder as the location.

Now you'll take a look at what the user interface looks like when you run the program. Although the project is not complete yet (you haven't added the code-behind file to process user input), you'll be able to see what the XAML markup looks like now.

11. Click the Start Debugging button.

The Taste of Summer program runs. Your screen should look like this:

Notice the text block object at the top of the screen, displaying the welcoming message "Taste of Summer!" The font you specified is 72-point Segoe Print in Medium Blue color. Below the text block object is an image object displaying a welcoming beach scene. I added the text "Select a Summer Taste..." to the JPG file in Microsoft Paint to give the user an indication of what they should do when they run the program. To be consistent, I specified the Segoe font in Paint and also used yellow to match the page's background color.

On the right side of the screen is a list box object with five items: Strawberry Shortcake, Strawberry-Rhubarb Jam, Cherries, Rhubarb, and Apples. If you click these items, or move between them with the arrow keys on your keyboard, the list box will highlight individual items.

However, nothing really significant happens when you select an item—the program's core logic still needs to be defined by a code-behind file. Likewise, the text box object is simply a light-green tile containing no text.

Now you'll add Visual Basic program code to manage the list box selections.

Use *Select Case* to process *ListBox* selections

1. In the Code Editor, click one of the lines of XAML markup associated with the list box object named *listboxPhotos*. (You'll find the seven lines of markup defining the *listboxPhotos* object near the beginning of the XAML you just entered.)

2. When you click the list box, its properties are loaded into the Properties windows, and you'll see *listboxPhotos* in the *Name* property.

   The event that you want to capture while the program runs is the *SelectionChanged* event, which fires whenever a list box item is selected by the user.

3. In the Properties window, click the Event Handler button (the lightning bolt) near the *Name* text box.

   The Event Handler button displays the events that the list box can respond to, including *SelectionChanged*.

4. Double-click next to the *SelectionChanged* event in the Properties window.

   Visual Studio inserts an event handler named *listboxPhotos_SelectionChanged* in the *SelectionChanged* text box, and opens the *MainPage.xaml.vb* code-behind file in the Code Editor.

5. Type the following Visual Basic statements in the Code Editor between the *Private Sub* and *End Sub* statements:

```
Dim bm As BitmapImage = New BitmapImage
Select Case listboxPhotos.SelectedIndex
    Case 0
        textboxInfo.Text =
          "Made with fresh strawberries, pound cake, whipped cream, and mint."
        bm.UriSource = New Uri("ms-appx:/Assets/Strawberry-Shortcake.jpg",
        UriKind.Absolute)
        imageViewer.Source = bm
    Case 1
        textboxInfo.Text =
          "Strawberry-Rhubarb jam will make summer last all year long."
        bm.UriSource = New Uri("ms-appx:/Assets/Jam.jpg", UriKind.Absolute)
        imageViewer.Source = bm
```

```
    Case 2
        textboxInfo.Text =
          "Fresh dark red cherries have a crisp bite and a tart summer taste."
        bm.UriSource =
          New Uri("ms-appx:/Assets/Cherries.jpg", UriKind.Absolute)
        imageViewer.Source = bm
    Case 3
        textboxInfo.Text =
          "Rhubarb grows quickly and makes good pies, crisp, and jam."
        bm.UriSource =
          New Uri("ms-appx:/Assets/Rhubarb.jpg", UriKind.Absolute)
        imageViewer.Source = bm
    Case 4
        textboxInfo.Text =
          "Fresh apples are good in a homemade pie or with wine and cheese."
        bm.UriSource = New Uri("ms-appx:/Assets/Apples.jpg", UriKind.Absolute)
        imageViewer.Source = bm
End Select
```

The preceding code block is known as a *Select Case* decision structure. It executes one set of statements based on a key variable or *test case*. The structure begins with the *Select Case* keywords and ends with the *End Select* keywords, and the test case is a variable, property, or other expression. Only one set of statements executes each time that the code block is run—the set that matches the test case. Then the Visual Basic compiler jumps to the line after the *End Select* statement and picks up execution there. In this way, a *Select Case* decision structure is a flow-control device—it evaluates a condition and runs just the statements that you need based on input from the user.

In this case, the program waits for the user to select an item in the list box named *listbox-Photos*. The item selected (an integer value between 0 and 4) is stored in the *SelectedIndex* property. The *Select Case* structure tests to see which of the items has been selected, and then updates the photographic image and text box accordingly.

Updating the *Source* property for an image object is quite simple in XAML markup (you simply set the string directly), but in the code-behind file it requires a few more steps. This is because the *Source* property requires an object that is of type *ImageSource*.

To create the setting in the proper format, you first need to create a new object named *bm*, which is a copy or *instance* of type *BitmapImage*. Next, you need to set the *bm* object's *UriSource* property to a uniform resource identifier (URI) that indicates the path name of the JPG file, and then assign the URI to the *Source* property of the image object. Windows 8 applications require that this path name assignment be an absolute path in URI format and that the string "ms-appx" is used to reference items within the Assets folder. Each time that the user makes a selection in the list box, these lines of code will ensure that the proper image and text description are loaded.

Now save your edits and run the Taste of Summer program.

6. Select File | Save All to save your changes.

7. Click the Start Debugging button.

The application runs in the Visual Studio IDE, and it looks exactly like it did when you last ran the program. The opening beach scene appears, along with a list box full of items and an empty green text box. But now that you've added your Visual Basic code, the list box and text box are fully functional.

8. Click Strawberry Shortcake in the list box.

Because Strawberry Shortcake is the first item in the list box, Visual Basic places the number 0 in the *SelectedIndex* property of the list box object. Visual Basic then fires the *Selection-Changed* event, which runs your new event handler. The *bm* instance is initialized first, and then the *Select Case* decision structure executes the code block corresponding to the first list box item. This code block loads a photo of the strawberry shortcake dessert into the image box and also displays a description of the item in the text box. Your screen should look like this:

9. Press the Down Arrow key twice to display the Cherries item.

The number 2 is placed in the *SelectedIndex* property and Visual Basic fires the *Selection-Changed* event. The *Select Case* structure loads a photo of fresh cherries in the image box, and also places a new item description in the text box. You'll see this page:

10. Select the remaining list box items one by one and verify that the event handler you created works properly.

   For each new item, the corresponding photo and description should appear on the page, and the output should be free of typos or formatting problems. If your display resolution is significantly different from the resolution that I am using, you may need to adjust the size or formatting of one or more items in the user interface.

11. When you're finished testing, close the application.

Evaluating Specific Conditions Using *If...Then...Else* Statements

The *If...Then...Else* statement offers an alternative decision structure for controlling which program statements are executed in an event handler. Like the *Select Case* decision structure, *If...Then...Else* evaluates a test case, and it also executes only one set of program statements based on the result. However, the test case for an *If...Then...Else* statement always needs to be a *conditional expression*—in other words, an expression that evaluates to either true or false. Conditional expressions may ask true-or-false questions about a property, a variable, a calculation, or some other piece of data in a program. Typically, these expressions make use of Visual Basic *comparison operators* such as = (equal to), <> (not equal to), > (greater than), < (less than), >= (greater than or equal to), and <= (less than or equal to).

In its most basic form, an *If…Then* statement has no *Else* clause, and it can be written on a single line. For example, the *If…Then* statement

```
If Fruit = "Apple" Then TextBox1.Text = "You selected an apple"
```

tests to see if the *Fruit* string variable matches the string "Apple"; if the two are equal, then Visual Basic assigns the string "You selected an apple" to the *Text* property of the *TextBox1* object. If the two are not equal (if the conditional expression evaluates to *False*), then no assignment is made and program execution continues with the next line. Occasionally, you will create more than one conditional expression on a line between the *If* and *Then* keywords, connected by the keywords *And* or *Or*.

If you want to perform some action when the conditional expression evaluates to *False*, add an *Else* clause to the *If…Then* statement. For example

```
If Fruit = "Apple" Then
    TextBox1.Text = "You selected an apple"
Else
    TextBox1.Text = "No fruit selected"
End If
```

performs the same action if the conditional expression evaluates to *True*, but assigns the string "No fruit selected" to the *Text* property if the expression evaluates to *False*. When you specify an *Else* clause, you may write your *If…Then…Else* statement on more than one line. However, if you do so, the entire code block must conclude with an *End If* statement. Programmers typically also indent the individual clauses of the structure for clarity, as I have done here.

Although in the preceding example only one line of code is executed after the conditional expression is evaluated, you are free to type as many lines of code as you would like in the indented areas. Longer code blocks in this style are typically referred to as *If…Then…Else* decision structures, rather than *If…Then…Else* statements, but either term works.

As a final nuance, you can test for multiple conditions in an *If…Then…Else* decision structure by using the helpful keyword *ElseIf* in the code block. For example, the code

```
If Fruit = "Apple" Then
    TextBox1.Text = "You selected an apple"
ElseIf Fruit = "Orange" Then
    TextBox1.Text = "You selected an orange"
Else
    TextBox1.Text = "No fruit selected"
End If
```

uses the *ElseIf* keyword to test for another case: if the *Fruit* string variable contains the text "Orange"—and if so, the text "You selected an orange" is assigned to the *Text* property. Note that you may include more than one *ElseIf* clause in your *If...Then...Else* decision structure.

The following exercise adds an *If...Then* statement to the Taste of Summer program to test if the current calendar month is June. If so, the *If...Then* statement adds the phrase "BEST THIS MONTH!" to the current contents of the text box. In addition to demonstrating how the *If...Then* statement works, the technique also shows you how to add very specific messages to the output of a program. In this case, the message would be most appropriate for early summer fruits, such as strawberries. (Seasons and harvest times naturally vary around the world, so adjust the conditional expression as you like for your particular setting.)

Add an *If...Then...Else* statement

1. In the Taste of Summer project, open *MainPage.xaml.vb* in the Code Editor (if it is not already visible) and scroll to the bottom of the *listboxPhotos_SelectionChanged* event handler.

2. Between the *End Select* and *End Sub* statements, create a blank line and type the following program code:

```
If (System.DateTime.Today.Month = 6) And
   (listboxPhotos.SelectedIndex <= 1) Then
      textboxInfo.Text = textboxInfo.Text & " BEST THIS MONTH!"
End If
```

This multiline *If...Then* statement contains two conditional expressions that are connected by the keyword *And*. Both conditional expressions must evaluate to *True* before Visual Basic will execute the indented line, which adds the phrase " BEST THIS MONTH!" to the *Text* property of the green text box object on the page.

The first test uses the *System.DateTime* object to check the current month, which is stored in this system resource as an integer value in the range of 1 to 12 (1 is equivalent to January, 2 is equivalent to February, and so on). If the current month is equal to 6 (or June), the first conditional expression evaluates to *True*. (Note that you can shorten the code *System.DateTime .Today.Month* to *Date.Today.Month* if you want to.)

The second test evaluates the *SelectedIndex* property, which contains an integer corresponding to the item the user selected in the list box. This particular list has early-summer harvest items as its first two members (Strawberry Shortcake and Strawberry-Rhubarb Jam). Since the list box object returns the numbers 0 and 1 when those items are selected, it is simple to create a conditional expression test that checks to see if the *SelectedIndex* property contains a number that is less than or equal to 1.

Also of interest in this code block is the string concatenation operator (&), which I introduced in Chapter 6, "Visual Basic Language Elements." This operator allows you to simply append the message " BEST THIS MONTH!" to the text that is already in the text box. I included a blank space in the appended message so that the two strings will be connected with an intervening space.

Warning Although the *SelectedIndex* property provides a very handy way to identify the list box items that a user has selected, there is also the potential for confusion when you use *SelectedIndex* in program code. For example, although you may remember *now* that the first item in the list box corresponds to Strawberry Shortcake and that the second item corresponds to Strawberry-Rhubarb Jam, will you remember this subtle information six months from now when you reopen the Taste of Summer project and add new items to the list box? In addition, the conditional expression that checks to see if the *SelectedIndex* property contains a number that is "less than or equal to 1" might cause you pause down the road when you revise the program. Will you remember what this *If...Then...Else* statement is trying to accomplish?

One solution is to add a comment to this part of the program that indicates just what you are testing in your conditional expressions, and how future edits might be accommodated. In addition, you should be sure to test your conditional expressions and flow control structures carefully, so that obscure syntax or unwanted errors don't creep into your code. (To learn more about tracking down unwanted errors in your programs, see Chapter 9, "Debugging Applications.")

Now save your edits and run the Taste of Summer program again.

3. Select File | Save All to save your changes.

4. Click the Start Debugging button.

   The application loads and runs, looking just as it did when you last ran the program.

5. Click Strawberry-Rhubarb Jam in the list box.

   Visual Basic places the number 1 in the *SelectedIndex* property of the list box object and runs the event handler. Inside the event handler, the *Select Case* decision structure updates the photo and displays information about strawberry-rhubarb jam in the text box.

   What happens next will depend on what month it is when you run this application. If it happens to be the month of June, the new *If...Then* decision structure will add the words "BEST THIS MONTH!" to the text box. However, if you're in a different month, the page will not be updated further. Here is what the page looks like in June, a good month for strawberries in northern climates:

Taste of Summer!

Strawberry Shortcake

Strawberry-Rhubarb Jam

Cherries

Rhubarb

Apples

Strawberry-Rhubarb jam will make summer last all year long. BEST THIS MONTH!

This type of timely message is just what you might want to use to draw the user a little deeper into your program's content. You might even add web-related features to your application in this part of the user interface, such as allowing your user to make a social media post or load an item into an Internet shopping cart.

6. Click the Strawberry Shortcake item.

   If it is June, then the Strawberry Shortcake item should display the same "BEST THIS MONTH!" message. However, the remaining items should not—they were not included in the second conditional expression.

7. Close the Taste of Summer program.

   If it is not the month of June, you'll need to modify the *If...Then* statement to create a condition that you can test for. Return to the Code Editor and change the month test to match the data that is stored on your computer. For example, if the current month is October, change the first conditional expression to the following:

```
If (System.DateTime.Today.Month = 10) And
    (listboxPhotos.SelectedIndex <= 1) Then
```

In the preceding statement, the only edit was changing the "6" to a "10."

8. Click the Start Debugging button again.

9. Test the new conditional expression (if you changed it) and verify that it works. Be sure to test each of the list box items.

As general word of caution, be aware that conditional expressions sometimes produce unexpected results; in other words, you might be surprised at what happens during some of the evaluations, especially when you use comparison operators. For example, if you use a less-than-or-equal-to operator (<=), what happens when you test values at the boundary (in this case, the number 1)? What happens if the list box is empty, or if new items are added, or if the existing items are rearranged? However, if you test each of the list box items one by one (both with mouse clicks and with the arrows keys on the keyboard), you can feel confident that your solution is working properly.

For more information about tools in the IDE that allow you to test conditional expressions and recover from run-time errors that occasionally surface, see Chapter 9.

10. Close the program when you are finished testing.

You'll continue working with Taste of Summer in the next section as well.

Using the Day of the Week in an *If...Then...* Statement

If you want to try a different calendar-related test at the bottom of the *listboxPhotos_Selection-Changed* event handler, try replacing the *If...Then...* decision structure you entered in the preceding exercise with the following code block, which displays the message "ON SALE TODAY!" if you select any item in the list box on a Monday:

```
If System.DateTime.Today.DayOfWeek = DayOfWeek.Monday Then
    textboxInfo.Text = textboxInfo.Text & " ON SALE TODAY!"
End If
```

It is easy to change the day of the week that you are testing for in this *If...Then...* statement. Simply adjust the *DayOfWeek.Monday* value in the first line to a different day of the week.

There is really no limit to what you can do with *Select Case* and *If...Then...Else* decision structures, especially when you use them to test system resources or property settings within your programs.

Controlling Program Flow Using *For...Next* and *For Each...Next* Loops

Occasionally in an event procedure, you'll want to execute a small subset of program statements a set number of times, creating what is known in programming circles as a *loop*. A loop is really just a shorthand way of writing out a long list of program statements. If your code is more compact, it is usually faster to write, easier to read, and more efficient during the process of compilation. As such, Visual Basic loops are handy mechanisms for flow control in event procedures, and are an important complement to decision structures.

In this section, you'll learn how to use *For...Next* and *For Each...Next* loops. The syntax for both of these looping structures is quite similar, although the loops have several differences.

For...Next Loops

The syntax for a *For...Next* loop looks like this:

```
For variable = start To end
    Statements to be repeated
Next [variable]
```

where *For*, *To*, and *Next* are required keywords. The equals operator (=) is also required.

The words shown in italic are placeholders for items that you will enter. This is a fairly standard way of showing Visual Basic syntax patterns in books and online materials, and it is useful for you to be exposed to it here. In this case, *variable* is a numeric variable that will keep track of the current loop count. You need to declare this variable before you use it, and typically it is a short integer variable. *variable* is shown in square brackets at the end of this code block because it is optional.

You replace *start* and *end* with numeric values representing the starting and stopping points for the loop. *Statements to be repeated* indicates the line or lines of program code that you will *loop through*, or execute over and over again.

For example, the following *For...Next* loop displays the word "Summer " 30 times in a text box object named *TextBox2* on the page. The words are displayed one after another with a single space in between. When a line in the text box is full, the repeating text pattern continues on subsequent lines.

```
Dim i As Short
For i = 1 To 30
    TextBox2.Text = TextBox2.Text & "Summer "
Next i
```

Notice that the routine uses the *i* short integer variable as its counter, and that this variable is declared before the loop. You can use this counter variable to create interesting effects, such as the following loop, which displays the pattern "Year 1 Year 2 Year 3 Year 4..." and so on up to "Year 50" in a text box object on the page:

```
Dim i As Short
For i = 1 To 50
    TextBox2.Text = TextBox2.Text & "  Year " & i
Next i
```

Note Although programmers often use a single-letter variable name in their *For...Next* loops, it can be useful to declare a more meaningful variable name—such as *Count*, *Month*, or *Year*—in your code to keep track of the loop count.

Complete the following exercise now to see what the first loop effects look like in the Taste of Summer program.

Add a *For...Next* loop

1. In the Taste of Summer project, display the *MainPage.xaml* page again in the Designer.

2. Click the *TextBox* control in the Toolbox, and create a new, wide text box object at the bottom of the page, beneath the photograph.

3. Set the following properties for the *TextBox* control to adapt it to the design of the project you've been building. Use either the Properties window or the Code Editor. (Apply these settings in addition to the ones that were defined when you created the object on the page.)

Object	Property	Setting
TextBox	Name	TextBox2
	Text	(empty)
	Background	LightGreen
	Foreground	Teal
	FontFamily	Segoe UI
	FontSize	18

Now you'll create a new event handler for the project. To practice creating special effects in the *TextBox2* object, you'll create an event handler that fires when the text box object is first loaded on the page at startup.

4. In the Properties window, click the Event Handler button to create a new event handler.

5. Double-click the *Loaded* text box in the Properties window.

Visual Studio inserts an event handler named *TextBox2_Loaded* in the text box and opens the code-behind file in the Code Editor.

6. Type the following Visual Basic statements between the *Private Sub* and *End Sub* statements:

```
Dim i As Short
For i = 1 To 30
    TextBox2.Text = TextBox2.Text & "Summer "
Next i
```

The *Loaded* event fires when an object in the user interface is first loaded by Visual Basic. It is thus a suitable event to use if you want an action to take place at startup (or when a new object is created while the program is running).

7. Select File | Save All to save your changes.

8. Click the Start Debugging button.

The application loads and runs, and the *For...Next* loop displays its repeating pattern of "Summer" in the new text box object at the bottom of the page. If you count the words, you'll see that the loop has printed "Summer" 30 times.

9. Click Apples in the list box.

Your screen should look like the following illustration:

10. Close the Taste of Summer program and display the Code Editor again.

Although this example is quite simple, it amply demonstrates the power of looping structures. In the next section, you'll learn how to use a loop to process items in the list box.

For Each...Next Loops

A *For Each...Next* loop is a special variation of the *For...Next* loop; it allows you to process the members of a *collection*, such as the items in a list box or the elements in an *array*. (An array is group of values represented by a unique name and declared in a specific data type; for more information, see Chapter 10, "Managing Data with Arrays and LINQ".) Collections are powerful mechanisms for controlling objects and other data in a Visual Basic program. The Microsoft .NET Framework maintains several standard object collections that you can use when you write your programs, and many of the objects in your application are actually stored in collections so that you can reference them individually or work with them as a group. For example, all the objects on a page are stored in something called the *Controls* collection.

A *For Each...Next* loop lets you step through the objects in a collection one by one and gather information or process individual items. For example, you might want to display, format, move, sort, rename, or resize an entire collection of objects at once.

Before you use a *For Each...Next* loop, you need to declare a variable that matches the data type of members in the collection:

```
Dim element As Object
```

The *element* variable declaration is not actually part of the *For Each...Next* loop, but it is included here to emphasize that the loop requires a variable to work with. Typically, the members of the collection are of type *Object*, and that type is often sufficient for most applications. However, if you are more specific in your variable declaration, you can often work with the underlying properties stored in *element*. For example, the items in a *ListBox* control are of type *ListBoxItem*, so if you use the declaration *Dim item As ListBoxItem* before you work with the items in a list box, you can access the properties and methods exposed by list box items.

The syntax for a *For Each...Next* loop is

```
For Each element In group
    Statements to be repeated
Next [element]
```

where *For Each*, *In*, and *Next* are required keywords, and *group* refers to a valid collection or array in the project or associated namespace. *Statements to be repeated* indicates the line or lines of program code that you will use to process individual members of the group.

> **Note** You can learn more about type considerations and the advanced features of *For Each...Next* loops by consulting the Visual Studio 2012 documentation, located at *http://msdn.microsoft.com* under the topic "For Each...Next Statement (Visual Basic)."

The following exercise demonstrates how you can use a *For Each...Next* loop to process items in a list box. You will configure the *TextBox2* object so that it records each list box item that you click, and you will add an Order All button that inserts all the list box items at once by using a *For Each... Next* loop.

1. Display the *MainPage.xaml.vb* code-behind file for the Taste of Summer project in the Code Editor, if it is not already visible.

2. Scroll to the bottom of the file and delete the *TextBox2_Loaded* event procedure.

   You used this event procedure to practice using a *For...Next* loop, but you don't need the event procedure now. (Note that when you delete the event handler from the Code Editor, the reference to *TextBox2_Loaded* is removed from the Properties window too.)

3. Return to the Visual Studio Designer and add a new *Button* control above the list box object on the page.

   This button will execute the *For Each...Next* loop.

4. Set the *Name* property of the button to **OrderButton**.

5. Set the *Content* property of the button to **Order All**.

6. Set the *Background* property of the button to **LightBlue**.

7. Set the *Text* property of the *TextBox2* object to **"Orders: "**.

8. This text box will now represent a basic tracking system that records each item selected in the list box. Be sure to type the two blank spaces after the colon (:) in the preceding step. Your user interface will look like this:

9. Now you'll add program code to two event procedures in the code-behind file.

10. Click your new Order All button, and then click the Event Handlers button in the Properties window.

11. Double-click the *Click* event in the Properties window to open a new event handler named *Button_Click_1* in the Code Editor.

12. Type the following program code for the event handler:

```
Dim item As Object
For Each item In listboxPhotos.Items
    TextBox2.Text = TextBox2.Text & item.Content.ToString() & ", "
Next
```

This *For Each...Next* structure loops through each item in the list box and adds its content to the *Text* property of the *TextBox2* object. The individual items are separated by commas, and the string concatenation (&) operator is used to combine the items so that the text box on the page keeps a running tally of the items clicked. Because the list box items are held in an *Object* variable, it is necessary to convert those items to type *String* before they are added to the text box. This is accomplished by using the *Content.ToString()* method. Collectively, the *For Each...Next* structure demonstrates how you can work with individual items in a list box and perform useful work while doing so.

This new tracking feature is potentially useful, so it makes sense to demonstrate how individual items can also be added to the text box. This can be accomplished with a single line of code in the *listboxPhotos_SelectionChanged* event handler that you created earlier in this chapter.

13. Scroll up so that the *listboxPhotos_SelectionChanged* event handler is visible in the Code Editor.

14. Near the bottom of the event handler, directly above the *End Sub* statement, type the following lines of Visual Basic code:

```
TextBox2.Text =
    TextBox2.Text & listboxPhotos.SelectedItem.Content.ToString() & ", "
```

This statement also adds to the text box object at the bottom of the page, but it only adds the list box item that was just selected. The item content is retrieved from the *listboxPhotos.SelectedItem.Content.ToString* statement, which you used in a slightly different form previously. The statement demonstrates that you can use the *SelectedItem* property in interesting ways, and it is worth investigating some of the other properties that you might manipulate by using this method.

Now you'll save and run the program.

15. Select File | Save All to save your changes.

16. Click the Start Debugging button.

The application loads and runs.

17. Click Strawberry Shortcake in the list box.

The program displays a picture and information about strawberry shortcake, and then adds the item to the "Orders:" text box at the bottom of the screen. This is the *listboxPhotos .SelectedItem.Content.ToString* statement at work.

18. Click Rhubarb in the list.

That item is added as well, and the new text is appended to the previous order. Now you'll see how the Order All feature works, which demonstrates the *For Each...Next* loop.

19. Click the Order All button.

Visual Studio runs the *Button_Click_1* event handler, and all five list items are added to the "Orders:" text box. Your screen should look like the following illustration:

The program should work as expected, tracking each selection made, including the "Order All" selection via the new button you added to the page. In this case, there is redundancy in the Orders list, but that was by design. However, you could just as easily limit orders to only new items, or items during a particular growing season, or time of day. Once you become familiar with text-processing operations and working with decision structures and event handlers, you can respond to a wide range of user input scenarios.

20. Close the program, and return to the Visual Studio IDE with the Taste of Summer application still loaded in the IDE.

You have one more flow control skill to learn in this chapter: managing error conditions with an exception handler.

Writing an Exception Handler to Manage Error Conditions

Overseeing how your program code executes involves careful planning and the use of interface elements and code structures that collectively manage the flow of your application. Event handlers, decision structures, and loops all perform important roles in this process, but there are times when even the best planning comes to naught, and a run-time error or other defect causes your program to stop running.

When your Visual Basic application encounters an unexpected problem that it can't recover from, Visual Studio generates an exception, and the compiler creates an *Exception* object in your program that contains specific information about the error that took place. You can use this information to recover from the error, and if the situation seems like something that might plague the program again, you can write an *exception handler* (or *error handler*) to manage and respond to the error before it forces the program to terminate.

In Visual Basic, an exception handler is created within the event handler that contains the potentially troublesome code. The exception handler is defined by a *Try...Catch* code block, which identifies the worrisome statements and tells Visual Basic what to do if they produce an error. In this respect, *Try...Catch* is a decision structure like *If...Then...Else*. It controls program flow based on error conditions that may or may not take place.

The syntax for a *Try...Catch* exception handler is as follows:

```
Try
     Statements that might produce a run-time error
Catch ex As Exception
     Statements to run if a run-time error occurs
Finally
     Optional statements to run whether an error occurs or not
End Try
```

where *Try* identifies the beginning of the exception handler, *Catch* identifies the statements to run if a run-time error occurs, *ex* is the name of a variable that holds information about the error, and *Finally* identifies statements that are executed whether an error occurs or not. The *Finally* clause of the exception handler is optional, and many exception handlers do not use this feature. (The *Catch* block is also optional, but only when a *Finally* block is provided.)

What type of statements should you put in the *Try* section of an exception handler? You can use exception handlers in any situation where actions that you are performing might produce a run-time error. Remember that run-time errors are not basic compilation errors, which are typically identified by Visual Studio while you are developing your code in the IDE or using commands on the Build menu. Instead, run-time errors are unexpected errors that halt program execution, like incorrect path names, disk drive errors, bad Internet connections, problems with permissions or security, printer problems, and overflow or out-of-memory errors.

To help users recover from run-time errors, statements in the *Catch* clause of an exception handler should temporarily disable features that are causing problems, or display messages for users so that they can fix the problem (for example, restoring an Internet connection) before continuing. A useful related feature is the optional *ex* variable that can be declared within the *Catch* statement. If you declare such a catch variable (which you can name *ex* or something else), you are able to use the *ex.Message* string, which returns a text string describing the run-time error that occurred. If this message is displayed for users to see, they may be able to fix the problem.

In the following exercise, you'll create a *Try...Catch* exception handler that traps any error that might take place when the user clicks the new Order All button in the Taste of Summer program. As you will recall, the button directs Visual Basic to place the item name of each item in the list box into the Orders text box at the bottom of the page. Although this code seems to be working just fine, there is one condition under which the button will produce a run-time error: if one of the list box items is empty (in other words, if the list box item's *Content* property is set to ""). If that unlikely situation takes place—perhaps because a later programmer or employee modifies the list box to add new seasonal items—the program should display an appropriate message and disable the button.

Add an exception handler

1. Display the Visual Studio Designer and adjust the Designer window so that the list box object is visible.

   You'll begin by intentionally introducing the empty list item error condition described previously.

2. Click the third item in the list box ("Cherries"), open the Properties window, and delete the text in the *Content* property.

   The item remains in the list box, but the item has no textual content. Now you'll run the program to see what happens when you click the Order All button.

3. Click the Start Debugging button.

   The application loads and runs.

4. Click the Order All button.

Visual Studio runs the *Button_Click_1* event handler, but this time the statement

```
TextBox2.Text = TextBox2.Text & item.Content.ToString() & ", "
```

produces a run-time error. The problem is that the expression *item.Content.ToString()* does not work if the *Content* property contains an empty or *Nothing* value. You'll see the following run-time error and exception message:

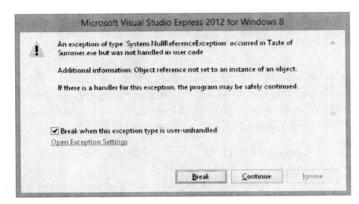

5. Click the Break button, and when the Visual Studio IDE returns, click the Stop Debugging button on the toolbar.

Now you'll add an exception handler to the *OrderButton_Click* event handler.

6. Display the Code Editor and scroll to the bottom of the *MainPage.xaml.vb* file.

Because you already have program code in this subprocedure, what you'll need to do is build the following *Try...Catch* exception handler under the existing variable declaration and around the *For Each...Next* loop. The keyword *Try* will go below the variable declaration, and *Catch* and the remaining exception handler statements will go below the *For Each...Next* loop.

7. Edit the *OrderButton_Click* event handler so that it looks like the following (the new program statements are formatted in bold to help you identify them):

```
Private Sub OrderButton_Click (sender As Object, e As RoutedEventArgs)
        Dim item As Object
    Try
        For Each item In listboxPhotos.Items
            TextBox2.Text = TextBox2.Text & item.Content.ToString() & ", "
        Next
    Catch ex As Exception
        TextBox2.Text =
            "Order All button disabled. Error processing items. "
        TextBox2.Text = TextBox2.Text & ex.Message
        OrderButton.IsEnabled = False
    End Try
End Sub
```

After you type the *Try* statement in the Code Editor and press the Enter key, Visual Studio adds the *Catch* and *End Try* statements to help you create the exception handler. However, the keywords are not put in the right place for your specific handler, so you'll need to move things around a little.

The *Catch* clause of the exception handler displays a message about the error condition for the user in a text box, and also uses the *ex.Message* string to provide details about the error from the *Exception* object. Finally, the *Catch* clause disables the Order All button so that the user is not able to click it again.

Now you'll save and test the exception handler.

8. Select File | Save All to save your changes.

9. Click Start Debugging.

   The application loads and runs.

10. Click the Order All button.

    Visual Studio runs the *OrderButton_Click* event handler again, but this time the new exception handler traps the run-time error. A helpful message appears in the text box, and the Order All button is disabled. Your screen should look like this:

Taste of Summer!

Strawberry Shortcake

Strawberry-Rhubarb Jam

Rhubarb

Apples

Select a Summer Taste...

Order All button disabled. Error processing items. Object reference not set to an instance of an object.

The exception handler should work as expected. Although the user might be annoyed with the message and the user interface is now only partially functional, the achievement is that the program has not completely *crashed*, or terminated abruptly. However, it you click the third list box item, you will notice that the code in the *listboxPhotos_SelectionChanged* event handler produces the same run-time error. The problem is the last line in the handler, which uses the same *Content.ToString()* code that you protected with the *Try...Catch* block. If you want, you can write an event handler for this situation, as well. Do you know how to do it?

Although it takes a little effort, you can make your programs quite error proof if you test your decision structures and flow control routines carefully, and write *Try...Catch* exception handlers for tests or conditions that could produce errors. With some effort, you can direct exception handlers to repair list boxes and other user interface elements, or present suitable error messages to the user. As you write programs that become more sophisticated and rely on external resources such as files, databases, and Internet connections, you'll need the flexibility and error protection that exception handlers provide.

11. Close the program and return to the Visual Studio IDE.

You're finished working in Visual Studio for now.

12. Select File | Exit to close Visual Studio and the Taste of Summer solution.

Congratulations! You've learned several valuable coding skills in this chapter, including how to control program flow and respond to errors if your program encounters them.

If you liked the design focus of this chapter, there's more to come. In Chapter 11, you'll learn more about fine-tuning the presentation of Windows 8 applications, including adding a tile to the Windows Start page, using a splash screen at startup, and designing applications for touch input and gestures. In Chapter 12, "Future Development Opportunities and the Windows Store," you'll learn more about selling and deploying applications.

Summary

This chapter explored controlling the design and program flow of Windows 8 applications. Some of the main design goals of Windows 8 apps is that they should be rich with content and information, and that they should present program elements in clear, well-organized tiles and panels containing graphical content. This chapter investigated several strategies for doing that, including using *ListBox*, *Image*, *TextBox*, and *TextBlock* controls to display colorful text and photographs.

From a Visual Basic programmer's point of view, the code-related skills necessary to manage input and program flow include writing well-organized event handlers and responding to error conditions if and when they occur. In this chapter, you learned how to use the *Select Case* and *If...Then...Else* decision structures to branch conditionally based on program circumstances, and how to use *For...Next* and *For Each...Next* loops to execute statements repeatedly and process object collections.

You also learned much more about processing input selections from the user, and how to work creatively with text strings using object properties and the string concatenation operator that you first encountered in Chapter 6. Finally, you used the *Try...Catch* exception handler to plan for run-time errors that might otherwise halt program execution.

In Chapter 8, "Using the .NET Framework," you'll learn how to add power and breadth to your applications by harnessing advanced features of the .NET Framework, a powerful programming interface that provides access to useful system resources, text-processing methods, mathematical formulas, and more. You will also revisit flow control and learn how to use a *Do...While* loop in a program.

Using the .NET Framework

After completing this chapter, you'll be able to

- Tap into the power of the Windows operating system using the .NET Framework class libraries.

- Use the Object Browser to learn about .NET Framework classes.

- Process text strings using methods in the *System.String* class.

- Calculate formulas using methods in the *System.Math* class.

- Generate random numbers using methods in the *System.Random* class.

- Use code snippets to insert ready-made code into your projects.

- Use a *Do...While* loop to execute a group of program statements repeatedly.

IN THIS CHAPTER, YOU'LL LEARN TO use the .NET Framework, a comprehensive, object-oriented class library that allows you to streamline a number of development tasks, including processing strings, building mathematical formulas, rendering graphics, connecting to databases, and requesting system information. The .NET Framework is installed as a core component of the Windows operating system, and Microsoft Visual Studio programs rely on many of its features to load and operate. Although the .NET Framework generally works behind the scenes, providing a variety of services to running applications, programmers can also take advantage of the framework's features directly, including those designed to support Windows 8 applications.

This chapter teaches you how to use important classes in .NET Framework class libraries, and how to browse through .NET classes with the Object Browser. You'll review popular string-processing methods in the *System.String* class, and you'll practice formatting the contents of string variables in useful ways. Next, you'll explore methods in the *System.Math* class, and you'll write a program that computes advanced mathematical formulas. While working with mathematical values, you'll learn how to use the *System.Random* class to generate a series of random numbers in your program, and also how to insert ready-made code snippets into your program. Looked at collectively, the features introduced in this chapter will give you a sense of how capable and wide-ranging the Visual Studio 2012 software is.

Programming Resourcefully: Using Class Libraries in the .NET Framework

Programmers don't like reinventing the wheel. If they take the time to create an event handler or a procedure to perform a given task, they want to use it again. And even more, if *another* programmer has already created an efficient routine to perform useful work, such as a conversion routine to translate file formats, most programmers will happily use it, provided that they can adapt the code to fit their particular situation. With all the emerging technologies developers need to learn, there is plenty to do without having to create every routine in your application from scratch.

Successful software publishers understand this situation, and they do their best to provide their developer customers with libraries of efficient, common routines that they can readily integrate into their projects. Microsoft took this situation into account when designing the Windows 8 operating system, so it's no surprise that Visual Studio provides an extensive collection of tested, coded solutions that developers can use right out of the box. The most significant example of this functionality is the .NET Framework, a large assortment of verified, ready-to-use assemblies and classes that Visual Studio programmers can employ to make their projects successful.

The newest version of the .NET Framework is 4.5. It is installed as a core component of the Windows 8 operating system. This framework provides support for Windows 8 applications, and it is tightly integrated into Visual Studio 2012, so that when you create new Microsoft Visual Basic or Microsoft Visual C# apps for the Windows Store, the .NET Framework class libraries on which they rely are already installed.

The .NET Framework libraries are organized into two sets of namespaces for Visual Studio 2012 developers that are constructing Windows 8 applications. The first set contains classes from a subset of the .NET Framework specifically designed for Windows 8 apps, and they can be identified by the name *System*. The second set contains classes related to the Windows Runtime API; you can identify them by the name *Windows*. You use the two sets of namespaces in the same way; in fact, they are essentially interchangeable regarding how you access them. Visual Studio automatically includes the assemblies associated with these namespaces in new Visual Basic 2012 projects. You can see (and modify) the list of the namespaces by selecting the Properties command on the Project menu, choosing the References category, and then examining the Imported Namespaces section of the resulting page. You can also use the *Imports* statement in code to specify which namespace you are referencing, or to define an *alias*, or shorthand notation, for a reference that would otherwise be lengthy and cumbersome.

 More Info To review the syntax of the *Imports* statement, which you can use to reference common namespaces, see the "Using the *CheckBox* and *RadioButton* Controls" section in Chapter 3, "Using Controls."

Object-Oriented Terminology

The .NET Framework is an *object-oriented class library*, which means that you refer to its contents using object-oriented concepts and syntax. As you have already learned, classes gather together all the data and behaviors that collectively define a programming feature, or *interface*, that developers can use in program code. The internal characteristics of a class are typically hidden from view, but the *properties*, *methods*, and *events* associated with classes are made available in a public way (via IntelliSense and other features) that makes it possible to take advantage of class features in Visual Basic program code.

.NET classes are organized into namespaces according to the task that they perform and the system component with which they are associated. Because there are so many namespaces, Microsoft has organized them into multilayered *hierarchies* that define parent namespaces and child namespaces. Namespaces can contain classes, related types, and other namespaces—every class or type must appear in some namespace.

Objects in Visual Studio programs are merely specific *instances* of classes. In other words, a class is a unique model or *blueprint* for a programmable feature that can be used, but an object is a *specific instance* of the class, with its own unique characteristics. For example, imagine three text box objects on a page in the Visual Studio Designer. Although each object was created using the same *TextBox* control in the XAML Toolbox (which in turn uses the *TextBox* class for its definition), each instance of the control is unique, maintaining its own name, content, dimensions, event handlers, and other defining characteristics.

Objects derive their characteristics from classes just like baked cookies derive their shape and physical characteristics from a kitchen cookie cutter. Object-oriented programming concepts like this explain how different classes and objects are connected in a project, and how comprehensive class libraries in the .NET Framework are organized and referenced. In fact, if you are not satisfied with the classes supplied to you with Visual Studio, you can modify them in useful ways, passing along the characteristics of one class to another through a system known as *inheritance*. You can also create your own class from scratch, with unique properties and event handlers that perform useful work in your programs.

With these concepts in mind, let's explore some of the useful class libraries in the .NET Framework. You'll begin by using the Visual Studio Object Browser to examine the classes in your own project, and then you'll tap into the breadth of built-in classes in the .NET Framework libraries for Windows 8 applications.

 More Info To learn more about the vocabulary of object-oriented terminology, see Chapter 10, "Object-Oriented Programming," in the free companion volume, *Start Here! Fundamentals of .NET Programming* (Microsoft Press, 2011). To learn how to create your own classes in a Visual Basic project and experiment with advanced features such as inheritance, see my *Microsoft Visual Basic 2012 Step by Step* (Microsoft Press, 2013).

Using the Object Browser

The Object Browser is a tool in the Visual Studio IDE that provides detailed information about the classes in your project, as well as the classes that you can use in the .NET Framework. Microsoft recommends that you become familiar with navigating namespace hierarchies using the Object Browser, and that you use the tool routinely as you develop a working knowledge of .NET Framework capabilities and syntax. You'll use the Object Browser in the following section to explore a new programming project and to investigate the *Microsoft.VisualBasic* namespace, a namespace with core Visual Basic language components and classes.

Use the Object Browser to explore *Microsoft.VisualBasic*

1. Start Visual Studio Express and click New Project to open a new Visual Studio application.

2. Choose Visual Basic / Windows Store under Templates, and then verify that the Blank App (XAML) template is selected.

3. Type **My Framework Power** in the Name text box.

4. Click OK to open and configure the new project.

   Visual Studio creates a new project with typical project files.

5. Right-click the *MainPage.xaml* file in Solution Explorer, and then select View Designer.

   Visual Studio loads *MainPage.xaml* into the Designer. Now you'll change the background color of the grid to green, and add a *TextBox* control and a *Button* control to the page. These elements will help you create a suitable test environment for experimenting with classes in the .NET Framework libraries.

6. Click the grid object (the page background) in the Designer, open the Properties window, and click the Brush category.

7. Open the edit menu for the *Background* property (the dark button to the right of the *Background* property in the Brush category), click Custom Expression, type **DarkGreen**, and press Enter.

   Visual Studio changes the background color of the grid to dark green. Because the grid covers the entire page, this change has the effect of changing the entire page's color.

8. Add a rectangular *TextBox* control to the page that is large enough for three lines of text.

9. Add a rectangular *Button* control to the page.

10. Set the following properties for the text box and button objects:

Object	Property	Setting
Text box	Name Text	TextBox1 ""
Button	Name Content	Button1 "Click to Test"

Your page will look like this:

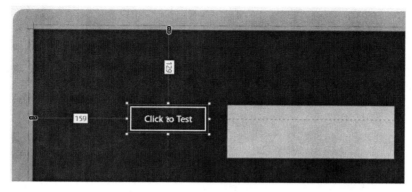

Now you'll open the Object Browser and look at your project's objects and classes, as well as the classes in the .NET Framework.

11. Click View | Object Browser.

Visual Studio opens the Object Browser in a window in the IDE. The Object Browser appears as a tabbed window, as most of the programming tools do by default. Your screen will look like this:

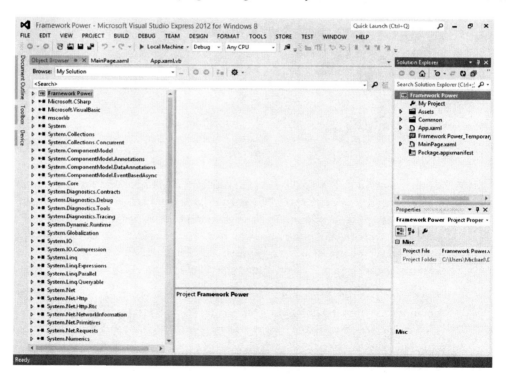

Note that you can resize, pin, dock, and close the Object Browser as you would the Properties window or any tool window. (For a refresher on how to manage essential window manipulation tasks, see Chapter 1, "Getting to Know Visual Basic 2012.")

As you can see, the Object Browser displays a lot of information. In the Objects pane on the left, icons identify hierarchical items such as the components of the .NET Framework. You can click these icons to displays the members of each group. What you see now are mostly the assemblies within the .NET Framework for Windows 8 applications. However, near the top of the list is a boxed "VB" icon, and this represents My Framework Power, your new Visual Studio project.

12. Verify that "My Solution" is selected in the Browse drop-down text box near the top of the Object Browser.

This option allows you to control which namespaces are displayed in the Object Browser; you should begin by examining the namespaces included in your application.

13. Click the expansion icon next to My Framework Power to see the namespace and classes associated with your application.

Expand the App and Application classes if they are not expanded in your Object Browser. Your window will look like this:

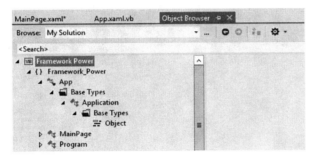

At this point, you'll see a fuller hierarchy of items in your application. At the top is the root namespace of your project, My_*Framework_Power*, and below that are three top-level classes: *App*, *MainPage*, and *Program*. These correspond to the three main areas of your project. At this point, you can continue your exploration of the project by clicking individual items. If more detailed information is available, you'll see it in the browser, and you'll also notice different icon shapes—each for a different type of information.

As you can see, the Visual Studio Object Browser provides an entirely new way to look at your application—from the point of view of an object-oriented programmer who is curious about the relationships among the classes, objects, properties, and events in the program.

Now you'll take a look at the *Microsoft.VisualBasic* namespace, which is also listed in the Object Browser. This namespace contains a number of items that are of use to Visual Basic programmers. Because this namespace is listed here, in the Object Browser, you know that it is available to your application—you just need to know how to use it!

14. Close the expansion icon next to the *My_Framework_Power* project, and then expand the *Microsoft.VisualBasic* assembly.

You'll see the *Microsoft.VisualBasic* namespace and its members.

15. Click Constants.

You'll see a list of string constants that are useful for working with string values, as shown in the following screen shot:

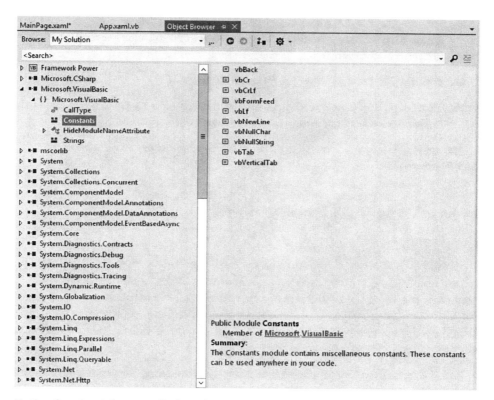

Notice that the right pane displays the 10 actual constants that *Microsoft.VisualBasic* provides, including *vbCr*, *vbCrLf*, *vbTab*, and so on. The "vb" in these constant names is an indication that they have roots in Visual Basic syntax and usage, and in fact these constants have been provided to Visual Studio programmers for some time. The description pane further indicates the module that these items are stored in, and it provides a summary comment.

16. Click the *vbCrLf* constant.

A message indicates that the constant is of type *String*, and that it represents a carriage-return character combined with a linefeed character. Programmers will typically append such a character to the end of a line of text when they are displaying it on the screen, printing, or manipulating text files. For example, the program statements:

```
Dim strTest As String
strTest = "Hello " & "friend" & vbCrLf
```

declare a variable of type *String*, concatenate two string values, and end the line with a combined carriage return–linefeed character.

Beyond this interesting string-processing feature, however, is a valuable new technique for discovering which framework elements are available to you.

17. Spend a few minutes exploring some of the other assemblies listed here for use in your programs. Expand the assemblies and namespaces, and examine the individual classes, methods, properties, and events.

18. When you're finished, close the Object Browser.

19. Click Save All to save your project, and then specify the *My Documents\Start Here! Programming in Visual Basic\Chapter 8* folder for the location.

Now let's examine how some of the .NET Framework features can be used in the new My Framework Power project.

Using Methods in *System.String*

Because so many input and output operations have to do with processing text strings, the .NET Framework class libraries feature string operations in several namespaces. The most significant for our purposes now is *System.String*, which is also referred to as the *String* class in the Visual Studio documentation. The *String* class exposes many members, including properties, methods, operators, fields, and constructors—several which are beyond the scope of this book. However, if you want to perform a string operation on one or more strings, and you would like to use a ready-made tool to accomplish your work, *System.String* is the place to look.

Table 8-1 lists several methods and one property in the *String* class that appear regularly in string-processing routines. Each is provided by the .NET Framework for your use and can be inserted into your programs right away. The third column in the table provides a sample Visual Basic routine to demonstrate how the elements work.

An interesting feature of the examples is that they also demonstrate how the behaviors (or methods) of the *String* class can be applied to variables of type *String*. For example, in the first row of Table 8-1, the *ToUpper* method is attached to the *BaseName* string variable, so that the content of the variable is changed to uppercase. You'll see several examples of this technique in this book.

TABLE 8-1 Popular Members of the *String* Class in the .NET Framework

String Method or Property	Description	String Example

ToUpper	Changes letters in a string to uppercase	`Dim BaseName, NewName As String`
		`BaseName = "Kim"`
		`NewName = BaseName.ToUpper`
		`'NewName = "KIM"`

ToLower	Changes letters in a string to lowercase	`Dim BaseName, NewName As String`
		`BaseName = "Kim"`
		`NewName = BaseName.ToLower`
		`'NewName = "kim"`

Length	Determines the number of characters in a string	`Dim River As String`
		`Dim Size As Short`
		`River = "Mississippi"`
		`Size = River.Length`
		`'Size = 11`

Contains	Determines whether the specified string occurs in the current string	`Dim region As String`
		`Dim result As Boolean`
		`region = "Germany"`
		`result = region.Contains("Ge")`
		`'result = True`

Substring	Returns a fixed number of characters in a string from a given starting point (the first element in a string has an index of 0)	`Dim Cols, Middle As String`
		`Cols = "First Second Third"`
		`Middle = Cols.SubString(6, 6)`
		`'Middle = "Second"`

IndexOf	Finds the starting point of one string within a larger string (the first element in the string has an index of 0; returns –1 if the string is not found)	`Dim BaseName As String`
		`Dim Start As Short`
		`BaseName = "Abraham"`
		`Start = BaseName.IndexOf("h")`
		`'Start = 4`

Trim	Removes leading and trailing spaces from a string	`Dim Spacey, Trimmed As String`
		`Spacey = "   Hello   "`
		`Trimmed = Spacey.Trim`
		`'Trimmed = "Hello"`

Remove	Removes characters from the middle of a string	`Dim RawStr, CleanStr As String`
		`RawStr = "Hello333 there"`
		`CleanStr = RawStr.Remove(5, 3)`
		`'CleanStr = "Hello there"`

Insert	Adds characters to the middle of a string	`Dim Oldstr, Newstr As String`
		`Oldstr = "Hi Felix"`
		`Newstr = Oldstr.Insert(3, "there ")`
		`'Newstr = "Hi there Felix"`

Compare	Compares strings and can disregard case differences	`Dim str1 As String = "Soccer"`
		`Dim str2 As String = "SOCCER"`
		`Dim Match As Integer`
		`Match = String.Compare(str1, str2, True)`
		`'Match = 0 [strings match]`

CompareTo	Compares a string to the current string and checks for case differences	`Dim str1 As String = "Soccer"`
		`Dim str2 As String = "SOCCER"`
		`Dim Match As Integer`
		`Match = str1.CompareTo(str2)`
		`'Match = -1 [strings do not match]`

Replace	Replaces all instances of a substring in a string with another string	`Dim Oldstr, Newstr As String`
		`Oldstr= "*se*ll"`
		`Newstr = Oldstr.Replace("*", "ba")`
		`'Newstr = "baseball"`

String Method or Property	Description	String Example
StartsWith	Determines whether a string starts with a specified string	```Dim str1 As String
Dim result As Boolean
str1 = "Hi Felix"
result = str1.StartsWith("Hi")
'result = True```
EndsWith	Determines whether a string ends with a specified string	```Dim str1 As String
Dim result As Boolean
str1 = "Hi Felix"
result = str1.EndsWith("Felix")
'result = True```
Split	Splits a string into substrings based on a specified separator and puts the substrings into a collection of variables called an array (see Chapter 10, "Managing Data with Arrays and LINQ")	```Dim AllText As String = "a*b*c*1*2*3"
Dim strArray() As String
strArray = AllText.Split("*")
'strArray = {"a", "b", "c", "1", "2", "3"}```

The following exercise demonstrates how you can use the *ToUpper*, *ToLower*, and *Compare* methods in a Visual Basic code-behind file.

Process text with .NET Framework methods

1. Click the button object on the page in the Visual Studio Designer, and then open the Properties window.

2. In the Properties window, click the Event Handler button to create a new event handler for the button object.

3. Double-click next to the *Click* event in the Properties window.

    Visual Studio creates an event handler named *Button1_Click*, and opens the *MainPage.xaml.vb* code-behind file in the Code Editor.

4. Type the following program statement in the Code Editor between *Private Sub* and *End Sub*:

    ```
    TextBox1.Text = TextBox1.Text.ToUpper()
    ```

    This simple, one-line event handler uses the *ToUpper* method of the *System.String* class to convert the contents of the text box object on the page to uppercase characters. Specifically, the *ToUpper* method generates a new uppercase string using the text found in the *TextBox1 .Text* string instance, and then uses that generated string to replace the existing *TextBox* content via the = assignment operator.

    You'll run the program now to see how the *ToUpper* method works.

5. Click the Start Debugging button.

The application launches and presents a page containing a button and a text box.

6. Type **This is a test** in the text box.

Your screen should look like this:

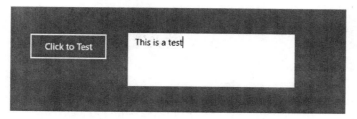

7. Click the Click to Test button.

Visual Basic uses the *ToUpper* method to convert the text string to uppercase. Your screen should look like this:

As you can see, the entire text string is converted to uppercase. Even the first character is replaced, but it just happens to be replaced with an identical character (the letter *T*).

8. Close the program and display the *Button1_Click* event handler again.

9. Edit the program statement that you just entered by changing the *ToUpper* method to *ToLower*.

As a complement to *ToUpper*, the *ToLower* method converts the contents of a string variable (or string property) to lowercase characters. If a character in the string is already lowercase, that character is also replaced, but with an identical (lowercase) character.

You'll run the program now to see how the *ToLower* method works.

10. Click the Start Debugging button.

The application runs.

11. Type **The door went SLAM!** in the text box.

Your screen should look like this:

12. Click the Click to Test button.

Visual Basic uses the *ToLower* method to convert the text string to lowercase. Your screen should look like this:

Now you have two new .NET Framework methods to use, and both offer popular methods to organize user input in a predictable format. For example, you may need to convert name, address, or state user input strings to uppercase so that any pattern-matching comparisons work as expected. (You never know what format users will enter data in.)

13. Close the My Framework Power program.

In the following exercise, you'll experiment with the *Contains* method to read text box input from the user and determine if it contains a search string.

Search a string for a pattern

1. Display the *Button1_Click* event handler in the Code Editor.

2. Delete the program statement containing the *ToLower* method and replace it with the following *If...Then...Else* decision structure:

```
Dim StringExists As Boolean
StringExists = TextBox1.Text.Contains("Los Angeles")
If StringExists Then
    TextBox1.Text = "Input string contains 'Los Angeles'"
Else
    TextBox1.Text = "String not found"
End If
```

This Visual Basic code declares a Boolean variable named *StringExists*, which will hold a value of *True* or *False*. The second line uses the *Contains* method to determine if the city name "Los Angeles" appears in the text box object on the page. If the city is present somewhere in the user input, then the *StringExists* variable is assigned the value of *True*, and the *If...Then...Else* structure displays "Input string contains 'Los Angeles'" in the text box. Otherwise, the message "String not found" is displayed.

> **Note** To learn more about the *If...Then...Else* decision structure, see Chapter 7, "Controlling Application Design, Layout, and Program Flow."

3. Click the Start Debugging button.

   The application runs in the Visual Studio IDE.

4. Type **Meet me in Los Angeles, OK?** in the text box.

   Your screen should look like this:

5. Click the Click to Test button.

   Visual Basic uses the *Contains* method and determines that the text string "Los Angeles" does appear in the user input that you typed. Your screen should look like this:

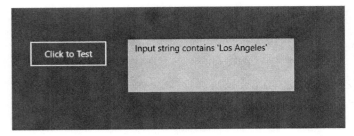

Note that the *Contains* method produced a value of *True* because the text string matched exactly. Had you typed "LOS ANGELES", the result would have been *False*.

6. Type **I will be driving to Minnesota this Summer** in the text box, and then click Click to Test.

Your screen should look like this:

The *Contains* method returned *False* since the string "Los Angeles" did not appear anywhere in the input.

7. Close the Framework Power program.

Continue experimenting with the *String* class in the .NET Framework if you like, using Table 8-1 as a guide to further explorations. Keep in mind that you can use more than one method or property from the .NET Framework in a routine, often to great effect.

For example, if you want to handle the issue of letter casing in your input, making sure that whether the input is uppercase, lowercase, or a mixture, the routine will produce the expected results, edit the code as follows (the only changes are in the second line):

```
Dim StringExists As Boolean
StringExists = TextBox1.Text.ToUpper.Contains("LOS ANGELES")
If StringExists Then
    TextBox1.Text = "Input string contains 'Los Angeles'"
Else
    TextBox1.Text = "String not found"
End If
```

There are a few things that you might note about this routine. First, the *ToUpper* and *Contains* methods are processed by the Visual Basic compiler from left to right in the second line, so *ToUpper* returns a string in uppercase, and then the *Contains* method searches through the string for the value "LOS ANGELES". The routine offers another example of the way that string properties and methods can be combined together to perform useful work.

Give it a try in Visual Studio now and see what happens!

Using Methods in *System.Math*

Now and then you'll want to do a little extra number crunching in your programs. You might need to round a number, calculate a complex mathematical expression, or introduce randomness into your programs. The math methods shown in Table 8-2 can help you work with numbers in your formulas. These methods are provided by the *System.Math* class of the .NET Framework, a class that lets you harness your computer's ability to perform calculations with tremendous speed and accuracy. The argument *n* in the table represents the number, variable, property, or expression that you want the method to evaluate.

TABLE 8-2 Useful Math Methods in the *System.Math* Class

Method	Purpose
Abs(n)	Returns the absolute value of n.
Atan(n)	Returns the arctangent, in radians, of n.
Cos(n)	Returns the cosine of the angle n. The angle n is expressed in radians.
Exp(n)	Returns the constant e raised to the power n.
Sign(n)	Returns -1 if n is less than 0, 0 if n equals 0, and +1 if n is greater than 0.
Sin(n)	Returns the sine of the angle n. The angle n is expressed in radians.
Sqrt(n)	Returns the square root of n.
Tan(n)	Returns the tangent of the angle n. The angle n is expressed in radians.

Note This is only a partial listing of the methods in the *System.Math* class. There are many more methods related to numerical calculations in the .NET Framework that Windows applications can use.

Give the math methods in the .NET Framework a try now by completing the following exercise.

Use the *System.Math* class to compute square roots

1. Display the *Button1_Click* event handler in the Code Editor.

2. Delete all seven lines of program code in the body of the event handler and replace them with the following statements:

```
Dim result As Double
result = System.Math.Sqrt(625)
TextBox1.Text = result
```

This routine declares a value named *result* of type *Double*, and calls the *Sqrt* method in the *System.Math* class to compute the square root of 625. The answer is displayed in the text box object on the page.

3. Click the Start Debugging button.

4. Click the Click to Test button.

Visual Studio calls the .NET Framework method and computes the result. Your screen should look like this:

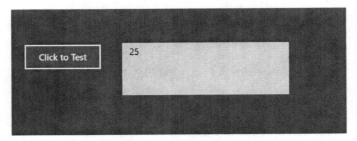

The square root of 625 *is* 25, as the program has calculated. The routine seems to be working correctly. But let's see what happens when you enter a much larger number for the calculation.

5. Close the program and display the *Button1_Click* event handler again.

6. Change 625 in the second line to 650250000.

That's a big number—over 650 million! And unfortunately, you can't include commas in large numbers like this when you are writing Visual Basic code. They confuse the compiler when you enter them. (Visual Basic thinks you are entering multiple arguments.)

7. Click Start Debugging again.

The application runs.

8. Click the Click to Test button.

Visual Studio computes the formula again, and displays the result of your more significant calculation. (The answer should be 25500.) Your screen should look like this:

Everything should now be working correctly.

9. Close the program.

Now you'll add a little *randomness* to your program by calculating random numbers using methods in the .NET Framework.

Working with Random Numbers

In computer terminology, a *random number* is a number that appears to be selected at random within a given range of values. For example, a programmer writing a game that randomly selects numbers between 1 and 100 would expect that numbers chosen at random would fall somewhere between 1 and 100, inclusively, and that a sequence of random numbers would be equally unpredictable—that is, there would be no discernible pattern among them.

I use the phrase "appears to be selected at random" because in computer programming, what you get when you generate a random number is actually a *pseudorandom substitute* for a number that would be truly unpredictable. Although this terminology seemingly borders on the philosophical, it is important to understand that when computer programs generate "random numbers," what they are actually doing is using a mathematical formula to produce values that seemingly follow no discernible pattern. Such numbers are a kind of substitute for "actual" random sequences or patterns that take place in nature, but are in the end artificially constructed. (You can learn much more about random numbers by searching for "random numbers" or "pseudorandom number generator" on the web.)

The .NET Framework provides the *System.Random* class to handle the creation of random numbers in Windows applications. Within this class are methods that can produce a sequence of numbers that meet statistical requirements for pseudorandomness—that is, they are created using a subtractive random number–generating algorithm, as defined by computer scientist Donald E. Knuth in his book *The Art of Computer Programming, Volume. 2: Seminumerical Algorithms, Third Edition* (Addison-Wesley, 1997).

There are many practical uses for random numbers in a program, including creating lottery programs, slot machines, roulette wheels, and games involving dice, coin flipping, shuffling cards, and so on. Randomness is even used in the fields of business, finance, mathematics, biology, and physics. For example, in physics, the theory of quantum mechanics uses randomness to explain how long it will take an unstable atom to decay.

The following exercise demonstrates how you can use the *Next* method in the *System.Random* class to generate a random number in the range of 1 to 100.

Generate a random number

1. Display the *Button1_Click* event handler in the Code Editor.

2. Delete all three lines of program code in the event handler and replace them with the following statements:

```
Dim generator As New Random
Dim randomValue As Integer
randomValue = generator.Next(1, 101)
TextBox1.Text = TextBox1.Text & " " & randomValue
```

This routine declares a *generator* variable of type *Random* in the project, and a *randomValue* variable of type *Integer* to hold the random number that is created. The *Next* method returns a new random number in the range of 1 to 101. The bottom number in the range, 1, can appear in the list of randomly generated numbers, but the highest valid number in the range is 100. (In other words, the range of random numbers is greater than or equal to 1, but less than 101.)

Each time that this routine is executed, a new random number is returned and assigned to the text box object on the page. Because the fourth line uses a pair of string concatenation operators *(&)*, the list of random numbers is added to each time the *Button1_Click* event handler is executed.

3. Click the Start Debugging button.

    The application starts.

4. Click the Click to Test button.

    Visual Studio calls the *Button1_Click* event handler and generates a random number.

5. Click the Click to Test button 20 more times.

    With each new call to the event handler, a new random number is generated. Your screen should look something like this:

This random number sequence is quite unpredictable. In fact, if you run the program again you will get completely different numbers.

6. Close the program.

You've learned to use another interesting feature of the .NET Framework class library.

Using Code Snippets to Insert Ready-Made Code

If you've enjoyed using the .NET Framework methods in this chapter, you might appreciate one additional example that uses the *System.Random* class to display random numbers on a page. This example also demonstrates an interesting feature of Visual Studio called the Insert Snippet command, which lets you insert ready-made code templates, or *snippets*, into the Code Editor from a list of common programming tasks. Visual Studio comes automatically configured with a library of useful code snippets, and you can add additional snippets from your own programs or from online resources such as MSDN. The following exercise shows you how to use this helpful feature. You'll also learn how to use a *Do...While* loop, a flow control structure that allows you to repeat a set of program statements until a particular condition is met.

Generate a set of random numbers with a *Do...While* loop

1. Display the *Button1_Click* event handler in the Code Editor.

2. Delete the last two program statements in the event handler so that only the following variable declarations remain:

```
Dim generator As New Random
Dim randomValue As Integer
```

3. Move the insertion pointer below the second *Dim* statement.

Now you'll use the Insert Snippet command to help you add some Visual Basic code to your application.

4. At the insertion point (below the second *Dim* statement), click the right mouse button to open a context menu in the Code Editor, and then click the Insert Snippet command, as shown in the following illustration:

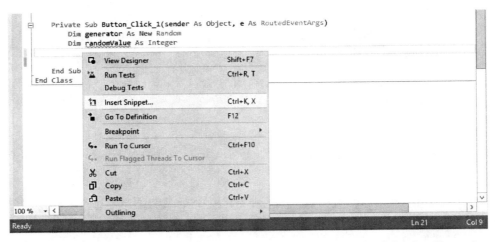

The Insert Snippet list box appears in the Code Editor, as shown in the following illustration. Depending on what version of Visual Studio you have installed, your snippet list may have some differences.

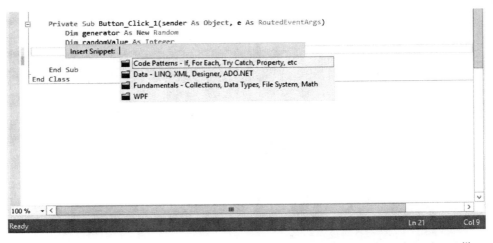

The Insert Snippet list box is a navigation tool that you can use to explore the snippet library and insert snippets into your program at the insertion point. To open a folder in the list box, double-click the folder name or press the Enter key when the folder name is highlighted. To return to the previous folder in the folder hierarchy, press the Backspace key.

5. In the list box, double-click the Code Patterns folder.

In this folder, you'll find snippets related to flow control structures in the Visual Basic language.

6. Double-click the Conditionals and Loops folder.

A list of loops and decision structures appears. The *For Each...Next, For...Next,* and *If...Then... Else* structures will be familiar to you from Chapter 7, but in this exercise you'll use a new looping structure called a *Do...While* loop.

7. Double-click the snippet entitled "Do...While Loop Statement."

Visual Studio inserts the following lines of code into the *Button1_Click* event handler at the insertion point:

```
Do While True

Loop
```

As an alternative to a *For...Next* loop, a *Do...While* loop executes a group of statements until a certain condition is *False. Do...While* loops are valuable because often you can't know in advance how many times a loop should repeat. In this case, the Insert Snippet command has provided you with the basic template for the loop. You just need to replace the *True* keyword with a valid looping condition and add the contents of the loop. Some of the snippets provided by Visual Studio are templates, like this one, and others insert elements from .NET Framework classes or other Visual Basic routines.

8. Replace the *True* keyword with the condition **randomValue <> 100**.

Visual Basic will translate this conditional expression to mean, "Loop as long as the integer variable *randomValue* does not contain 100." In this exercise, you will direct Visual Basic to generate random numbers between 1 and 101 and place them in the text box until the number 100 appears. At that point, the *Do...While* loop will terminate.

9. Between the *Do While* and *Loop* statements, type the following code:

```
randomValue = generator.Next(1, 101)
TextBox1.Text = TextBox1.Text & " " & randomValue
```

These are the same two statements you used earlier to generate and display random numbers in the text box. This time, however, you have placed them within the *Do...While* loop so that they will run over and over again until the number 100 appears. Your event handler should look like this:

```
Private Sub Button_Click_1(sender As Object, e As RoutedEventArgs)
    Dim generator As New Random
    Dim randomValue As Integer
    Do While randomValue <> 100
        randomValue = generator.Next(1, 101)
        TextBox1.Text = TextBox1.Text & " " & randomValue
    Loop

    End Sub
End Class
```

Well done. But because the results of this execution are not fully predictable (you don't know how many numbers will be generated), it makes sense now to add vertical scroll bars to the text box object, so that long lists of numbers can be more easily inspected by the user.

To add scroll bars to a text box, you need to use XAML markup, as scroll bars are not listed among the properties of a *TextBox* control in the Properties window.

10. Return to the Visual Studio Designer and click the text box object on the page.

First, you'll resize the text box object so that it is big enough to allow the vertical scroll bar to fully appear.

11. Using the resizing handles, resize the text box object so that its height is about twice what it is now.

You want the text box to be big enough that it can display about eight lines of text.

Now you'll add scroll bars to the text box object.

12. Open the XAML tab of the Code Editor, and locate the XAML markup for the *TextBox* control.

13. After the markup *x:Name="TextBox1"*, enter the following property setting:

```
ScrollViewer.VerticalScrollBarVisibility="Visible"
```

This property setting adds a vertical scroll bar to the text box and makes the scroll bar visible when the user places the mouse over the text box. (Otherwise, the scroll bar is not visible—this is an aspect of the Windows 8 application design guidelines, to minimize user interface "chrome.")

Your Designer and XAML code will look like this:

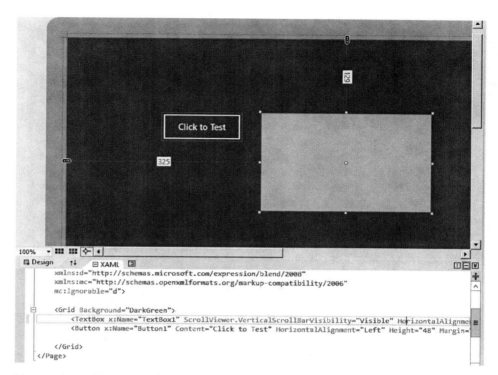

```
      xmlns:d="http://schemas.microsoft.com/expression/blend/2008"
      xmlns:mc="http://schemas.openxmlformats.org/markup-compatibility/2006"
      mc:Ignorable="d">

      <Grid Background="DarkGreen">
          <TextBox x:Name="TextBox1" ScrollViewer.VerticalScrollBarVisibility="Visible" HorizontalAlignme
          <Button x:Name="Button1" Content="Click to Test" HorizontalAlignment="Left" Height="48" Margin=

      </Grid>
</Page>
```

Now you're ready to save changes and run the program.

14. Select File | Save All to save your changes.

15. Click the Start Debugging button.

16. Click the Click to Test button.

Visual Studio calls the *Button1_Click* event handler and generates a list of random numbers.

As you can see, the routine looped many times before it finally generated the number 100. Your screen should look something like this:

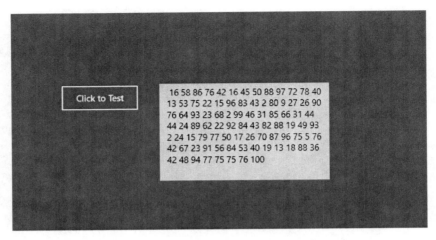

17. Click the Click to Test button again to run a second set of numbers.

    As the values are randomly generated, they are added to the list box, and the second set of random numbers follows a different sequence than the first. As soon as the text box is full, you can use the new scroll bar feature to examine any numbers that are not immediately visible.

18. Scroll to the bottom of the text box using the new scroll bar.

    Your text box with the new scroll bar should look like this:

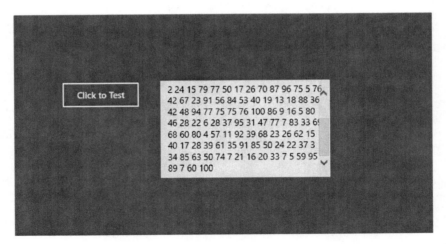

    Experiment with the scroll bar by clicking within the bar and by dragging the scroll bar indicator up and down. Scroll bars can be useful features, and you'll want to add them to your programming skill set.

19. Close the program, and then select File | Exit to close Visual Studio.

Congratulations! You've learned to generate random numbers using a *Do...While* loop, and also how to use the Insert Snippet command to add useful code templates to your programs.

 Tip To insert new snippets or reorganize the snippets that you have, click the Code Snippets Manager command on the Tools menu. The Code Snippets Manager dialog box gives you control over the contents of the Insert Snippet list box and also contains a mechanism for gathering new snippets online.

Summary

This chapter explored how to use the .NET Framework class libraries to add coding breadth to your Visual Basic applications. You learned how to use the Visual Studio Object Browser to explore the namespaces and classes in your projects, and to locate information about constants, properties, and methods in .NET Framework libraries. You've also learned how to use methods in the *System. String*, *System.Math*, and *System.Random* classes to add processing power to your Visual Basic code. Along the way, you learned how to use code snippets to add predefined code to your programs quickly, and how to use the *Do...While* loop to execute statements repeatedly until a specific condition has been met.

Although the .NET Framework generally works behind the scenes, providing services to running applications, it is also a key component of the product offerings of Visual Studio, allowing you to build formulas, render graphics, connect to databases, process strings, request system information, and much more. In the next chapter, you'll continue your exploration of Visual Basic and Visual Studio 2012 by learning how to track down and fix errors in your programs with the powerful debugging tools provided by the Visual Studio IDE.

Chapter 9

Debugging Applications

After completing this chapter, you'll be able to

- Identify different types of errors in your programs.

- Use Microsoft Visual Studio debugging tools to set breakpoints and correct mistakes.

- Use the Autos and Watch windows to examine variables during program execution.

- Use a visualizer to examine *String* data types and complex data types within the IDE.

- Use the Immediate window to change the value of variables and properties during program execution.

- Remove breakpoints.

IN THE PAST FEW CHAPTERS, YOU'VE had plenty of opportunity to make programming mistakes in your code. Unlike human conversation, which usually works well despite occasional grammatical mistakes and mispronunciations, communication between a software developer and the Microsoft Visual Basic compiler is successful only when the precise rules and regulations of the Visual Basic programming language are followed.

In this chapter, you'll learn more about the software defects, or *bugs*, that stop Visual Basic programs from running. You'll learn about the different types of errors that turn up in programs and how to use the Visual Studio debugging tools to detect and correct these defects. What you learn will be useful as you experiment with the programs in this book and when you write longer programs in the future.

Why focus on debugging now? Some programming books skip this topic altogether or place it near the end of the book (*after* you've learned all the language features of a particular product). There is a certain logic to postponing the discussion, but I think it makes the most sense to master debugging techniques *while* you learn to program so that detecting and correcting errors becomes part of your standard approach to writing programs and solving problems. At this point in this book, you know just enough about XAML controls, decision structures, and statement syntax to create interesting programs—but also enough to get yourself into a little bit of trouble! As you'll soon see, however, Visual Studio 2012 makes it easy to uncover your mistakes and get your programs working again.

Finding and Correcting Errors

The defects you've encountered in your programs so far have probably been simple typing mistakes or syntax errors. But what if you discover a nastier problem in your program—one you can't find and correct by a simple review of the objects, properties, and statements you've used? The Visual Studio IDE contains several tools that help you track down and fix errors in your programs. These tools won't stop you from making mistakes, but they often ease the pain when you encounter one.

Three Types of Errors

Three types of errors (or exceptions) can occur in a Visual Basic program: syntax errors, run-time errors, and logic errors. The following list describes each:

- A *syntax error* is a mistake (such as a misspelled property or keyword) that violates the programming rules of Visual Basic. Visual Basic will point out several types of syntax errors in your programs while you enter program statements, and it won't let you run a program until you fix each syntax error.

 Tip A syntax error recognized by the Visual Basic compiler when you try to build your project is sometimes known as a *compiler error*. You can often learn more about this type of programming mistake by reading about the problem in the Output window, which appears automatically when you build a project.

- A *run-time error* is a mistake that causes a program to stop unexpectedly during execution. Run-time errors occur when an outside event or a hidden problem (that is, an undetected syntax error) forces a program to stop while it's running. For instance, if you experience Internet connectivity problems while a program is running, or if you try to read a disk drive and it doesn't contain a CD or DVD, your code will generate a run-time error.

- A *logic error* is a human error—a mistake that causes the program code to produce the wrong results. Most debugging efforts are focused on tracking down logic errors introduced by the programmer.

If you encounter a syntax error, you often can solve the problem by using the MSDN documentation to learn more about the error message, and you can fix the mistake by paying close attention to the exact syntax of the functions, objects, methods, and properties that you have used. In the Code Editor, incorrect statements are underlined with a jagged blue line, and you can learn more about the error by holding the mouse pointer over the statement. The following screen shot shows the error message that appears in Visual Studio when I type the keyword *Case* incorrectly as "Csae" and then hold the mouse pointer over the error. This error message appears as a ScreenTip.

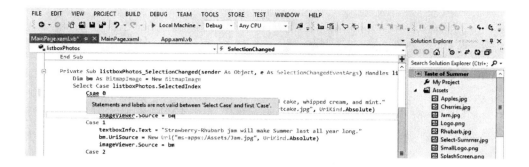

Tip By default, a jagged green line indicates a warning, a jagged red line indicates a syntax error, a jagged blue line indicates a compiler error, and a jagged purple line indicates some other error. The color of these items and most of the features in the user interface can be adjusted by selecting the Options command on the Tools menu, clicking the Fonts And Colors option under Environment, and adjusting the default values under Display Items.

If you encounter a run-time error, you often can address the problem by correcting your typing. For example, if a file containing electronic artwork loads incorrectly into an image object, the problem might simply be a misspelled file name. However, many run-time errors require a more thorough solution. You can add an *exception handler*—a special block of program code that recognizes a run-time error when it happens, suppresses any error messages, and adjusts program conditions to handle the problem—to your programs. I introduced the syntax for exception handlers in Chapter 7, "Controlling Application Design, Layout, and Program Flow."

Identifying Logic Errors

Logic errors in your programs are often the most difficult to fix. They're the result of faulty reasoning and planning, not a misunderstanding about Visual Basic syntax. Consider the following *If...Then* decision structure, which evaluates two conditional expressions and then displays one of two messages based on the result.

```
If Age > 13 And Age < 20 Then
    OutputBox.Text = "You're a teenager"
Else
    OutputBox.Text = "You're not a teenager"
End If
```

Can you spot the problem with this decision structure? A teenager is a person who is between 13 and 19 years old, inclusive, but the structure fails to identify the person who's exactly 13. (For this age, the structure erroneously displays the message "You're not a teenager.") This type of mistake isn't a syntax error (because the statements follow the rules of Visual Basic); it's a mental mistake or logic error. The correct decision structure contains a greater-than-or-equal-to operator (>=) in the first comparison after the *If...Then* statement, as shown here:

```
If Age >= 13 And Age < 20 Then
```

Believe it or not, this type of mistake is the most common problem in a Visual Basic program. Code that produces the expected results most of the time—but not all the time—is the hardest to identify and to fix.

Debugging 101: Using Debugging Mode

One way to identify a logic error is to execute your program code one line at a time and examine the content of one or more variables or properties as they change. To do this, you can enter *debugging mode* (or break mode) while your program is running and then view your code in the Code Editor. Debugging mode gives you a close-up look at your program while the Visual Basic compiler is executing it. It's kind of like pulling up a chair behind the pilot and copilot and watching them fly the airplane. But in this case, you can touch the controls.

While you're debugging your application, you'll use buttons on the Standard toolbar and the Debug toolbar, as well as commands on the Debug menu and special buttons and windows in the IDE. You can open the Debug Toolbar by clicking View | Toolbars | Debug. The following illustration shows the commands on the Debug menu that are available when a project is loaded, including Start Debugging, Step Into, Toggle Breakpoint, and New Breakpoint. You'll learn to use this menu in the exercises that follow.

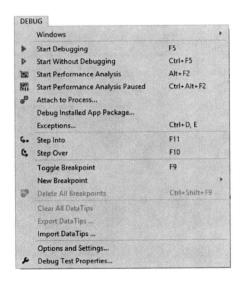

In the following lesson, you'll set a breakpoint—a place in a program where execution stops. You'll then use debugging mode to find and correct the logic error you discovered earlier in the *If...Then* structure. (The error is part of an actual program.) To isolate the problem, you'll use the Step Into button on the Debug toolbar to execute program instructions one at a time, and you'll use the Autos window to examine the value of key program variables and properties. Pay close attention to this debugging strategy. You can use it to correct many types of glitches in your own programs.

Debug the Debug Test program

1. Start Visual Studio.

2. On the File menu, click Open Project.

   The Open Project dialog box opens.

3. Open the Debug Test project in the *My Documents\Start Here! Programming in Visual Basic\ Chapter 9* folder.

   The project opens in the IDE.

4. If the *MainPage.xaml* page isn't visible in the Designer window, open it now.

   The Debug Test program prompts the user for his or her age. When the user clicks the Test button, the program informs the user whether he or she is a teenager. The program still has the problem with 13-year-olds identified earlier in the chapter, however. You'll open the Debug toolbar now and set a breakpoint to find the problem.

5. If the Debug toolbar isn't visible, click the View menu, point to Toolbars, and then click Debug.

   The Debug toolbar appears below or to the right of the Standard toolbar.

6. Click the Start Debugging button on the Standard toolbar.

   The program runs and the Debug Test page appears.

7. Remove the 0 from the Age text box, type **14**, and then click the Test button.

   The program displays the message, "You're a teenager." So far, the program displays the correct result.

8. Type **13** in the "How old are you?" text box, and then click the Test button again.

   The program displays the message, "You're not a teenager," as shown in the following screen illustration:

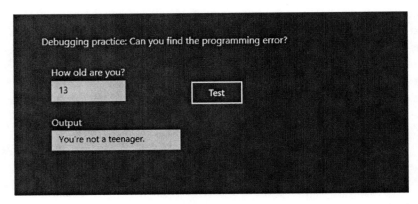

This answer is incorrect, and you need to look at the program code to fix the problem.

9. Close the program, and then open the *MainPage.xaml.vb* code-behind file in the Code Editor.

10. Move the mouse pointer to the Margin Indicator bar (the gray bar just beyond the left margin of the Code Editor window), next to the statement *Age = AgeBox.Text* in the *Button_Click_1* event handler, and then click the bar to set a breakpoint.

The breakpoint immediately appears as a red dot in the left margin of the Code Editor. See the following illustration for the breakpoint's location and shape:

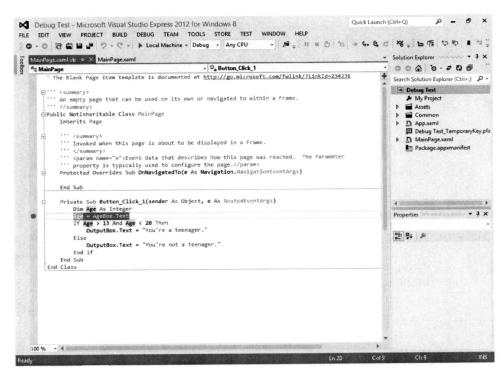

11. Click the Start Debugging button to run the program again.

The page opens just as before, and you can continue your tests.

12. Type **13** in the "How old are you?" text box, and then click Test.

Visual Studio opens the Code Editor again and displays the *Button_Click_1* event handler—the procedure currently being executed by the compiler. The statement that you selected as a breakpoint is highlighted in yellow, and an arrow appears in the Margin Indicator bar, as shown in the following illustration:

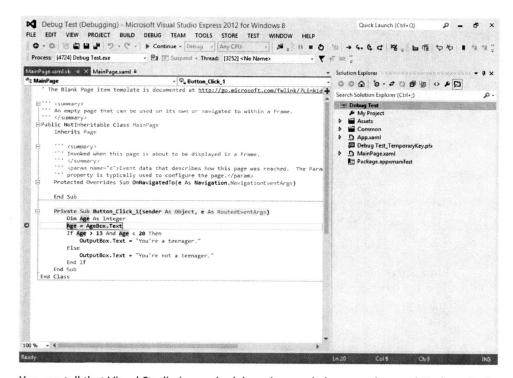

You can tell that Visual Studio is now in debugging mode because the word "Debugging" appears in its title bar. In debugging mode, you have an opportunity to see how the logic in your program is evaluated.

 Tip You can also enter debugging mode in a Visual Basic program by placing the *Stop* statement in your program code where you'd like to pause execution. This is an older, but still reliable, method for entering debugging mode in a Visual Basic program.

13. Place the pointer over the *Age* variable in the Code Editor.

Visual Studio displays the message "Age | 0" and a tiny pin icon next to the value. While you're in debugging mode, you can display the value of variables or properties by simply holding the mouse pointer over the value in the program code. *Age* currently holds a value of 0 because it hasn't yet been filled by the *AgeBox* text box—that statement is the next statement the compiler will evaluate.

The pin icon feature lets you place the value of an expression at a convenient location within the IDE while you are debugging. The pinned expression is called a *DataTip*, and there are three commands on the Debug menu that are related to this feature. Try using a DataTip now to watch the value of the *Age* variable.

14. Click the pin icon to create a DataTip for the *Age* variable in the IDE.

15. Now hold the mouse over the DataTip until three small buttons are displayed next to the *Age* variable.

Your screen will look like the following:

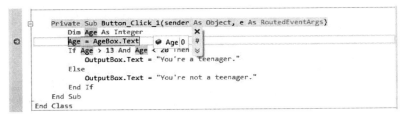

```
    Private Sub Button_Click_1(sender As Object, e As RoutedEventArgs)
        Dim Age As Integer                    ✕
        Age = AgeBox.Text        📌 Age 0     📌
        If Age > 13 And Age < 20 Then  ⌄
            OutputBox.Text = "You're a teenager."
        Else
            OutputBox.Text = "You're not a teenager."
        End If
    End Sub
End Class
```

Until you remove this DataTip, it will display the value of the *Age* variable in the IDE. If you click the Close button (the top button), you will remove the DataTip from the IDE. If you click the Unpin From Source button (the middle pushpin button), the *Age* variable will remain in its current position in the IDE, even if you scroll the Code Editor window up or down. If you click the Expand To See Comments button (the bottom button), you can add a descriptive comment to the *Age* variable in a special text box that appears.

16. Click the Close button next to the DataTip to remove the *Age* variable and its value of 0 for now.

As you can see, this is a handy way to watch variables change in a program as it runs, and you should feel free to use DataTips whenever you debug your code. Before you use them exclusively, however, experiment with some additional techniques in the following steps.

Note If you add more than a few DataTips to your program code, you can manage the DataTips collectively by using the Clear All DataTips, Export DataTips, and Import DataTips commands on the Debug menu. These features can be useful in large development projects where you have many variables and expressions to assess and evaluate in your code-behind files. In particular, the Export DataTips and Import DataTips commands will allow you to transfer DataTips from one project to the next.

17. Continue by clicking the Step Into button on the Debug toolbar.

The Step Into button executes the next program statement in the event handler (the line that's currently highlighted). By clicking the Step Into button, you can see how the program state changes when just one more program statement is evaluated. If you hold the pointer over the *Age* variable now, you'll see that it contains a value of 13.

18. On the Debug menu, point to Windows, and then click Autos.

The Windows submenu provides access to the entire set of debugging windows in Visual Studio. The Autos window shows the state of variables and properties currently being used (not only the properties you are currently setting, but others as well). As you can see in the following screen shot, the *Age* variable holds a value of 13 and the *AgeBox.Text* property holds a string of "13".

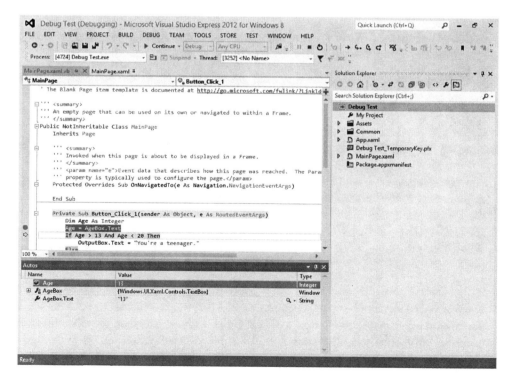

19. Click the Step Into button twice more.

The *If* statement evaluates the conditional expression to *False*, and the compiler moves to the *Else* statement in the decision structure and highlights it with yellow. Here's your bug—the decision structure logic is incorrect because a 13-year-old *is* a teenager. Do you recognize the problem? The first comparison needs the greater-than-or-equal-to operator (>=) to specifically test for this boundary case of 13. You'll stop debugging now so that you can fix this logic error.

20. Click the Stop Debugging button on the Debug toolbar.

21. In the Code Editor, add the equal to sign (=) to the first condition in the *If* statement so that it reads as follows:

```
If Age >= 13 And Age < 20 Then
```

22. Run the program again and test your solution, paying particular attention to the numbers 12, 13, 19, and 20—the boundary (or *fringe*) cases that are likely to cause problems.

Remember that you still have a breakpoint set, so you'll enter debugging mode when you run the program again. Use the Step Into button to watch the program flow around the crucial *If* statement, and use the Autos window to track the value of your variables as you complete the tests. When the user interface page opens again, enter a new value and click the Test button. (You'll learn how to remove the breakpoint later in the chapter.)

23. When you're finished experimenting with debugging mode, click the Stop Debugging button on the Debug toolbar to end the program.

Congratulations! You've successfully used debugging mode to find and correct a logic error in a program.

Tracking Variables by Using a Watch Window

The Autos window is useful for examining the state of certain variables and properties as they're evaluated by the program, but items in the Autos window *persist*, or maintain their values, only for the current statement (the statement highlighted in the debugger) and the previous statement (the statement just executed). (Technically, this interval is described as the *buffer* between statements.) When your program goes on to execute code that doesn't use the variables, they disappear from the Autos window.

To view the contents of variables and properties *throughout* the execution of a program, you need to use a Watch window—a special debugging tool that tracks important values for you so long as you're working in debugging mode. In Visual Studio Express 2012, you can open up to four Watch windows, numbered Watch 1, Watch 2, Watch 3, and Watch 4. When you are in debugging mode, you can open these windows by pointing to the Windows command on the Debug menu, pointing to

Watch, and then clicking the window you want on the Watch submenu. You can also add expressions, such as *Age >= 13*, to a Watch window.

The following exercise opens a Watch window; it assumes that the Debug Test project is still open.

Open a Watch window

1. Click the Start Debugging button on the Standard toolbar to run the Debug Test program again.

    I'm assuming that the breakpoint you set on the line *Age = AgeBox.Text* in the previous exercise is still present. If that breakpoint isn't set, stop the program now, and set the breakpoint by clicking in the Margin Indicator bar next to the statement, as shown in Step 10 of the previous exercise, and then start the program again.

2. Type **20** in the Age text box, and then click Test.

    The program stops at the breakpoint, and Visual Studio enters debugging mode, which is where you need to be if you want to add variables, properties, or expressions to a Watch window. One way to add an item is to select its value in the Code Editor, right-click the selection, and then click the Add Watch command.

3. Select the *Age* variable, right-click it, and then click the Add Watch command.

    Visual Studio opens the Watch 1 window and adds the *Age* variable to it. The value for the variable is currently 0, and the Type column in the window identifies the *Age* variable as an *Integer* type.

    Another way to add an item is to drag the item from the Code Editor into the Watch window.

4. Select the *OutputBox.Text* property, and then drag it to the empty row in the Watch 1 window.

    When you release the mouse button, Visual Studio adds the property and displays its value. (Right now, the property is an empty string.)

5. Select the expression *Age < 20*, and then add it to the Watch window.

    Age < 20 is a conditional expression, and you can use the Watch window to display its logical, or Boolean, value. Your Watch window should look like this:

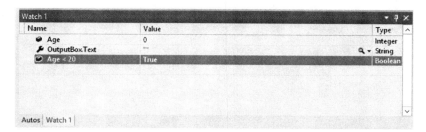

Now step through the program code to see how the values in the Watch 1 window change.

6. Click the Step Into button on the Debug toolbar.

> **Tip** Instead of clicking the Step Into button on the Debug toolbar, you can press the F11 key on the keyboard.

The *Age* variable is set to 20, and the *Age < 20* condition evaluates to *False*. These values are displayed in red type in the Watch window because they've just been updated.

7. Click the Step Into button three more times.

The *Else* clause is executed in the decision structure, and the value of the *OutputBox.Text* property in the Watch window changes to "You're not a teenager." Your Watch 1 window should look like this:

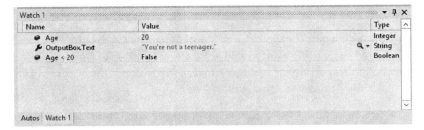

The conditional test is operating correctly. Because you're satisfied with this condition, you can remove the test from the Watch window.

8. Click the Age < 20 row in the Watch window, and then press the Delete key.

Visual Studio removes the value from the Watch window. As you can see, adding and removing values from the Watch window is a speedy process.

> **Tip** Note that the values you add to a Watch window will remain in the window until you delete them—even between programming sessions. This is a convenience feature—Visual Studio saves your debugging information and lets you pick up right where you left off the next time you load the project.

Leave Visual Studio running in debugging mode for now. You'll continue using the Watch window in the next section.

Visualizers: Debugging Tools That Display Data

Although you can use a DataTip, a Watch window, or an Autos window to examine simple data types such as *Integer* and *String* in the IDE, you'll eventually be faced with more complex data in your programs. For example, you might be examining a variable or property containing structured information from a database (a dataset) or a string containing HyperText Markup Language (HTML) or Extensible Markup Language (XML) formatting information from an XML document. So that you can examine this type of item more closely in a debugging session, Visual Studio offers a set of tools in the IDE called *visualizers*. The icon for a visualizer is a small magnifying glass.

The Visual Studio IDE offers a number of standard visualizers, such as the text, HTML, and XML visualizers (which work on string objects), and the dataset visualizer (which works for *DataSet*, *DataView*, and *DataTable* objects). Microsoft has also designed Visual Studio so that third-party developers can write their own visualizers and install them into the Visual Studio debugger.

In the following exercise, you'll see how the text visualizer works. (For this exercise, I assume that you are still in debugging mode and that the Watch window is open with a few expressions in it from the Debug Test program.)

Open a text visualizer in the debugger

1. Look on the right side of the Watch window for a small magnifying glass icon.

   A magnifying glass icon indicates that a visualizer is available for the variable or property that you are examining in a Watch window, an Autos window, or a Locals window. If you completed the previous exercise, the *OutputBox.Text* property should show a visualizer now.

2. Click the visualizer arrow.

   When the property you are examining is a text (string) property, Visual Studio offers three visualizers: a simple text visualizer, which displays the selected string expression as readable text; an XML visualizer, which converts XML markup to a viewable document with highlighting and structure; and an HTML visualizer, which converts HTML code to a webpage. The Watch window should look like this:

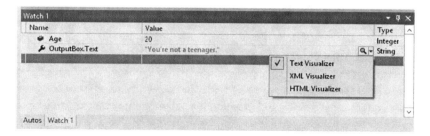

3. Select the Text Visualizer option.

Visual Studio opens a dialog box and displays the contents of the *OutputBox.Text* property. Your screen should look like this:

Although this particular result offers little more than the Watch window did, the benefits of the visualizer tool become immediately obvious when you examine variables or properties containing database information or web documents. (You'll practice working with structured data from an XML document in Chapter 10, "Managing Data with Arrays and LINQ.")

4. Click Close to close the Text Visualizer dialog box.

Leave Visual Studio running in debugging mode. You'll continue using the Watch window in the next section, too.

 Tip In debugging mode, visualizers also sometimes appear in the Code Editor next to interesting variables or properties. If a visualizer appears, feel free to click it to get more information about the underlying data, as you did in the previous exercise. I'll remind you about this capability again in Chapter 10.

Using the Immediate Window

So far, you've used the Visual Studio debugging tools that allow you to enter debugging mode, execute code one statement at a time, and examine the value of important variables, properties, and expressions in your program. Now you'll learn how to change the value of a variable by using the Immediate window.

The following exercise demonstrates how the Immediate window works. The exercise assumes that you're debugging the Debug Test program in debugging mode.

Use the Immediate window to modify a variable

1. Click the Debug menu, point to Windows, and then click Immediate.

   When you select the command, Visual Studio opens the Immediate window and prepares the compiler to receive commands from you *while the Debug Test program is paused*. This is a very handy feature because you can test program conditions on the fly, without stopping the program and inserting program statements in the Code Editor.

2. In the Immediate window, type **Age = 17**, and then press Enter.

   You've just used the Immediate window to change the value of a variable. The value of the *Age* variable in the Watch window immediately changes to 17, even though the number in the *AgeBox* text box is 20 on the page. Your Watch 1 and Immediate windows should look like this:

   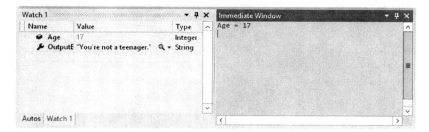

3. Type the following statement in the Immediate window, and then press Enter:

   ```
   OutputBox.Text = "You're a great age!"
   ```

   The *Text* property of the *OutputBox* object is immediately changed to "You're a great age!" In the Immediate window, you can change the value of properties, as well as variables.

   The Watch 1 and Immediate windows should look like this:

   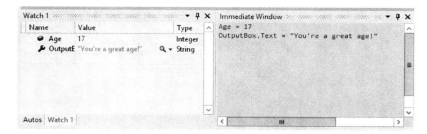

As you can see, both of the changes that you made to program values are reflected in the Watch 1 window, and this gives you the opportunity to test the program further.

4. Click the Step Into button two times to display the Debug Test form again.

Notice that the *Text* property of the *OutputBox* object has been changed, as you directed, but the *Text* property of the *AgeBox* object still holds a value of 20 (not 17). This is because you changed the *Age* variable in the program, not the property that assigned a value to *Age*. Your screen should look like the following illustration:

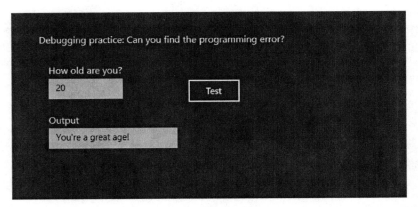

The Immediate window has many uses—it provides an excellent companion to the Watch window, and it can help you experiment with specific test cases that might otherwise be very difficult to enter into your program.

Removing Breakpoints

If you've been following the instructions in this chapter carefully, the Debug Test program is still running and has a breakpoint in it. Follow these steps to remove the breakpoint and end the program. You're finished debugging the Debug Test project.

Remove a breakpoint

1. Press Alt+Tab to return to the Code Editor, and then click the red circle associated with the breakpoint in the Margin Indicator bar.

The breakpoint disappears. That's all there is to it! But note that if you have more than one breakpoint in a program, you can remove them all by clicking the Delete All Breakpoints command on the Debug menu. Visual Studio saves breakpoints with your project, so it's important to know how to remove them; otherwise, they'll still be in your program, even if you close Visual Studio and restart it.

2. Click the Stop Debugging button on the Debug toolbar.

The Debug Test program ends.

3. On the View menu, point to Toolbars, and then click Debug.

The Debug toolbar closes.

4. Click Save All to save your changes to the project, and then select File | Exit to close Visual Studio.

You've learned the fundamental techniques of debugging Visual Basic programs with Visual Studio.

Summary

The complex nature of Windows programming means that you'll run into syntax errors and other logic problems from time to time as you build your applications. This chapter introduced the programming tools in the Visual Studio IDE that help you locate and correct programming mistakes.

You learned how to open the Debug toolbar and how to use commands on the Debug toolbar and the Debug menu. You learned how to set a breakpoint in a Visual Basic code-behind file, and how to use the Autos and Watch windows to examine variables and property settings during program execution. You also learned how to use DataTips and visualizers to examine data types within the IDE, and how to use the Immediate window to change the value of variables or property settings while a program is paused.

In the next chapter, you'll continue your exploration of Visual Basic and Visual Studio 2012 by learning how to manage data effectively in a program using arrays and an important technology known as Language Integrated Query (LINQ).

Chapter 10

Managing Data with Arrays and LINQ

After completing this chapter, you'll be able to

- Use arrays to store numeric and string data.

- Use a *For...Next* loop to access array elements and display them in a text box.

- Use methods in the *Array* class to sort and reverse array elements.

- Understand LINQ syntax.

- Use LINQ to retrieve data from one or more arrays.

- Use LINQ to retrieve data from XML documents.

BECAUSE THERE IS SO MUCH DATA in the world—employee records at the office, price and product information online, confidential patient records at the clinic—it makes sense that software developers are spending a lot of time thinking about how data is managed in their programs. In Microsoft Visual Studio, an important technology used for extracting and managing data is known as *Language Integrated Query (LINQ)* (pronounced *link*). LINQ is extremely useful because it allows you to retrieve data in the same way from almost *any* data source, whether it is stored in arrays, lists, databases, or Extensible Markup Language (XML) documents.

In this chapter, you'll learn how to store different types of data in arrays, and how to use methods in the *Array* class to sort and reorganize the contents of an array. Building on these skills, you'll learn how to use LINQ to retrieve data from one or more arrays, and to use the selected information efficiently in a program. You'll learn how to write LINQ *query expressions* in Visual Basic code, and how to use essential LINQ keywords, including *From*, *Where*, and *Select*. If you've had any exposure to SQL statements that extract information from structured tables in a database, you'll find that LINQ syntax is similar in many respects. After you learn the fundamentals of managing array data with LINQ, you'll learn how to open XML documents in a program, and how to use the data in XML documents as a source for LINQ queries.

In a sense, this chapter will only scratch the surface of what you can do with LINQ and the impressive data management features available to Windows 8 applications. However, by taking your first steps, you'll discover how powerful data management with arrays and LINQ can be, and some of the opportunities that await you as a Visual Basic programmer.

Using Arrays to Store Data

As you learned in Chapter 6, "Visual Basic Language Elements," a variable is a temporary storage location for data in your program that is assigned a unique name and created (or declared) to hold a specific type of data. An *array* is a similar storage mechanism, but an array associates a *collection* of values with a unique name. Like variables, arrays are created using the *Dim* statement, and they are typically declared using a specific data type (*String, Integer, Double, Char*, and so on).

Arrays allow you to organize collections of values that are impractical to arrange using traditional variables. For example, imagine creating a nine-inning baseball scoreboard in a program. To save and recall the scores for each inning of the game, you might be tempted to create two groups of 9 variables (a total of 18 variables) in your code. You'd probably name them something like *Inning1HomeTeam, Inning1VisitingTeam*, and so on, to keep them straight. However, working with these variables individually would take considerable time and space in your event handlers, and the code would be confusing to read. Fortunately, Microsoft Visual Basic allows you to organize groups of similar variables into an array that has one common name and one or more easy-to-use *indices* to reference individual elements. For example, you can create one two-dimensional array (2 units high by 9 units wide) named *BaseballScoreboard* to contain the scores for a nine-inning baseball game. Let's see how this works.

Declaring Arrays

You create, or *declare*, arrays in program code just as you declare simple variables. As usual, the place in which you declare the array determines its *scope*, or where it can be used, as follows:

- If you declare an array locally in an event handler, you can use it only in that handler.

- If you declare an array near the top of a page's code-behind file, you can use the array throughout the page's event handlers and procedures.

When you declare an array, you typically include the information shown in Table 10-1 in your declaration statement.

TABLE 10-1 Syntax Elements for an Array Declaration

Syntax Elements in Array Declaration	Description
Array name	The name you'll use to represent your array in the program. In general, array names follow the same rules as variable names. (See Chapter 6 for more information about variables.)
Data type	The type of data you'll store in the array. In most cases, all the variables in an array are the same type. You can specify one of the fundamental data types, or if you're not yet sure which type of data will be stored in the array or whether you'll store more than one type, you can specify the *Object* type.
Number of dimensions	The number of dimensions that your array will contain. Most arrays are one-dimensional (a list of values) or two-dimensional (a table of values), but you can specify additional dimensions if you're working with a complex mathematical model, such as a three-dimensional shape. The number of dimensions in an array is sometimes called the array's rank. You reference values in different array dimensions by using array indices.
Number of elements	The number of elements that your array will contain. The elements in your array correspond directly to the array index. The first array index is always 0 (zero). In a multidimensional array, you provide the number of elements for each dimension.

Arrays that contain a set number of elements are called *fixed-size arrays*. Arrays that contain a variable number of elements (arrays that can expand during the execution of the program) are called *dynamic arrays*. In this chapter, you'll just learn about fixed-size arrays, since the focus in this chapter is primarily creating and sorting arrays, and managing array data with LINQ queries. (Fixed-size arrays give you everything that you need to perform these tasks and more.) To learn more about dynamic arrays and their important uses, however, see my book *Visual Basic 2012 Step by Step* (Microsoft Press, 2013).

Declaring a Fixed-Size Array

The basic syntax for a fixed-size array is

```
Dim ArrayName(Dim1Index, Dim2Index, ...) As DataType
```

where *Dim* is the keyword that declares the array and *ArrayName* is the name for the array. Between the required parentheses, *Dim1Index* is the upper bound of the first dimension of the array (which is the number of elements minus 1), and *Dim2Index* is the upper bound of the second dimension of the array (the number of elements minus 1). Additional dimensions may be included in a similar format as long as they are separated by commas. Finally, *DataType* is a keyword corresponding to the type of data that will be included in the array.

For example, to declare a one-dimensional string array named *Waiters* that has room for seven employee names (corresponding to array elements 0 through 6), you would type the following in a code-behind file:

```
Dim Waiters(6) As String
```

You can also explicitly specify the lower bound of the array as zero by using the following code:

```
Dim Waiters(0 To 6) As String
```

This "0 to 6" syntax may be included simply to make your code more understandable—newcomers to your program will understand immediately that the *Waiters* array has seven elements numbered 0 through 6 if you use this syntax. However, since the lower bound of the array must always be zero, you can't use this syntax to create a different lower bound for the array.

In the previous section, I mentioned that a programmer could concisely declare a two-dimensional array named *BaseballScoreboard* with room for two rows and nine columns of integer data. Here is how you would make that declaration using a *Short* integer data type and allowing for two baseball teams and nine innings:

```
Dim BaseballScoreboard(1, 8) As Short
```

Although the array indices *(1, 8)* might be confusing at first, remember that all arrays begin with a lower bound of 0 for each dimension. The preceding declaration creates a *Short* integer array with array elements numbered 0 through 8 in the first row (scores for the visiting team), and elements numbered 0 through 8 in the second row (scores for the home team).

Using an Array

When you create an array, Visual Basic sets aside room for it in memory. Conceptually, it is a little like Visual Basic setting aside a blank, lined index card for you to write information on, with exactly the right amount of space for your data. After you declare the array, all you need to do is jot down the information you want to track, and Visual Basic holds it in memory until the program terminates. (At that point, the contents of your array will be destroyed, or, in this analogy, recycled.)

Your seven-element *Waiters* array of type *String* might be imagined like this:

```
Waiters(0): _____
Waiters(1): _____
Waiters(2): _____
Waiters(3): _____
Waiters(4): _____
Waiters(5): _____
Waiters(6): _____
```

In this conceptual example, each array element is represented by an array index, enclosed in parentheses. The index allows you to reference each element in the array individually. The blank lines shown in this conceptual example are not *actually* the way that string arrays are stored in memory. I'm just using the lines to signify that when you declare an array, arrangements are made in computer memory so that the information will have a safe place to reside under a given array name.

Note To refer to an element in an array, you use the array name and an array index corresponding to the element that you want to use. The index must be an integer or an expression that results in an integer. For example, the index could be a number such as 5, an integer variable such as *num*, or an expression such as *num-1*. The counter variable in a *For...Next* loop is often used, as you'll see in the Array Tests sample program in the following section.

Be sure that the integer value used refers to an actual element within the declared bounds of the array. For example, in the *Waiters* array just shown, the array index must be between 0 and 6, inclusively. If you specify an index that is outside the bounds of the array, you will receive a *System.IndexOutOfRangeException* run-time error.

For example, the following statement assigns the value "Ben" to the array element with an index of 5 in the *Waiters* array:

```
Waiters(5) = "Ben"
```

This statement produces the following result in the conceptual *Waiters* array:

```
Waiters(0): _____
Waiters(1): _____
Waiters(2): _____
Waiters(3): _____
Waiters(4): _____
Waiters(5): Ben
Waiters(6): _____
```

Likewise, the following statement assigns the number 4 (representing four runs) to row 0, column 2 (the top of the third inning) in the *BaseballScoreboard* array example declared in the previous section:

```
BasesballScoreboard(0, 2) = 4
```

The important thing to note here is that when you work with a multidimensional array like *BaseballScoreboard*, you need to use multiple indices to reference individual array elements. If you are using a *For...Next* loop to help you reference elements in the array (a topic introduced following), for a two-dimensional array you will need two *For...Next* loops, one nested inside the other, if you want to step through each array element. (The counter variables in the two *For...Next* loops will represent a pair of indices for each element in the array.)

Assigning Initial Values to an Array

It is also possible to declare an array and assign it initial values. To declare an array in this manner, you use what is called an *array literal*. An array literal consists of a list of comma-separated values that are enclosed in braces ({}). When using this syntax, you can either supply the array type or let Visual Basic use *type inference* to determine what type the array should be. For example, to declare a one-dimensional array named *Waiters* of type *String* and fill it with seven names, you would use the following syntax:

```
Dim Waiters() As String = {"Ben", "Sue", "Lee", "Kim", "Pat", "Eve", "Sal"}
```

Conceptually, this would produce the following result in computer memory:

```
Waiters(0): Ben
Waiters(1): Sue
Waiters(2): Lee
Waiters(3): Kim
Waiters(4): Pat
Waiters(5): Eve
Waiters(6): Sal
```

Note that in this example, the size of the array is determined automatically by Visual Basic when *Waiters* is declared in program code. In addition, you don't *have* to indicate the array data type (although I did so here), because Visual Basic can use type inference to determine the correct type for you. If all the values in an array literal assignment are of the same type, it will be pretty clear to the compiler what data type should be used for the array. However, if there is a mixture of types, such as an assortment of integer, single-precision, and double-precision numbers, Visual Basic will select a data type for the array that is large enough to accommodate all the values. In many cases, this will be the data type *Object* because *Object* variables (and arrays) are designed to hold any type of data. (Visual Basic will also create an array of type *Object* if the compiler's Option Infer setting is set to Off. See Chapter 1, "Getting to Know Visual Basic 2012," for help adjusting this setting.)

The following statement declares an array named *Prices* and uses an array literal to add four values to the array when it is created. Since no type is specified, Visual Basic evaluates the array elements and determines that in this case, the *Object* type is most appropriate.

```
Dim Prices() = {1000, 1350.50, 299.99, 5000}
```

Again, note that if the compiler's Option Infer setting is set to On, you will get a slightly different result. The *Double* type will be specified when the preceding statement is executed.

A multidimensional array can also be declared in this way, although you need to take care to list the elements in the proper order (that is, row 0, row 1, row 2, and so on). For example, the following statement declares a two-dimensional array named *Building* and assigns six measurements to the array:

```
Dim Building = {{10, 20}, {50, 60}, {77, 112}}
```

This array has three rows and two columns. Array element (0, 0)—that is, row 0, column 0—now contains a value of 10. Array element (0, 1)—that is, row 0, column 1—now contains a value of 20. Array element (2, 1)—that is, row 2, column 1—now contains a value of 112. Also, notice that there are four sets of braces used in the declaration; these braces clarify which elements are being assigned and keep them in the proper order.

Now that you've learned about arrays and how they can be declared and used, it is time for a sample project that puts arrays to work. In the following exercise, you'll build a program named Array Tests that will give you the chance to see how fixed-size arrays are used in a program. This project will also be the foundation of the work that you do with LINQ queries later in the chapter.

Create string arrays in a program

1. Start Visual Studio Express and click New Project to open a new Visual Studio application.

2. Choose Visual Basic | Windows Store under Templates, and then verify that the Blank App (XAML) template is selected.

3. Type **My Array Tests** in the Name text box.

4. Click OK to open and configure the new project.

   Visual Studio creates a new project with typical project files.

5. Double-click the *MainPage.xaml* file in Solution Explorer to display the default user interface page.

   Visual Studio loads *MainPage.xaml* into the Designer.

   Now you'll change the background color of the grid to light blue and add a *TextBox* control and a *Button* control to the page. These elements will help you create a nice-looking test environment to experiment with arrays.

6. Click the grid object (the page background) in the Designer, open the Properties window, and click the *Brush* category.

7. Open the edit menu for the *Background* property (the dark button to the right of the *Background* property under the Brush category), click Custom Expression, type **LightBlue**, and press Enter.

   Visual Studio changes the background color of the grid to light blue.

8. Change the Designer's Zoom control to 100% if that is not the current setting.

   A zoom of 100% will be suitable for this sample program, which only takes up part of the page.

9. Add a rectangular *TextBox* control to the page and make it large enough for at least 15 lines of text (place the control in the middle of the page, near the top).

10. Add a rectangular *Button* control to the page.

11. Set the following properties for the text box and button objects:

Object	Property	Setting
Text box	Name Text	DataPanel " "
Button	Name Content	DisplayArray "Show Array Contents"

Your page will look like this:

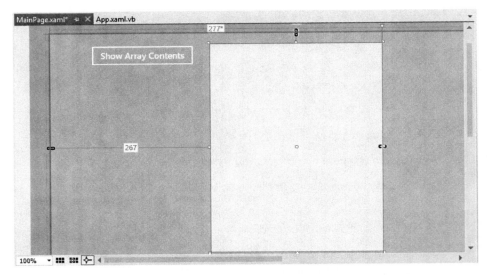

12. Right-click the *MainPage.xaml* file in Solution Explorer, and then click View Code to view the code-behind file for *MainPage.xaml.vb* in the Code Editor.

You'll declare two fixed-size arrays in this program near the top of the Blank Page template (below the statements *Public NotInheritable Class MainPage* and *Inherits Page*) so that the arrays will be available to all of the event handlers associated with the page.

13. Move the insertion point below the *Inherits Page* statement, and then type the following two lines of Visual Basic code (keep "Rosemary"} on the second line—it just wrapped here due to the constraints of this book's margins):

```
Dim Waiters() As String = {"Ben", "Sue", "Lee", "Kim", "Pat", "Eve", "Sal"}
Dim Drivers() As String = {"George", "Kim", "Sal", "Robert", "Jenna",
"Rosemary"}
```

These statements declare two string arrays, named *Waiters* and *Drivers*, that will contain the names of restaurant employees that have been trained to wait tables and drive a delivery truck, respectively. The arrays are being declared and assigned initial values at the same time through the array literal syntax described earlier in the chapter. The sizes of the arrays are determined automatically when the statements are compiled—*Waiters* contains seven elements and *Drivers* contains six elements. Your Code Editor should look like this:

Now you'll create an event handler for the *DisplayArray* button object, so that it displays the contents of the *Waiters* array in the text box using a *For...Next* loop.

14. Double-click the *MainPage.xaml* file in Solution Explorer to display the Designer, and then click the *DisplayArray* button containing the text "Show Array Contents."

The properties of the button object appear in the Properties window.

15. In the Properties window, click the Event Handler button to create a new event handler for the *DisplayArray* button object.

16. Double-click next to the *Click* event in the Properties window.

Visual Studio creates an event handler named *DisplayArray_Click*, and opens the *MainPage .xaml.vb* code-behind file again in the Code Editor.

17. Type the following program statements in the Code Editor between *Private Sub* and *End Sub*:

```
Dim i As Short
For i = 0 To 6
    DataPanel.Text = DataPanel.Text & Waiters(i) & vbCrLf
Next i
```

These lines begin by declaring a variable *i* of type *Short* for use as a counter in a *For...Next* loop that displays the contents of the *Waiters* array. The *For...Next* code block loops seven times, and during each pass the counter *i* is incremented by 1. Notice how the counter is used to access each element in the *Waiters* array, and how the contents of the array are appended to the contents of the *DataPanel* text box on the page. The string concatenation operator (*&*) is used twice during each pass through the loop to join the current contents of the text box to the array element and a linefeed character, which is stored in the *vbCrLf* constant.

As you can see, a *For...Next* loop is tailor-made to access the contents of a fixed-size array, because the index of the array elements corresponds with the loop counter variable.

Run the program now to see how the *Waiters* array works.

18. Click the Start Debugging button.

The application launches and displays a page containing a button and a text box.

19. Click Show Array Contents.

Your screen should look like this:

The seven elements of the *Waiters* array, representing employees who have been trained to wait tables at a local restaurant, appear in the text box. The main page's code-behind file declared the *Waiters* array and filled it with *String* data, and the event handler for the *DisplayArray* button displayed the contents of the array on the page.

20. Click Show Array Contents again.

The contents of the *Waiters* array are displayed a second time in the text box. However, this time, the array elements are appended to the current contents of the text box, so the list appears twice.

21. Close the program and display the Visual Studio IDE.

22. Click Save All to save your project, and then specify the *My Documents\Start Here! Programming in Visual Basic\Chapter 10* folder for the location.

Now you'll learn how to use methods in the *Array* class to reorder the contents of the *Drivers* array.

Using Methods in the Array Class

When you create arrays in Visual Basic, you are building on the foundation of the .NET Framework–defined *Array* class. This *Array* class also provides a collection of methods that you can use to manipulate arrays while they are loaded in memory. The most useful methods include *Array.Sort*, *Array.Find*, *Array.Reverse*, *Array.Copy*, and *Array.Clear*. You can locate other interesting methods by experimenting with the *Array* class in the Code Editor (by using Microsoft IntelliSense) and by checking the Visual Studio 2012 documentation at *http://msdn.microsoft.com*.

The *Array* class methods work much like the .NET Framework methods discussed in Chapter 8, "Using the .NET Framework." Each method is called by name and (in this case) requires a valid array name as an argument. For example, to alphabetically sort the *Waiters* string array that you created in the last exercise, you would use the following syntax:

```
Array.Sort(Waiters)
```

This statement would sort the *Waiters* array alphabetically, placing "Ben" in the first element, "Eve" in the second element, and so on.

When Visual Basic executes the *Array.Sort* method, it creates a temporary storage location for the array that is being sorted in memory. Then Visual Basic uses a sorting routine to reorganize the array in *alphanumeric* order (meaning that strings are sorted in alphabetical order, from *A* to *Z*, and numeric values are sorted in ascending order, from small numbers to big numbers). After the sort is complete, the contents of the original array are discarded and the contents of the sorted list are loaded in the array's elements, with the smallest value in array location 0 and the largest value in the last array location.

Before you call the *Array.Sort* method, of course, it is important that you declare the array in your program and that you fill it with appropriate data. Programmers often use *Array.Sort* to organize a list of names or values before they display them or store them in a file or database.

A companion to *Array.Sort* is the *Array.Reverse* method, which reverses the order of elements in an array. This action is especially useful if the array is already in alphanumeric order; for example, if you have just used the *Array.Sort* method to sort the list. In other words, by using the *Array.Reverse* method, you can easily shuffle an array of string values that is in alphabetical order (from *A* to *Z*) to reverse alphabetical order (from *Z* to *A*). Likewise, if a numeric array contains values that are in ascending order, *Array.Reverse* will change the pattern to descending order.

In the following exercise, you'll see how the *Array.Sort* and *Array.Reverse* methods can be used to reorder the *Drivers* string array, which you declared and filled with data in the last exercise.

Use the *Array.Sort* and *Array.Reverse* methods

1. Display *MainPage.xaml* in the Designer and create two new button objects on the page below the *DisplayArray* button.

2. Set the following properties for the new button objects:

Object	Property	Setting
Button	*Name* *Content*	SortArray "Sort Drivers Array"
Button	*Name* *Content*	ReverseArray "Reverse Drivers Array"

Your page will look like this:

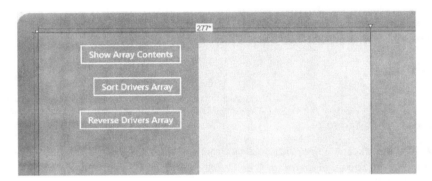

3. Click the *SortArray* button to display the properties of the object in the Properties window.

4. In the Properties window, click the Event Handler button to create a new event handler for the *Click* event of the *SortArray* button.

5. Double-click next to the *Click* event in the Properties window.

   Visual Studio creates an event handler named *SortArray_Click* and opens the *MainPage.xaml.vb* code-behind file in the Code Editor.

6. Type the following program statements in the Code Editor, between *Private Sub* and *End Sub*:

```
Array.Sort(Drivers)
Dim Count As Short
For Count = 0 to 5
    DataPanel.Text = DataPanel.Text & Drivers(Count) & vbCrLf
Next Count
```

The first line in this event handler sorts the *Drivers* string array, which results in an array organized in alphabetic (*A* to *Z*) order. The remaining lines declare a *Short* integer variable named *Count*, and display the contents of the *Drivers* array in the *DataPanel* text box by using *Count* as the array index. Since this particular array holds six elements, I configured the *For...Next* loop to cycle six times (from 0 to 5).

7. Return to *MainPage.xaml* in the Designer and click the *ReverseArray* button.

   In the Properties window, the list of events for the *Button* control should still be listed, as you just used it to create an event handler for the *SortArray* button. (If the *Button* events are not listed, click the Event Handler button.)

8. Double-click next to the *Click* event in the Properties window.

   Visual Studio creates an event handler named *ReverseArray_Click* and opens the *MainPage.xaml.vb* code-behind file in the Code Editor.

9. Type the following program statements in the Code Editor, between *Private Sub* and *End Sub*:

```
Array.Reverse(Drivers)
Dim Count As Short
For Count = 0 to 5
    DataPanel.Text = DataPanel.Text & Drivers(Count) & vbCrLf
Next Count
```

   This event handler is exactly the same as the *SortArray_Click* event handler, except that it calls the *Array.Reverse* method instead of the *Array.Sort* method. (In fact, if you want, you can copy and paste the code—you just need to change "Array.Sort" to "Array.Reverse".)

   Now you'll run the program to see how the *Array* class methods work.

10. Click the Start Debugging button.

    The application launches and displays a page containing buttons and a text box.

11. Click Sort Drivers Array.

    Your screen should look like this:

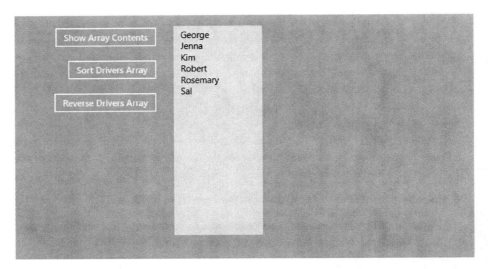

The six elements of the *Drivers* array, representing restaurant employees who can drive a delivery truck for the business, appear in the text box. The program declared the *Drivers* array and filled it with *String* data, and the event handler for the *SortArray* button sorted the contents and displayed them on the page.

12. Click Reverse Drivers Array.

The contents of the *Drivers* array are reversed and displayed in the text box a second time. As described earlier, the array elements are appended to the current contents of the text box, so that you can clearly see what is happening in the arrays as you test them.

Your screen should look like this:

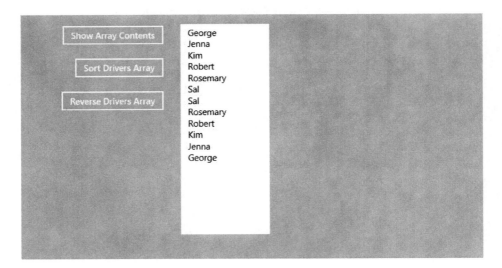

13. Click Show Array Contents to add the contents of the *Waiters* array to the text box.

   If the contents of the arrays run below the bottom border of the text box, you can use the arrow keys to see the content that is hidden.

   As you can see, arrays function very quickly, and they can be manipulated with relatively short event handlers and routines. This is the case even when arrays grow very large and contain hundreds or even thousands of elements. They are remarkable data-processing tools and complement nicely what you can do with text files and databases.

14. Close the program and display the Visual Studio IDE.

15. Click Save All to save your changes.

   Now you'll build on these skills by using LINQ to extract information from arrays and XML Documents.

Introducing LINQ

LINQ allows a Visual Studio programmer to perform complex *queries* to retrieve data from arrays, lists, collections, databases, XML documents, and other data containers that can be integrated into a Windows development project. Although this broad definition of LINQ's capabilities might sound rather complicated, LINQ is really just a tool to select, or *extract*, information from a data source. Like *Structured Query Language (SQL)*, LINQ was designed to help businesspeople and programmers ask questions about valuable data collections that are typically too large or cumbersome to inspect manually (that is, item by item). For example, How many employees at Blue Yonder Airlines have worked at the company for 25 years or more? Or, How many customers of City Power & Light owe more than $500 to the utility and have not made a payment in 5 months?

The questioning character of these database inquiries is where the term *query* comes from in LINQ. But it is not necessary to have extremely large data collections on hand to begin working with LINQ in your programs. In fact, most programmers don't realize how *simple* it is to get started with LINQ. As soon as you understand the fundamentals of basic LINQ query expressions, you can retrieve or filter data from very modest data sources, such as arrays or structured XML documents. In the following sections, you'll learn how to use basic LINQ syntax and how to get started with LINQ data selection in your programs.

Understanding LINQ Syntax

A LINQ expression query is a Visual Basic code block that usually includes the keywords described in the following list. You'll see that I include *Dim* in this list, although it is not technically part of the LINQ syntax, because *Dim* is often used to create a storage variable for LINQ expressions.

- **Dim**   When you build a LINQ query, you first need a storage variable to hold information related to elements in the query. The *Dim* keyword is often used to declare the variable that holds information returned by LINQ. In the following syntax, you'll see that no specific variable type is required with *Dim*, because LINQ uses something called an anonymous type to infer the data type automatically. (This is helpful because you can't know for sure what type of data will be returned by the query.) Moving forward, you should know that an *anonymous type* is an object data type that is built automatically by Visual Basic and not given a name for the program to use. Just like an anonymous donor, who gives a gift but is not named in public records, an anonymous type provides an object that can be used in a program without the syntax that defines a type.

  The following line of code declares a variable named *queryData* to hold the results of a LINQ query. It also declares an iteration variable named *person* to represent each element of the data source individually. (Declaring the *person* variable is somewhat similar to declaring a counter variable for a *For...Next* loop.) The *Waiters* data source specified here will be discussed in the next section.

  ```
  Dim queryData = From person In Waiters
  ```

- **From**   In the preceding statement, you may also have noticed the *From* keyword. In a LINQ query, the *From* keyword is required to identify where the data you plan to use will come from. You can include more than one data source in a LINQ query, and this capability accounts for some of the power and flexibility of LINQ. In the following statement (which is simply copied from the preceding—you will only include this statement once in your code), the string array *Waiters* is specified as the data source for the query:

  ```
  Dim queryData = From person In Waiters
  ```

- **Where**   The optional *Where* statement filters the result returned by the LINQ query. You may include one or more *Where* statements, or none at all. Typically, the iteration variable is used in a *Where* statement. For example, the following statement would filter the LINQ query so that only array elements that match the text "Sue" will be returned. Note that this statement uses the *person* iteration variable defined in the preceding *Dim* statement.

  ```
  Where person = "Sue"
  ```

- **Select**   The *Select* statement is also optional; it allows you to return only selected fields or portions of the data source, to further refine your results. This is most effective when the data source that you are using has numerous fields, or when you specify more than one data source and want to limit the results returned by the query.

There are many more options available for the *Select* statement, but the basic use of *Select* is quite straightforward. In the following example, a new LINQ query named *CrossTrained* is declared that searches two string arrays (*Waiters* and *Drivers*) to see if there is any overlap between the two arrays. The iteration variables *person* and *driver* represent each array element during the query; Visual Basic compares the arrays element by element, and if there is a match (if *person* is equal to *driver*), that item is selected and stored with other matches in the *Crosstrained* variable.

```
Dim Crosstrained = From person In Waiters, driver In Drivers
    Where person = driver
    Select person
```

Now let's take a look at some program code to see how LINQ works in a Visual Basic code-behind file. You'll also learn how to use a *For Each...Next* loop to display the results of a LINQ query in a program. The sample project that you will be using is My Array Tests, which should still be loaded in Visual Studio if you completed the exercises earlier in this chapter.

 Tip When you work in the Code Editor, you'll discover a time-saving feature associated with LINQ. Since LINQ is fully integrated into Visual Studio and the Visual Basic language, the IDE supplies IntelliSense to help you build your LINQ code block as soon as you specify the data source that you will be using with the *From* clause.

Create a LINQ query to extract data from one array

1. Display *MainPage.xaml* in the Designer and create three new button objects on the page below the *ReverseArray* button.

   You'll create three buttons to handle the final three examples in this chapter, all of which create LINQ queries.

2. Set the following properties for the new button objects:

Object	Property	Setting
Button	Name Content	LinqSingleName "LINQ Name Query"
Button	Name Content	LinqArrayOverlap "LINQ Cross-training Query"
Button	Name Content	XmlQuery "LINQ XML Query"

Now widen the text box object (*DataPanel*) on the page so that it can display lines that are a little longer.

Your page should now look like this:

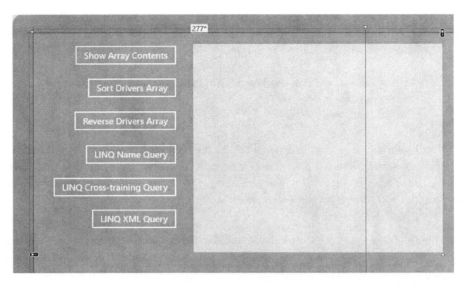

3. Click the *LinqSingleName* button to display the properties of the object in the Properties window.

4. In the Properties window, click the Event Handler button.

5. Double-click next to the *Click* event of the button object in the Properties window.

    Visual Studio creates an event handler named *LinqSingleName_Click* and opens the *MainPage.xaml.vb* code-behind file.

6. Type the following program statements in the Code Editor, between *Private Sub* and *End Sub*. The first two lines comprise a complete LINQ query. (Note that I've placed a blank line after the query, just to clarify for the compiler that the query is complete.)

```
Dim queryData = From person In Waiters
                Where person = "Sue"

For Each person In queryData
    DataPanel.Text = DataPanel.Text & "LINQ query found a person named " &
        person & vbCrLf
Next
```

The first two lines of this event handler are the same lines defining a LINQ query shown previously, in the description of basic LINQ syntax. The *Dim* keyword creates a variable (*queryData*) to hold the results that are returned by LINQ. *Waiters* is a string array previously declared and assigned data in the program; this is the data source for the LINQ query. The *person* variable is an iterative variable that represents each item in the *Waiters* array as it is processed by the LINQ query.

The *Where* clause filters the results of the query, passing along only array items that match the string "Sue". Keep in mind that additional *Where* clauses could be added to further refine the data returned by this query. (In a much larger array, there may be many items that are identical, and you may wish to test other values.)

The final four lines of the event handler form a *For Each...Next* loop that steps through the *queryData* variable item by item and displays a separate line in the text box for each value returned. Only the items that match "Sue" will appear. If "Sue" doesn't exist in the array at all, the *For Each...Next* loop will not execute.

You'll run the program now to see how your first LINQ query works.

7. Click the Start Debugging button.

    The application launches and displays a page containing a collection of buttons and a text box.

8. Click LINQ Name Query.

    Visual Basic loads the *LinqSingleName_Click* event handler and runs the LINQ query to find array items that match "Sue" in the *Waiters* array. One matching item is found, and the *For Each...Next* loop displays a message about it in the text box. Your screen should look like this:

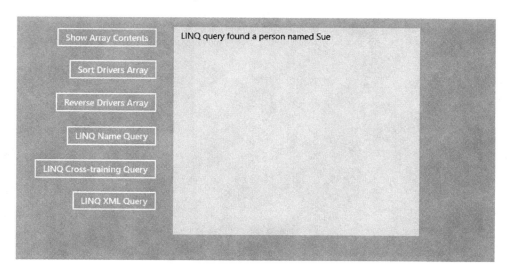

9. Close the program and return to the Visual Studio IDE.

You have demonstrated a fundamental use of LINQ: to search for individual items within a data collection. But before you leave this example, you'll try modifying the *Waiters* array so that it contains two "Sue" items. It is important to verify that the LINQ query you have will return multiple data items, not just one item that matches.

10. Scroll to the top of the Code Editor and locate the statement that declares the *Waiters* array:

```
Dim Waiters() As String = {"Ben", "Sue", "Lee", "Kim", "Pat", "Eve", "Sal"}
```

11. Replace the "Eve" element with "Sue", keeping everything else in the array as it is.

Your array declaration should now look like this:

```
Dim Waiters() As String = {"Ben", "Sue", "Lee", "Kim", "Pat", "Sue", "Sal"}
```

Now run the program again to see how the unchanged LINQ query works with slightly different data.

12. Click the Start Debugging button.

The application launches and displays the familiar My Array Tests page.

13. Click LINQ Name Query.

Visual Basic runs the *LinqSingleName_Click* event handler again, but this time finds two matching array items in its LINQ query. Your screen should look like this:

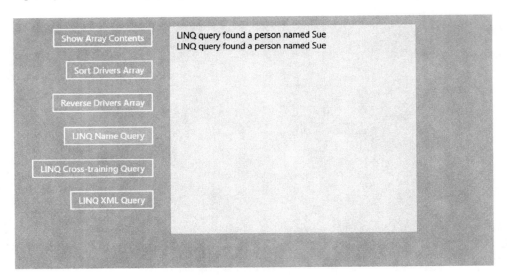

14. Your program should work correctly because the LINQ query has been designed to return each data item that matches the string "Sue", and there are two such items in the revised array.

15. Close the program and return to the Visual Studio IDE.

16. Near the top of the code-behind file, change the statement that declares the *Waiters* array back to its original form:

```
Dim Waiters() As String = {"Ben", "Sue", "Lee", "Kim", "Pat", "Eve", "Sal"}
```

Now you're ready to compose a LINQ query that searches through both the *Waiters* and *Drivers* string arrays, and returns any employee names that are in both lists. This can be useful if, for example, you want to know which employees are capable of working both as truck drivers and as waiters in the restaurant business.

Create a LINQ query to find overlapping elements in two arrays

1. Display the Designer, and then click the *LinqArrayOverlap* button to display the properties of the object.

2. In the Properties window, click the Event Handler button (if necessary) to display the events available for the *Button* control.

3. Double-click next to the *Click* event of the *LinqArrayOverlap* object.

   Visual Studio creates an event handler named *LinqArrayOverlap_Click* and opens the code-behind file.

4. Type the following statements in the Code Editor to define your second LINQ query:

```
Dim Crosstrained = From person In Waiters, driver In Drivers
                   Where person = driver
                   Select person

For Each person In Crosstrained
    DataPanel.Text = DataPanel.Text & "LINQ found " & person &
        " in both lists" & vbCrLf
Next
```

This code block declares a variable named *Crosstrained* that will contain the results of the LINQ query. I have used the term *Crosstrained* because the list will represent employees that appear in both arrays—that is, those who have been cross-trained to work as either waiters or drivers.

Notice that the *From* clause in the LINQ query specifies two data sources for the query, and that both sources are string arrays. The *person* variable is again the iterative variable that represents each item in the *Waiters* array as the data is processed, and the *driver* variable represents elements in the *Drivers* array.

Here you also see a *Where* clause at work, filtering the results so that only employees who appear in both the *Waiters* array and the *Drivers* array are returned by the LINQ query. Those items are processed by the *For Each...Next* loop, which steps through the *Crosstrained* variable item by item and displays a separate line in the text box for each item.

Now you'll run the program now to see how the query works.

5. Click the Start Debugging button.

   The application launches and displays the My Array Tests page.

6. Click LINQ Cross-Training Query.

   Visual Basic loads the *LinqArrayOverlap_Click* event handler and runs the second LINQ query to locate items that appear in both the *Waiters* and *Drivers* arrays. Two overlapping items are found, and the *For Each...Next* loop displays messages about them in the text box. Your screen should look like this:

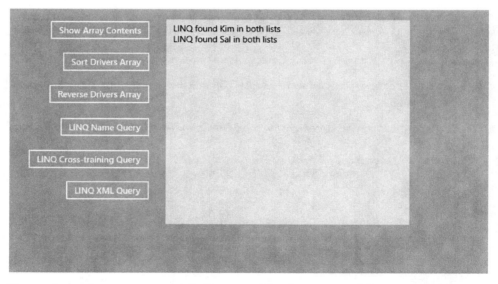

The results are impressive, especially if you consider that LINQ could just as easily be processing thousands of items with little more in the way of program code. Once you understand the meaning and flow of basic LINQ syntax, you can begin very quickly to write sophisticated query expressions.

7. Close the program and return to the Visual Studio IDE.

8. Click the Save All button to save your changes to the project.

You have one more demonstration routine to write: an event procedure that returns data from an XML document that is included in your project's Assets folder.

Debugging Programs Containing Arrays and LINQ Data

As you learned in Chapter 9, "Debugging Applications," the Visual Studio IDE provides several tools that help you track down errors in, or *debug*, your Visual Basic programs. As you expand your programming skills to include the use of arrays and LINQ queries, the Visual Studio debugging tools will become especially useful. For example, you can use a DataTip or a Watch window to inspect the entire contents of an array while your program is in break mode. If you place a *Stop* statement in a *For...Next* loop that processes an array in some way, you can enter break mode and use the Step Into button on the Debug toolbar to watch the array's contents change as you move through the loop.

Likewise, complex LINQ queries can be demystified and debugged if you place a *Stop* statement after the final *Select* statement in a query and use break mode to step through the remaining lines of the event handler. This can be especially useful in *For Each...Next* loops that process query variables, like the *Crosstrained* and *person* variables you used in the last exercise. The Locals window is also very useful when you evaluate and debug LINQ queries.

Finally, as you begin working with XML documents in Visual Basic applications, try using an XML visualizer to examine XML document structure and element formatting while you work on your program. As discussed in Chapter 9, a visualizer is represented by a small magnifying glass icon that appears in the Code Editor for certain program elements during break mode. If you see this tool next to a variable that contains XML data in your code, click the icon and you'll see a dialog box with helpful information about the document's contents. For example, try this technique to examine the *AllRunners* variable in the *XmlQuery_Click* event handler in the following exercise. The *AllRunners* variable contains the contents of the *ListOfRunners.xml* file.

Working with XML Documents

Arrays are interesting and important data sources for LINQ queries, but they represent only the beginning of what you can do with LINQ in Visual Basic programs. Other important sources of data supported by Visual Studio and LINQ include relational databases, Excel worksheets, and XML documents. You can even find third-party software vendors who will sell you LINQ providers that allow you to work with data from Google, Amazon, Microsoft Active Directory, and so on.

As your final LINQ example in this chapter, you will learn how to add an XML document to your project's Assets folder, and to use the XML document as a source for data in a LINQ query. An *XML document* is a structured text file that conforms to the specifications for XML. As already discussed in this book, XAML files also conform to the general rules for XML documents, and they are in essence a special type of XML document designed to instantiate .NET objects in a Windows application.

XML documents do not have a set list of predefined elements that they need to contain. Instead, they allow you to create your own names for elements in a document. The elements just need to conform to basic syntax rules for tagging, and to fit together in a hierarchy under a single top-level element. In a Visual Basic application, you can use any hierarchical data structures that exist in XML documents, so it is beneficial to create and maintain them.

XML documents have several advantages over proprietary data formats, such as that used by Microsoft Access (*.mdb* format). First, XML is easily readable by humans, so special database tools are not required to open and understand XML data files. Second, XML is based on an open, public standard, and it has been adopted by Microsoft and other software publishers for information exchange and use on the web. Third, XML files are easily included in Visual Studio programming projects. Essentially, XML files are simply text files, so if you need an efficient, flexible data source in your project that can easily be updated and installed with your application, XML documents may be a good choice.

The XML document that you will use in this chapter is named *ListOfRunners.xml*. The file is meant to represent information about a list of long-distance runners, and the file includes fields named *FirstName*, *LastName*, *Gender*, and *Age*. (This is the type of information that a race organizer might use to register runners for a competition, or to record race results and determine prize winners.) Although the XML document contains only the information for 18 athletes now, it is the kind of file that could be expanded to contain hundreds or even thousands of records. This is just the type of information that a programmer might want to include in a programming project, and that you can use to practice building LINQ queries.

You can find the *ListOfRunners.xml* file in the *My Documents\Start Here! Programming in Visual Basic\Chapter 10* folder on your hard disk. *ListOfRunners.xml* is simply a text file, and you can edit the file in a text editor (such as Notepad or WordPad) or in the Visual Studio IDE, which is designed to open and edit XML documents. If you open *ListOfRunners.xml* in Internet Explorer, the various document elements will appear in different colors, and the document's logical structure will be navigable via a collapsible/expandable tree.

The following illustration shows *ListOfRunners.xml* in Internet Explorer 10:

```xml
<?xml version="1.0"?>
<AllRunners>
    <Runner Age="27" Gender="M" LastName="Brewer" FirstName="Alan"/>
    <Runner Age="33" Gender="M" LastName="Kiel" FirstName="Oliver"/>
    <Runner Age="24" Gender="F" LastName="Scemla" FirstName="Isabelle"/>
    <Runner Age="46" Gender="F" LastName="Simpson" FirstName="Katherine"/>
    <Runner Age="48" Gender="M" LastName="Bryant" FirstName="Chris"/>
    <Runner Age="19" Gender="F" LastName="Kol" FirstName="Ayla"/>
    <Runner Age="45" Gender="M" LastName="Carvallo" FirstName="Carlos"/>
    <Runner Age="63" Gender="M" LastName="Krebs" FirstName="Peter"/>
    <Runner Age="26" Gender="F" LastName="Stewart" FirstName="April"/>
    <Runner Age="36" Gender="F" LastName="Smith" FirstName="Samantha"/>
    <Runner Age="29" Gender="M" LastName="Lo" FirstName="Renee"/>
    <Runner Age="43" Gender="M" LastName="Thorpe" FirstName="Steven"/>
    <Runner Age="31" Gender="F" LastName="Dickson" FirstName="Holly"/>
    <Runner Age="52" Gender="M" LastName="Grisso" FirstName="Geoff"/>
    <Runner Age="39" Gender="F" LastName="Ortman" FirstName="Danni"/>
    <Runner Age="17" Gender="F" LastName="Hagege" FirstName="Adina"/>
    <Runner Age="40" Gender="F" LastName="Yamagishi" FirstName="Makoto"/>
    <Runner Age="20" Gender="M" LastName="Winston" FirstName="Greg"/>
</AllRunners>
```

Using XML Documents in a Visual Basic Project

Before you can use an XML document in a Visual Basic project, you need to include the document in the project's Assets folder. The procedure to add an XML document to the folder is the same as the process for including electronic artwork, audio files, or video files to the Assets folder. You simply right-click the Assets folder in Solution Explorer, click Add | Existing Item, and then locate the XML document in the Add Existing Item dialog box.

The following exercise shows you how to load an XML document and use it as a data source for a LINQ query.

Create a LINQ query that retrieves XML data from an XML document

1. With the My Array Tests project still loaded in the Visual Studio IDE, right-click the Assets folder in Solution Explorer, and then click Add | Existing Item.

    The Add Existing Item dialog box appears.

2. Browse to the *My Documents\Start Here! Programming in Visual Basic\Chapter 10* folder, click the *ListOfRunners.xml* document, and then click Add.

Visual Studio adds the XML document containing runner information to the My Array Tests project. Now you are ready to use the document as a data source for a LINQ query.

3. Display the *MainPage.xaml* user interface page in the Designer, and then click the *XmlQuery* button to display the properties of the object.

4. In the Properties window, click the Event Handler button (if necessary) to display the events available for the *Button* control.

5. Double-click next to the *Click* event of the *XmlQuery* object.

   Visual Studio creates an event handler named *XmlQuery_Click* and opens the code-behind file.

6. Type the following statements in the Code Editor to define your final LINQ query:

```
Dim AllRunners = XElement.Load("Assets/ListOfRunners.xml")
Dim runnerQuery = From athlete In AllRunners.Descendants("Runner")
                  Where athlete.Attribute("Age").Value >= 35
                  Select FName = athlete.Attribute("FirstName").Value,
                         LName = athlete.Attribute("LastName").Value

For Each person In runnerQuery
    DataPanel.Text = DataPanel.Text & person.FName & " " & person.LName &
        vbCrLf
Next
```

A unique *Dim* statement initiates this event handler—it uses the *XElement.Load* method to load the *ListOfRunners.xml* document into the *AllRunners* variable. Notice how this statement relies on the fact that you have already inserted the XML document into the Assets folder in your project.

The routine then declares a variable named *runnerQuery* to hold the results of the LINQ query. The *From* clause indicates that the XML document stored in the *AllRunners* variable will be used as the source for data, and that the descendants of the top-level *Runner* element will all be included. (If you examine *ListOfRunners.xml* again, you will see that it begins with the top-level element *Runner*.) The *athlete* variable is the iterative variable that represents each element in the XML document as the data is processed.

The *Where* clause filters data such that only runners who are 35 years old or older appear in the final list. For names that match the age filter, the *FirstName* and *LastName* elements for each runner are returned and displayed in the text box on the page. Note the particular syntax of the *Attribute* and *Value* properties; these allow XML data elements within the XML document hierarchy to be returned. The process is just a little more complicated than the array processing work accomplished earlier in the chapter, because there is more structure in these XML documents than there was in the single-dimension array.

Finally, the XML data items returned by the LINQ query are processed by the *For Each...Next* loop, which steps through the *runnerQuery* variable item by item, displaying a line in the text box for each runner who is 35 or older.

Run the program now to see how the XML document query works.

7. Click the Start Debugging button.

The application launches and displays the My Array Tests page.

8. Click LINQ XML Query.

Visual Basic loads the *XmlQuery_Click* event handler and runs the LINQ query to extract runners aged 35 and older from the *ListOfRunners.xml* file. Nine matching names were found, and the *For Each...Next* loop displays each name in the text box. Your screen should look like this:

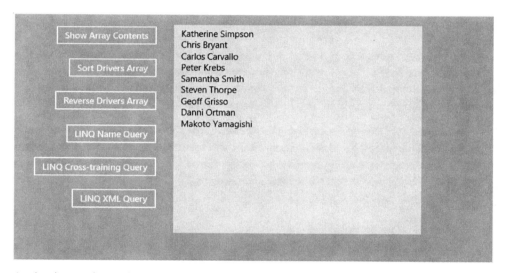

Again, the results are interesting. About half of the runners in the XML document are aged 35 and older; this represents about 50 percent of the group. The query returned information that will be useful to the race coordinator and others involved with marketing upcoming events. However, you could easily extract different information by changing the *Where* clause in the event handler; now that the query has been written, changing the filter criteria is quite easy.

9. Close the program and return to the Visual Studio IDE.

10. Click the Save All button to save your changes to the project, and then exit Visual Studio.

You're finished working in Visual Basic for now. Congratulations on building useful data management skills with arrays and LINQ.

Summary

This chapter explored using arrays and LINQ to manage data in a Visual Basic program. Working with data is a fundamental task in computer programming, and as you continue working with Visual Basic, you'll have many opportunities to learn about connecting to data sources and processing data efficiently.

Arrays allow you to store a collection of values in memory while your program is running. You declare an array with the *Dim* statement, and you store information in an array by using an array index and assigning data to the array in the appropriate type. If you use special array literal syntax, you can also assign initial values to an array at the same time that you declare it. After you create an array, you can manipulate array elements by using methods in the *Array* class, including *Array.Sort* and *Array.Reverse*. This chapter also demonstrated how you can process array elements by using one or more *For...Next* loops.

Building on what you learned about with arrays, this chapter also explored using LINQ to perform selection queries on the data stored in arrays and XML documents. Although LINQ has some amazing capabilities (and advanced programming books often devote several chapters to the topic), it is actually quite easy to get started with LINQ and the fundamental LINQ keywords *From*, *Where*, and *Select*. You used LINQ in this chapter to extract data from one array, to find overlapping items in two arrays, and to retrieve XML data matching filter criteria from an XML document.

In Chapter 11, "Design Focus: Five Great Features for a Windows 8 Application," you'll return again to the user interface of Windows 8 applications and learn how to add some final touches to your Visual Basic project, including preparing a splash screen for your app, setting program permissions, and optimizing your app for touch input and gestures.

Design Focus: Five Great Features for a Windows 8 Application

After completing this chapter, you'll be able to

- Create a colorful tile for your app on the Windows Start page.

- Create a splash screen for your app that appears at startup.

- Set permissions and capabilities for your app to enhance security.

- Use a project template to showcase your app's content.

- Optimize your app for touch input and gestures.

IN THIS CHAPTER, YOU'LL RETURN TO the user interface of Windows 8 applications, and learn more about designing apps with the qualities and characteristics of programs distributed via the Windows Store. You'll learn how to create a custom tile for your app on the Windows Start page, and how to create a unique splash screen for your project that appears when you first run your app. You'll learn how to edit the *Package.appxmanifest* file in your project to control important permissions and capabilities that are essential security considerations for you and the users of your software. You'll also learn more about creating Microsoft Visual Basic applications by using the Grid App template, which offers a ready-made design for building apps with multiple pages and useful navigation tools. Finally, you'll learn more about the support for touch input and gestures in a Windows 8 application, and how you can design your user interface to take advantage of these and other capabilities.

Although there is still much to learn about Visual Basic programming and the design of Windows 8 applications, you're off to an excellent start in this book. Add the following techniques to your impressive collection of programming skills, and then move on to more advanced techniques in Visual Basic and Windows development. A number of exciting opportunities await you.

Creating a Tile for Your App on the Windows Start Page

One of the fundamental features of the Windows 8 UI is the *Start page*, where you launch a Windows application by clicking a colorful, rectangular *tile* representing the program that you want to run. When you create a new Windows Store app in Microsoft Visual Studio 2012, Visual Studio automatically adds a default application tile named *Logo.png* to your project's Assets folder. When you deploy the project on your computer, Visual Studio places this tile on the Start page, and you can use it to launch your app.

For example, the following illustration shows the Windows Start page containing the default tile for the Media Sample project created in Chapter 3, "Using Controls," as well as the 1965 project that you will create in this chapter. Do you see how much more inviting the second tile is?

In the preceding screen shot, the Media Sample tile contains a plain gray background and a very basic X logo, while the 1965 tile contains a striking green background and an interesting cloud logo comprised of both text and image effects. I created the 1965 tile using Microsoft Paint, and you'll do so as well in the following section.

Note Paint is a basic graphics editor that has been included in Windows for years, and it is just the sort of thing for this type of editing work. However, if you have a more sophisticated graphics editing program, you can use that instead—you'll just need to translate the following instructions to the software that you own. The only requirement is that your graphics editor should be able to create an image with precise dimensions. (You'll need the ability to create images with the dimensions 150×150 pixels, 30×30 pixels, and 310×150 pixels.)

Create a tile for the Start page

1. On the Windows Start page, point to the upper-right corner of the screen to display the Search charm, and then click it.

   Windows opens the Search box.

2. Type **Paint** and press Enter.

   As you type the application name, the Search tool begins its search, and usually highlights the Paint program after just a few letters. When Paint is highlighted, press Enter, and Windows will launch the handy tool. Maximize Paint if it is not running in full-screen (maximized) mode.

   You'll see the following screen:

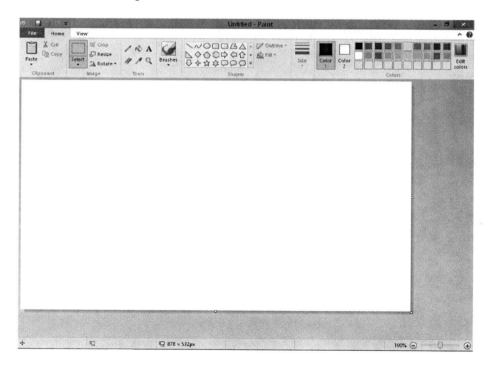

Complete application programs for the Windows Store should have three images prepared in different sizes. (In fact, creating all three types is a submission requirement for the Windows Store.) The three tile sizes will allow for different viewing options and screen resolutions. As noted previously, the dimensions you need are 150×150 pixels, 30×30 pixels, and 310×150 pixels.

The 150×150 image is the standard-sized tile. The 30×30 image is not used on the Start page itself, but for situations when Windows displays the All Programs list, search results, or other circumstances in which a smaller tile is desired. The 310×150 image is for situations when a wide-format tile is needed.

Although I will only create a 150×150-pixel image in this exercise, the procedure for creating the 30×30 and 310×150 images is virtually identical to the steps that you will take here. When you work with the *Package.appxmanifest* file, it is also quite apparent where the alternate formats are specified.

To use Paint to create a 150×150-pixel image, first turn on Rulers, Gridlines, and the status bar, so that you can create a Paint canvas (or drawing surface) in the appropriate size.

3. In Paint, click the View Ribbon tab, and then click the Rulers, Gridlines, and Status Bar check boxes.

    Your screen will look like this:

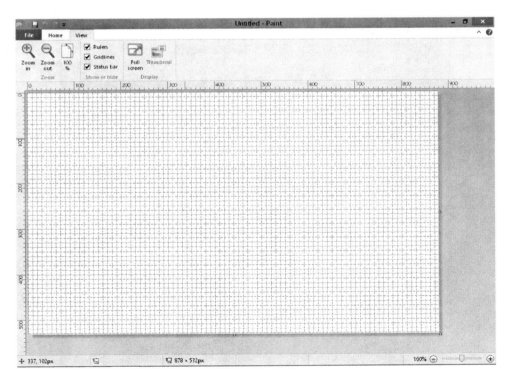

The rulers shown along the top and left edges of the Paint canvas display measurements in pixels, and a thin red line appears on both rulers, corresponding to the location of the mouse pointer and the horizontal and vertical axes of the point on the grid. You can use these to create the proper canvas dimensions.

4. Move the pointer to the lower-right corner of the canvas, and the mouse pointer will turn into a resizing pointer.

5. Hold down the mouse button to select and resize the canvas, and then drag the mouse up and to the left to create a much smaller image.

6. As you drag the canvas corner (always keeping the mouse button down), notice the dimension indicator at the bottom of the screen in the middle of the status bar. Your task is to set the dimensions of the canvas to exactly 150×150 pixels. When you have a canvas of that size, release the mouse button.

    It may take a little practice to get an exact size of 150×150 pixels. To make your task easier, you can zoom in on the canvas with the Zoom In tool before you start resizing, as larger canvas sizes sometimes make precise editing movements easier to accomplish.

    Your screen will look like the following. Notice that the dimension indicator and the Zoom In tools are circled.

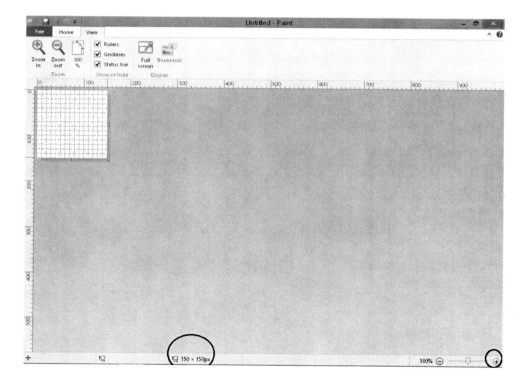

This 150×150-pixel canvas (currently blank) is the size that you need to create the default tile in a Windows 8 application. You'll save the blank tile now, so that you will have a correctly sized (blank) version available as you create additional tiles for projects.

7. Choose File | Save As | PNG Picture, browse to the *My Documents\Start Here! Programming in Visual Basic\Chapter 11* folder and open it, type **Blank_Logo_150x150**, and then click Save.

You've created a blank logo file for the app tile, which you can use over and over again. (I've included this file in the Chapter 11 sample files as well.) Now that you've created this file, you'll never need to resize the Paint canvas again for a 150×150-pixel tile icon; that work is already done.

Now you'll create a tile that has some visual interest.

8. Choose File | Save As | PNG Picture, and in the *My Documents\Start Here! Programming in Visual Basic\Chapter 11* folder, specify the new file name **My_1965_Logo** and click Save.

Paint creates a copy of the *Blank_Logo_150×150.png* file under a new name. In this exercise, you'll create a tile for a sample Windows app named 1965. (You can substitute a different name if you want.) The Windows app itself has no content other than the tile and the splash screen you'll create in the next exercise.

The Windows 8 style guidelines recommend that Start page tiles be colorful and clean, with simple graphics and text effects. In other words, you want to avoid overly complex bitmaps or drawings in tiles, although in some situations a colorful photograph can make an excellent tile.

You can also add live content to Start page tiles if you use a pop-up communication feature known as *toast notification* to send updates to your tile from your application or another source. Although this feature is beyond the scope of this chapter, it is an exciting feature of the Windows 8 user interface that is used by some commercial Windows 8 apps, such as mail programs, weather apps, and newsreaders.

At this point, you'll create a rather simple tile with a green background that contains both text and an image. First, you'll create a text effect.

9. Click the Home ribbon tab, and then click the Text tool.

10. Click the center of the canvas, and then select the Segoe UI font from the Font Family drop-down list box.

11. Select 28-point in the Font-Size text box.

12. Click the Italic button, and then type **1965**.

13. Click somewhere on the canvas away from the text input box to lock in your text.

14. Click the Select tool, select the year, and then move it to the exact middle of the tile.

Your screen will look like this:

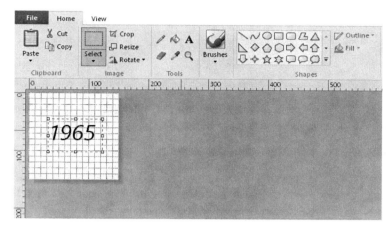

Now you'll add a thought-cloud icon to the tile from Paint's Shapes panel. This will add additional interest to the Start tile for the project.

15. With the Home ribbon tab still active, click the Cloud Callout shape in the lower-right corner of the Shapes group.

The insertion pointer now becomes a shape-drawing tool when you hold it over the canvas.

16. Click the Size command, and then click the second width from the top; this will be the line width for the Cloud Callout shape.

17. On the canvas, draw a cloud shape over the text "1965" so that your tile looks like the following:

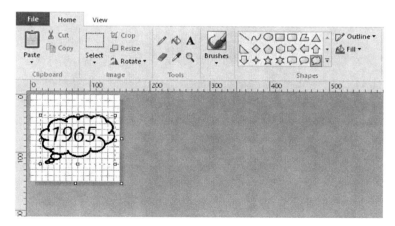

18. Move and adjust the shape so that it is centered well and does not overlap the numbers on the tile.

Note If the cloud completely covers the text, the Fill command may be set to Solid Color. You don't want this particular effect now, so if this is the case, set the Fill command to No Fill for the cloud shape.

19. Click somewhere on the canvas a bit away from the text input box to lock in your changes.

Now you'll use a Fill tool to add green color to the tile. You'll add color to the outside of the cloud shape, to keep the "1965" text clean and legible.

20. Click the Edit Colors button on the right side of the Colors group.

The Edit Colors dialog box appears. Although you could have simply used one of the default colors in Paint, it makes sense to specify an exact color, because your tile needs to work with the color data in the Visual Studio program you are about to create.

In Visual Studio, the Dark Green color has a color value of Red: 0, Green: 100, Blue: 0. Enter those values now for the fill color in Paint.

21. In the Red text box, change the value to 0 and press Tab. In the Green text box, change the value to 100 and press Tab. In the Blue text box, change the value to 0.

22. Your dialog box should look like this:

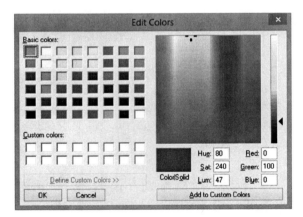

23. Click OK.

24. Click the Fill With Color tool, and then click somewhere on the canvas outside of the cloud.

Paint fills the shape with dark green. Your screen should look like this:

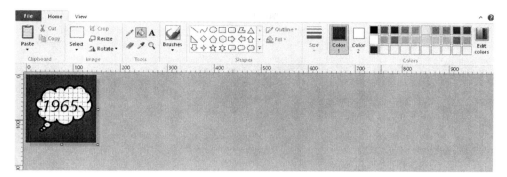

Your Windows app tile is now complete. Now you'll create a new Visual Basic app and add the *My_1965_Logo.png* file to it.

25. Choose File | Save to save your changes, and then close Paint.

Now you'll use the new image in a Visual Studio project. Note that if you didn't create the image by following the preceding steps, you can use the image that I created for you. It is named *1965_Logo.png*.

Add a custom Start page tile to a Visual Studio project

1. Start Visual Studio Express and click New Project to open a new Visual Studio project.

2. Choose Visual Basic | Windows Store under Templates, and then verify that the Blank App (XAML) template is selected.

3. Type **My 1965** in the Name text box.

4. Click OK to open and configure the new project.

    Visual Studio creates a new project with typical project files.

5. Double-click the *MainPage.xaml* file in Solution Explorer to display the default user interface page.

    Visual Studio loads *MainPage.xaml* into the Designer. Now you'll change the background color of the grid to dark green.

6. Click the grid object (the page background) in the Designer, open the Properties window, and click the Brush category.

7. Click the *Background* property, click the Solid Color Brush button (the second button in the set of five buttons below the *Background* property), and then enter values of R: **0**, G: **100**, and B: **0** in the Editor. Press Enter after the last value.

Your Properties window will look like this:

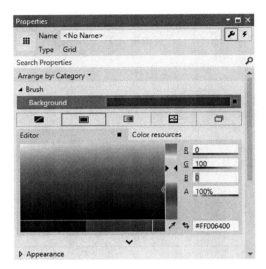

Visual Studio changes the background color of the grid to dark green. Note that you've now matched colors between the app's Start tile and the background of the program. This sort of consistency takes a few steps to achieve, but it is the type of setting that a customer would appreciate in their Windows 8 app.

8. Open Solution Explorer and open the Assets folder for the project.

Your screen should look like this:

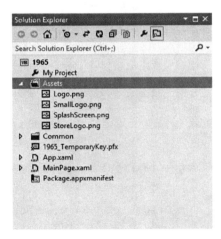

9. Click *Logo.png* in the Assets folder, and then press Delete.

If you're using the default settings in Visual Studio, you'll be warned now that "'Logo.png' will be deleted permanently."

10. Click OK to delete the file.

You'll be replacing it with *My_1965_Logo.png*.

11. Right-click the Assets folder in Solution Explorer, click Add | Existing Item, and then browse to the *My Documents\Start Here! Programming in Visual Basic\Chapter 11* folder. Click My_1965_Logo and then click Add.

If you didn't create the *My_1965_Logo.png* file, you can use the *1965_Logo.png* file that I created. Visual Studio adds the image you select to the Assets folder, where it can be used freely in the project.

12. Point to the file now in the Assets folder.

Visual Studio shows you a preview of the image, so that you can verify that you have the right item and that the colors are compatible:

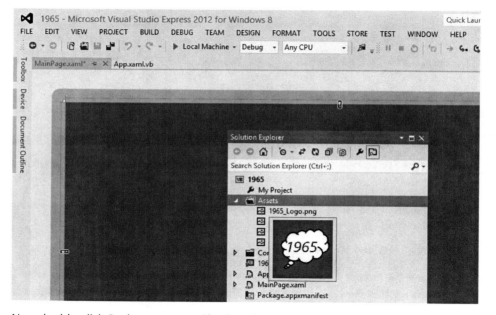

13. Now double-click *Package.appxmanifest* in Solution Explorer.

In what is called the *Manifest Designer*, Visual Studio shows you a collection of properties for the deployment package of the app that you are building. You'll use this Manifest Designer several times in this chapter to adjust settings for your Windows 8 app. The end result will be a manifest file that travels with your app and contains important deployment instructions.

Your screen should look like this:

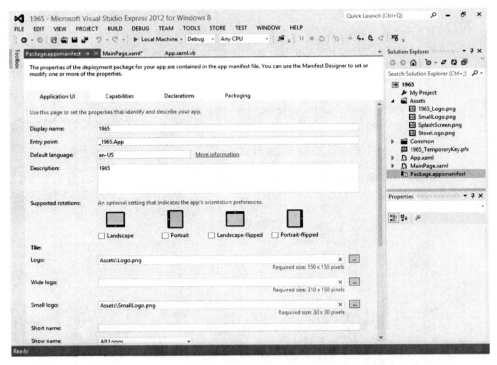

14. On the Application UI tab (the page currently selected in the designer), scroll down to the Tile section.

Here you'll find Logo, Wide Logo, and Small Logo text boxes. This is the place that you specify the various tile images you will be using to customize your app.

15. In the Logo text box, select "Assets\Logo.png" and press Delete.

This is the default tile that you removed from the Assets folder previously. Note the reminder message that the Logo needs to be 150×150 pixels. You carefully followed this guideline in Paint at the beginning of this section. However, if you do specify an image of the wrong size, Visual Studio will notify you about it here.

16. In the Logo text box, type **Assets\My_1965_Logo.png**.

Your work is now complete. At a later time, you can create appropriate Wide Logo and Small Logo files. Keep in mind that they should have essentially the same design and fill color patterns as *My_1965_Logo.png*, but each image will be a different size. You will also give the files unique names, like *1965_Wide_Logo.png* and *1965_Small_Logo.png*. But rather than go through those steps here, we'll move on to add a few more interesting features to your app.

17. Click Save All to save your project, and then specify the *My Documents\Start Here! Programming in Visual Basic\Chapter 11* folder for the location.

18. Click Start Debugging to run the program.

The Visual Basic app launches and briefly displays its gray splash screen. (You'll customize that in the next exercise.) Then the grid loads and displays the dark-green background. Since you haven't added any controls or program logic to the app, you won't see anything else at this point.

19. Close the application, and then open the Start page.

You'll see the new tile on the Start page, looking just as colorful as many of the commercial apps and accessories that surround it.

Now you've learned how to add a professional-looking tile to your Visual Basic app. If you click the tile, you'll see that it works perfectly to launch the program, and even displays a transitional effect as it loads. Best of all, the green background color of the tile matches the background color of your application as it runs—a nice touch.

Tip To create additional 150×150-pixel tiles, remember to use the boilerplate (blank) tile that you created in the first exercise. Hopefully this will be a handy image file for you. It is much easier to create a tile when you already have an appropriately sized canvas.

Now you'll learn how to add a splash screen to a Windows 8 application.

Creating a Splash Screen for Your App

A *splash screen* is a transitional image that appears when your application first launches. Every Windows 8 app must have a splash screen, which consists of an image (or text) and a surrounding background color. The basic image has much in common with the Start page tile you just created, and both items are designed to add interest to the startup process for a Windows 8 app. To create these items, the programmer typically needs to use a stand-alone graphics program that is not included in Visual Studio.

You'll create a splash screen in this section using Paint, because it comes free with Windows and is therefore handy and ubiquitous. However, there is one drawback to using Paint to create a splash screen for a Windows 8 app: Paint cannot produce transparent images, and this type of artwork gives you more flexibility when you're creating splash screen transitions. For example, if your image is transparent, you don't need to worry about matching the background color of the image to the splash screen color (a value specified on the Application UI page in the Manifest Designer). However, Paint is more than up to the task of creating your first splash screen in this chapter. To keep consistent with your Start page tile, your splash screen effect will contain an image and the text "1965," and it will be surrounded by a dark-green background color.

Before you begin, keep in mind that a splash screen appears for just a few moments. This is not the place to put elaborate program instructions or copyright information. And you'll want to avoid placing advertisements and version information on splash screens too. Instead, use the splash screen to offer a preview of the functionality of your app in some unique way. Consider an image or photo that will be easily localizable and that can be displayed effectively in different screen resolutions. In short, remember that the purpose of the splash screen is to provide a welcoming transition to your program from the Windows UI.

Tip If you *are* interested in creating a transparent splash screen image, consider using a graphics editor such as Adobe Elements or Adobe Illustrator. You can also find shareware utilities on the web that will allow you to create transparent images suitable for splash screens.

Create a splash screen to run at startup

1. Open Paint to create your new splash screen. (If you left Paint open from the preceding exercise, simply open a new [blank] document in Paint now.)

2. Click the View ribbon tab, and then verify that the Rulers, Gridlines, and Status Bar check boxes are all checked.

3. Resize the canvas so that it is exactly 620×300 pixels.

   All Windows 8 apps must have a splash screen that is 620×300 pixels in size. These are the default dimensions, which are used when the computer is using so-called *1x scaling*. However, note that Microsoft also asks commercial developers to create additional splash screens for 1.4x and 1.8x scaling (that is, additional images sized to 868×420 pixels and 1116×540 pixels for devices that use other standard scale factors to display content).

Although I won't discuss creating the secondary splash screens here, you can easily build them on your own as you prepare your app for the Windows Store. Follow the same basic steps shown here, except create larger images. An easy way to do this is to adjust the image size in Paint using the File | Properties command.

After you've resized your screen to 620×300 pixels, it should look like this:

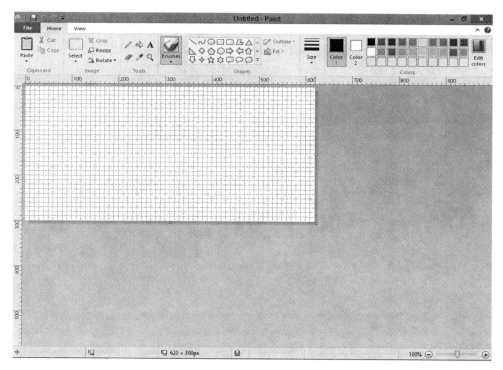

Now you'll create a larger version of the "1965" text and thought cloud that you created in the preceding section.

4. Click the Home ribbon tab, and then click the Text tool.

5. Click the center of the canvas, and then click the Segoe UI font in the Font Family drop-down list box.

6. Type **60** in the Font-Size text box and press Enter.

7. Click the Italic button, and then type **1965**.

8. Click somewhere on the canvas away from the text input box to lock in your text.

9. Click the Select tool, select the year, and then move it to the middle of the tile.

   Now you'll add a thought-cloud icon to the tile, as you did in the previous exercise. This will add consistency to the project.

10. With the Home ribbon tab still active, click the Cloud Callout shape in the Shapes group.

    The insertion pointer now becomes a shape-drawing tool when you hold it over the canvas.

11. Click the Size panel, and then click the third width from the top, which will be used as the line-drawing width for the shape.

12. In the canvas, draw a cloud shape over the text "1965" so that your splash screen looks like this:

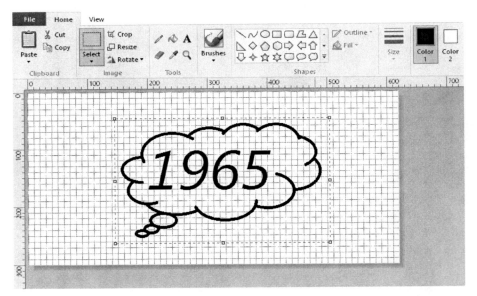

13. Move and adjust the shape so that it looks good and the art elements are not overlapping on the canvas.

14. Click somewhere on the canvas away from the text input box to lock in your text.

    Your splash screen is now complete.

15. Choose File | Save As | PNG Picture, and in the *My Documents\Start Here! Programming in Visual Basic\Chapter 11* folder, specify the new file name **My_1965_SplashScreen**. Then click Save.

16. Close Paint.

    Now you'll return to Visual Studio and add the new splash screen to the project.

17. Open Visual Studio, and then open the Assets folder in Solution Explorer to display the assets for the My 1965 project.

You'll see the following files:

18. Click SplashScreen.png in the Assets folder, and then press Delete.

You'll see the warning, "'SplashScreen.png' will be deleted permanently."

19. Click OK to delete the file.

Don't worry—you'll be replacing the default splash screen with *My_1965_SplashScreen.png*.

20. Right-click the Assets folder in Solution Explorer, click Add | Existing Item, and then browse to the *My Documents\Start Here! Programming in Visual Basic\Chapter 11* folder. Click My_1965_SplashScreen, and then click Add.

If you didn't create the new splash screen, you can use the one that I created for you in the Chapter 11 sample files. It is named *1965_SplashScreen.png*.

Visual Studio adds the new image to the Assets folder. Now you'll record the new file's use in the Manifest Designer.

21. If the Manifest Designer is not still open, double-click Package.appxmanifest in Solution Explorer.

You have already filled out one section in the Application UI page with information about the project tile. The splash screen entries for the project are at the bottom of the Application UI page.

22. Scroll to the bottom of the Application UI page, and then change the current Splash Screen entry from "Assets\SplashScreen.png" to **Assets\My_1965_SplashScreen.png**.

23. In the Background Color text box, type **darkGreen**.

24. Click the Save All button to save your changes to the manifest.

25. The changes that you have made will include the new splash screen in the project and display it when the 1965 project starts. The "darkGreen" color value matches the color you have already set for the tile on the Start page and for the background color in your application.

26. Click Start Debugging to run the program.

The Visual Basic app launches and now displays the new splash screen, as shown in the following screen illustration:

The image comes and goes in less than 2 seconds. After the splash screen finishes, you'll see the dark-green color of the application's user interface (technically, the background color of the main page's grid object). Again, since you have added no controls or program logic to the app, you won't see anything else at this point.

Did you notice the white background of the *My_1965_SplashScreen.png* file? Now is the time to consider whether you want to keep the white background, return to Paint and add a matching background color (using Paint's Fill With Color tool), or create a transparent image that will simply appear on top of the dark-green color you specified in the Manifest Designer. If the image were transparent—again, something not possible with Paint, but an effect you could add with another graphics program—you could simply blend your image into the background color. The choice is up to you.

27. Close the application, and then display the Visual Studio IDE.

Feel free to run the splash screen effect a few more times to examine it. With splash screens, sometimes it takes a few run-throughs to see just what is happening.

Congratulations—you've learned how to add a splash screen to your app, which is another hallmark of programs sold via the Windows Store. You can now add this colorful effect to your other Visual Basic projects.

Settings Permissions and Capabilities for Your Windows 8 App

The applications that you have created so far in this book have assumed that you are a trustworthy user of your computer with full access to the system and no intention of harming anything in your working environment. Unfortunately, you can't be so trusting when you are creating applications that will be distributed commercially. It's important to offer the users of your programs the necessary permissions and capabilities to do their work, but nothing further. Fortunately, Visual Studio makes this easy by allowing developers to control the features or devices that a user has access to while they are working in the application.

How does application security work in the Windows 8 operating system? Basically, a Windows 8 app runs in a security container with limited access to the computer's hardware, the network, and the file system. The authorized permissions and capabilities for each Visual Studio application are stored in the *Package.appxmanifest* file for the project so that Windows can learn what capabilities the application will need to function. This information is also used during the installation of programs from the Windows Store, so that appropriate security permissions are set. Occasionally, these settings will also require that the user grant appropriate permissions before the program runs. (For example, using a computer's built-in web camera or microphone will require special permission.)

Table 11-1 presents some of the important permissions and capabilities settings that you can control in your Windows 8 application. (The items are presented in the order that they appear on the Capabilities tab of the *Package.appxmanifest* file.) You'll learn how to set these permissions and capabilities in the following exercise.

TABLE 11-1 Permissions and Capabilities Settings

Capability	Description
Documents Library Access	Allows your app to access the user's Document Library, and to add, change, or delete files. Your app can access only file types that it has declared in the Declarations section of *Package.appxmanifest*.
Enterprise Authentication	Allows an app to connect to intranet resources that require domain credentials.
Internet (Client)	Allows your app to access the Internet and public networks. Most apps that require Internet access should use this capability.
Internet (Client & Server)	Allows your app to access the Internet and public networks, and allows incoming connections from the Internet to your app. This is a superset of the Internet (Client) capability. You do not need to declare both.

Capability	Description
Location	Allows your app to access the user's current location.
Microphone	Allows your app to access the user's microphone.
Music Library	Allows your app to access the user's music library, and to add, change, or delete files. It also allows access to music libraries on HomeGroup computers, and music file types on locally connected media servers.
Pictures Library Access	Allows your app to access the user's picture library, and to add, change, or delete files. It also allows access to picture libraries on HomeGroup computers, and picture file types on locally connected media servers.
Proximity	Allows your app to access the user's near-field communication (NFC) device.
Removable Storage	Allows your app to access removable storage devices, such as an external hard drive or USB flash drive, and to add, change, or delete files. Your app can access only file types that it has declared in the manifest. Your app can't access removable storage devices on HomeGroup computers.
Shared User Certificates	Allows your app to access software and hardware certificates, such as smart card certificates.
Text Messaging	Allows your app to access text-messaging functionality.
Videos Library Access	Allows your app to access the user's video library, and to add, change, or delete files. It also allows access to video libraries on HomeGroup computers, and video file types on locally connected media servers.
Webcam	Allows your app to access the user's camera.

Set permissions and capabilities for your app

1. If the Manifest Designer is not currently open in Visual Studio, open it now.

   You open the Manifest Designer by double-clicking the *Package.appxmanifest* file in Solution Explorer.

2. Click the Capabilities tab.

   You'll see the following page, which includes a list of the permissions and capabilities that you can control in a Windows 8 app:

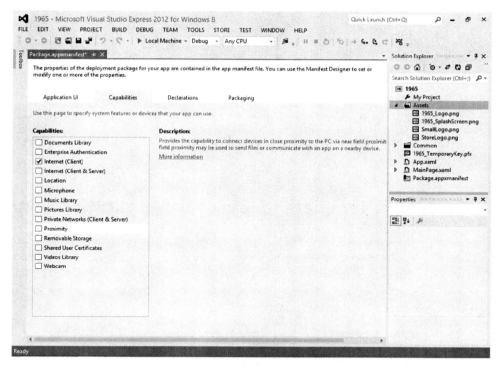

Notice that the check boxes containing permissions and capabilities are in the same order as they are in Table 11-1. You can learn additional information about each setting by clicking the item and reading information in the Description field on the page.

Currently, this application only allows client Internet access; the user is allowed basic Internet access if you provide it via controls in the application user interface. To remove this capability, you would remove the check mark from the Internet (Client) check box.

Some capabilities require that you configure additional settings on the Declarations tab of the Manifest Designer. For example, if you click Documents Library, an error symbol appears on the Capabilities tab; if you hold the mouse pointer over this error symbol, a message indicates that when you grant access to the Documents Library for the local PC, you need to indicate which files types can be accessed. This is done on the Declarations tab.

3. Read about the various permission and capabilities, and keep them in mind as you create Windows 8 apps.

Visual Studio developers often adjust these settings early in the programming process so that they apply to testing scenarios. However, they can be adjusted as necessary throughout the development process.

4. Return the permissions and capabilities in this project back to the original (default) settings if you changed them.

In addition to considering important security issues, you've learned another valuable use for the *Package.appxmanifest* file. Remember that this file travels with the project and informs the operating system about the capabilities and settings for your app.

5. Save your changes, and then choose File | Close Project to close the My_1965 application.

You're finished with this demo program. The next project that you open will be a built-in template.

Using a Project Template to Showcase Application Content

As your Windows 8 apps become more sophisticated, you'll add extra pages to the user interface and concern yourself more directly with navigation from page to page and from element to element. In Windows 8 apps, application content and navigation strategies go hand in hand; your programs should be designed around interesting data, and each screen should organize content into clear sections offering an appropriate level of detail.

There are several options for linking your pages together. In a hierarchical interface, or *hub design*, the main page (the hub) displays several categories of content, each corresponding to a more specific *section page*, which contains additional information and links to lower-level *detail pages*. The detail pages typically contain the most specific information, including detailed text descriptions, photos, video clips, and links to related material.

Windows 8 apps do not need to be large and complex to perform useful work; however, in situations where an app's user interface *does* stretch to several pages, you should organize the content in meaningful ways and offer familiar navigation tools that provide access to the information. In a Windows 8 app, the most useful navigation commands and gestures include panning, zooming, filtering, pivoting, and the ability to switch views quickly and efficiently.

Careful user interface design is important for marketing reasons as well as usability. Well-organized pages allow you to infuse your company identity and brand into your application. For example, a distinctive layout, color palette, logo, and artwork style can create a recognizable look and feature set for your application and your business. As you build commercial software, you should begin to think about how your application fits in with other products and marketing materials in your company, including print materials, web sites, slide shows and demos, videos, and so on.

A good way to get started with multipage applications and navigation tools is to experiment with a few of the built-in Visual Studio project templates. These templates provide ready-made content and links that are general enough to be adapted to a variety of situations. The Visual Studio templates are not trivial to customize, but you'll find MSDN resources online that will help you adapt the templates to your unique situation. In the following section, you'll open the Grid App (XAML) template and learn more about working with multipage projects and navigation tools. The Split App (XAML) template is also useful, offering a similar selection of linked pages.

Use the Grid App template to display product information

1. Choose File | New Project to open a new project template in Visual Studio.

   The New Project dialog box appears.

2. Click the Grid App (XAML) template under the Visual Basic | Windows Store category.

   Your screen should look like this:

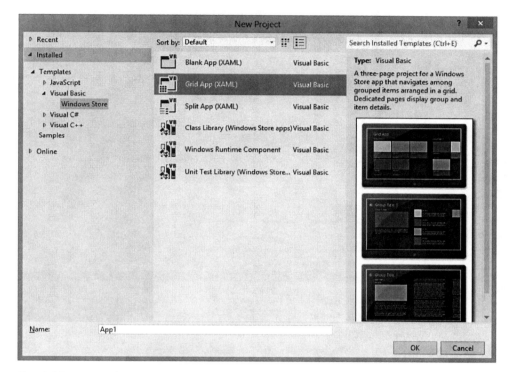

The Grid App is a three-page project template that demonstrates how information can be organized using a grid pattern and linked content pages. The three pages are organized into a hierarchy that includes a hub page (*GroupedItemsPage.xaml*), a section page (*GroupDetailPage.xaml*), and a detail page (*ItemDetailPage.xaml*).

The template scheme is general enough to be used in a variety of contexts. For example, you might use the Grid App template to showcase products, display menu items in a restaurant, catalog musical instruments, organize CDs or videos, track employees, display different groupings of plants or animals, and so on.

3. Type **My Sample Grid** in the Name text box.

4. Click OK to create a new project based on the Grid App template.

   Visual Studio loads the template and displays the components of the project in Solution Explorer. The three pages that make up the default app's user interface are listed.

5. Double-click the *GroupedItemsPage.xaml* file in Solution Explorer.

Your screen should look like this:

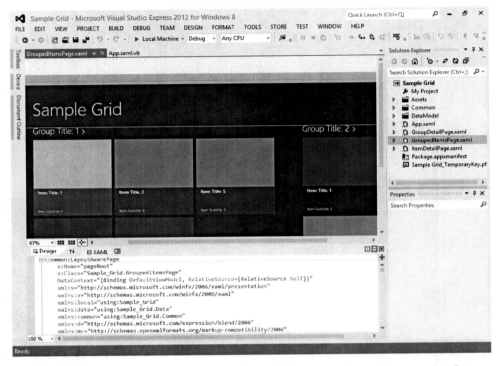

GroupedItemsPage.xaml is the main page of the Grid App template—the page that first appears when you start the application. For example, each group could represent a genre in a music-listening program, and each item in the group could represent an album from that genre.

If you examine the XAML tab of the Code Editor, you'll see that each of the items in the user interface are being defined by XAML markup. You can modify this markup to change the template to an actual, working program. Currently, the project contains numerous placeholder strings for items in the user interface. These include "Sample Grid", "Group Title", "Item Title", and so on.

The project also includes a DataModel folder, containing both a data model and a method that generates data for the application using hard-coded strings. You can replace the sample data shown in the following screen shot with your own data to customize the application. You can do this by opening the *SampleDataSource.vb* file in the DataModel folder and scrolling down to find the code that creates the sample items in the template. (Essentially, this code is contained in a procedure that takes up the second half of the *SampleDataSource.vb* file.)

The editing tasks to customize this template will take you a little time, but you'll learn a lot about Visual Studio and Windows 8 apps in the process.

6. Double-click the *GroupDetailPage.xaml* file in Solution Explorer.

Your screen should look like this:

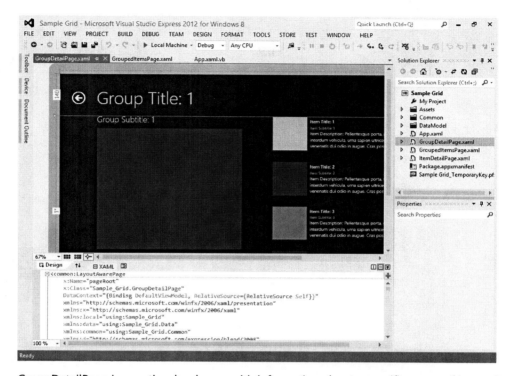

GroupDetailPage is a section-level page with information about a specific group of items. On this page are short descriptions of products or other components that you can select to learn more about a subcategory of information.

Near the top of the Designer you'll see the text "Group Title: 1," which serves as a title for the page. To the left of the title you'll see a navigation button on the page.

7. Click the navigation button now.

Since you're in design mode, the button doesn't operate as a navigation tool, but it is selected on the page, and the properties of the object appear in the Properties window. This object functions as a Back button in the program, and the purpose of the button is to display the previous page of information, much like the Back button in a web browser.

Since you selected the button in the Designer, you can see the button's XAML definition in the Code Editor. Not only does this button have a name (*backButton*), but it also has an event handler that runs when the button is selected (*GoBack*), as well as style settings and other programmatic features. By examining the Back button and other user interface elements in the template, you can learn how the program works and how to customize it.

The *GroupDetailPage.xaml* file is connected to a code-behind file named *GroupDetailPage*
.xaml.vb. As you examine both files, you'll see many familiar items, as well as some new keywords and programming concepts. The challenge with working with any template or sample
project is investigating the code without fully understanding everything that you are seeing.
Such are the ups and downs of working with sample code and learning by doing.

However, keep in mind that you are not alone and that the MSDN online help resources will
help you unpack even the trickiest Windows 8 projects. For more information about the files
in the Grid App and Split App templates, visit *http://msdn.microsoft.com* and search for the
topic "C#, VB, and C++ project templates for Windows Store apps."

Now you'll run the template to see how it works.

8. Click Start Debugging.

The project starts and the template user interface appears. The project name that you gave
the template appears at the top of the main page. Your screen will look like this:

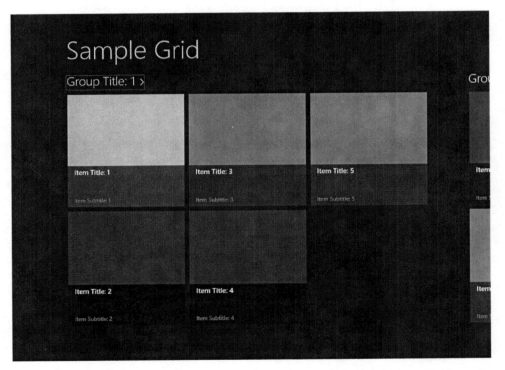

Although the project is still in template form (you haven't replaced the group and item placeholders with meaningful text or images), all the navigation links are functional. You'll see how
they work now.

9. Use the arrow keys to scroll to the right.

If you have a touch-enabled device, you can try panning or sliding to the left or right now as well. You can try these movements by tapping the screen with your finger and dragging the user interface in the direction that you would like to scroll.

You can also use the scroll bar at the bottom of the page to navigate a page that contains more information than will fit on the screen at one time. The Grid App template is designed to display information for several groups at once.

As you scroll or slide to the right, you'll see additional information. Ideally, of course, you will customize these items with your own content, and then remove anything that you do not need.

Now you'll explore the page hierarchy of the Grid App template.

10. Click the header "Group Title: 2" on the page.

You'll see the *GroupDetailPage.xaml* page, which displays information about the second group in the template. Your screen will look like this:

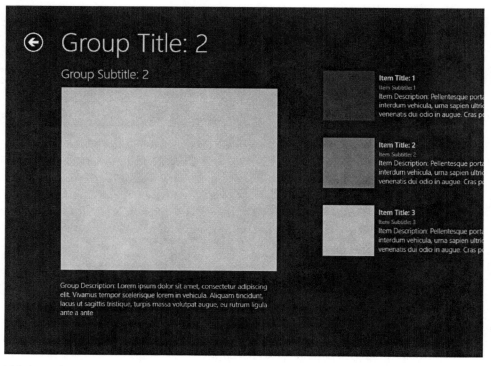

This is a subgroup (or section) page that is linked to the main hub and three detail sections. Latin placeholder text and empty photo tiles are used to demonstrate how your application might combine text and pictures to provide information about a subgroup and members.

11. Click "Item Title: 2" on the page.

The *ItemDetailPage.xaml* page appears, with detailed information about the second item in group two. Your screen will look like this:

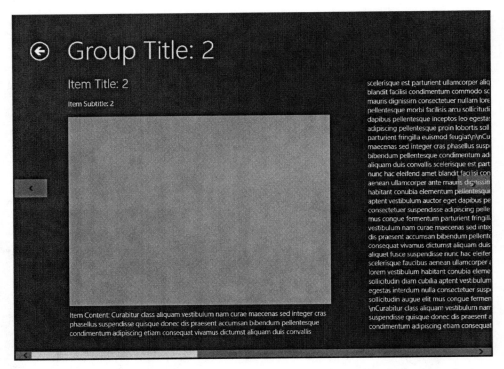

In addition to the item content, there are also navigation tools visible on the page. At the bottom of the screen is a scroll bar, and at the top of the screen (on the left side) is the Back button discussed earlier. Displayed very faintly on the left and the right are also Back and Next buttons that allow the user to scroll to the previous item or the next item in the group. If you hold the mouse over one of these buttons, it will brighten. (The subtle design of these buttons attempts to minimize chrome and emphasize content, two design goals of Windows 8 apps.)

12. Click the Next button on the right side of the page to view Item Title: 3.

13. Click the (lower) Back button twice to return again to Item 2 and Item 1.

At this point, you may begin to notice something rather interesting about the Grid App template. If you examine the six subgroups and the items contained in each subgroup, you will notice that there are not actually separate pages in the project for every possible group collection or item collection. Instead, all the data is displayed by just three pages, and the information on each page is loaded by XAML controls that are bound to a specific data source in the project that holds information about the project's content. So, all the information pertaining to the six subgroups is displayed by the GroupDetailPage page, and all the information pertaining to the items within each subgroup is displayed by the ItemDetailPage page.

14. Continue to navigate the different groups and item collections in the template, and consider the potential that such a tool might offer you.

15. When you're finished, close the program and display the Visual Studio IDE again.

You're through working with the template. Since you haven't made any substantial changes to the program, you can simply discard the project.

16. Choose File | Close Project, and then click Discard to discard any edits that you made.

As you write more substantial Windows 8 applications, keep the Grid App template in mind. It provides a straightforward method to develop multipage designs and showcase your app's content. The Split App template, a two-page design with a similar tile-based layout, offers similar possibilities to Visual Basic programmers.

Optimizing Your App for Touch Input and Gestures

As you have learned in this book, Windows 8 apps should be designed so that they can receive input in a variety of ways, including mouse, keyboard, touch, pen (stylus), and so on. The good news is that much of this input is handled automatically by Windows 8 and Visual Studio 2012. When you create a Windows 8 app using XAML controls and the other tools in Visual Studio, basic input functionality is automatically included to the extent that it is supported by the hardware devices that you are using. So, for example, if you have a desktop PC that has a mouse and keyboard attached, then the input controls in your Windows 8 app will automatically support these devices. However, you will only have access to touch input in your programs if you have a device that supports touch.

As we have all heard, the computer industry is going through a transition of sorts right now in terms of hardware and user expectations about input. Although traditional desktop applications have typically supported only mouse and keyboard for input, millions of handheld devices are now flooding the market and putting a premium on touch input and gestures. With the release of Windows 8, Microsoft has announced that touch input should become a standard feature of Windows applications, and that touch should be designed into programs early in the development process. However, traditional mouse and keyboard input is also essential, and it is important to consider support for enhanced features such as the right mouse button and tilt wheel, as well as third-party devices like the pen or stylus.

As you move beyond the basics of simple mouse and keyboard input in a Visual Basic application, you'll want to consider carefully the significance of touch input and how you might customize touch input for Windows 8 users. Although much of the support for touch and gestures comes automatically in Windows 8 apps, there are important considerations about design that you should think about as you write programs for the Windows Store. In the following section, you'll learn the basics about touch input, and some of the pitfalls to avoid when designing Windows 8 apps that support touch and gestures.

Touch Input is Built In

Touch is a considered a primary mode of interaction in Windows 8, so Visual Studio 2012 has been optimized to make touch input straightforward, precise, and trouble free. The XAML controls in the Visual Studio Toolbox have been designed to support touch input as well as traditional mouse and keyboard interaction. The built-in support for touch input in XAML controls includes gestures such as tap, slide, swipe, press and hold, pinch, and stretch. Also included is support for useful touch procedures such as panning, zoom, rotating, and dragging. Not all controls support touch equally, of course; but in areas where touch functionality is useful, you'll find that most of the support for this type of input is already enabled in the software.

In addition, the event handlers for controls that support touch have built-in events that support touch interaction. Most XAML controls also have property settings that are related to touch input and gesture support.

The Tap

The most fundamental touch input is the *tap* gesture, shown in the following illustration. Tapping on a screen element should always invoke its primary action in touch-enabled user interfaces; for example, a user might tap a photograph to enlarge it or open it for editing in a graphics program. Keep in mind that while a mouse or a pen might offer very precise on-screen input, fingers typically are not as accurate, so your screen elements should be large enough to support tap gestures and other touch input.

The Slide

Another foundational gesture in a Windows 8 app is the panning movement, or *slide*, shown following. A slide is a one-finger motion that moves the page right or left, and often supports moving items from one location to another. This gesture is typically equivalent to scrolling with the mouse or using the arrow keys on a keyboard. You can also use a slide gesture in moving, drawing, or writing operations.

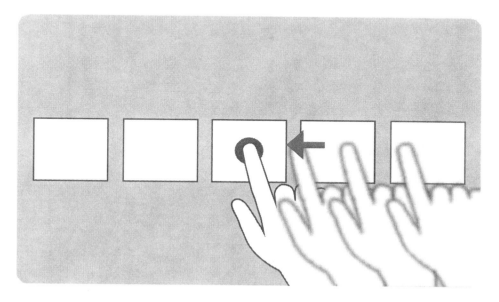

Zooming and Resizing

Input gestures often involve using two or even three fingers to manipulate objects in a Windows 8 app. The on-screen objects following help to demonstrate the zoom-in or *stretch* gesture, a technique used to increase the magnification of the page so that objects can be examined more clearly. The opposite of this gesture is called a *pinch*, which produces the opposite visual effect: a zoom-out.

On this touch-enabled screen, notice what the objects look like before zooming:

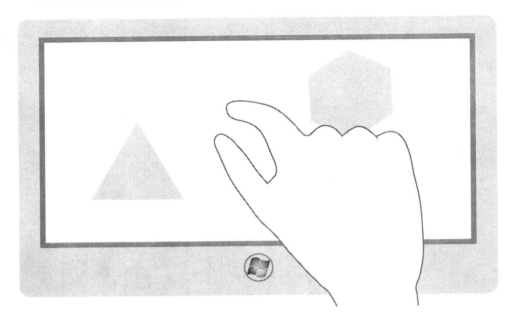

And notice what they look like after zooming (or stretching):

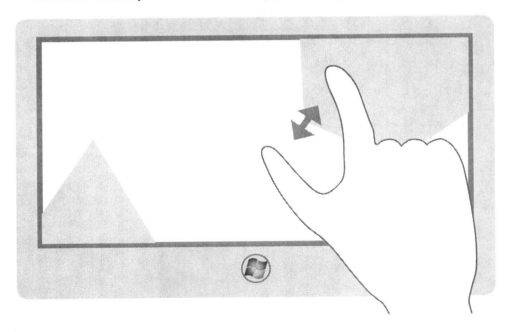

Programmers can also use the stretch or pinch gestures to allow individual objects to be resized on a page. Note that some objects, but not all objects, can be resized. Resizing capability depends on what the programmer wants to allow the user to do.

Designing for Touch

Designing for touch involves more than simply designing the user interface for finger input and touch gestures. It also requires thinking about how the touch-enabled device will be held by the user. For example, if the device is held on the user's lap, then the user may have both hands free to manipulate the objects on the screen. However, if the user is holding the device in two hands, the lower parts of the screen will likely be partially obscured by the hands, and only the top half of the device will be completely visible. Depending on how the device is held, some types of input will be harder or easier.

Furthermore, since most people are right-handed, they will tend to hold the touch-enabled device with their left hand and touch it with their right. Accordingly, objects placed on the right side of the screen will be easier to touch than objects on the left. In addition, some users may have motor impairments or other disabilities that may influence how they interact with touch-enabled devices.

Even as you work to consider how touch input and gestures might be best used in an application, don't forget about traditional input devices and how users might innovatively use them in a Windows 8 app. For example, consider adding support for the right mouse button or a tilt wheel in your application. These are very common input features and are commonly used in Windows applications; users will often expect to see them supported. Visual Studio and the Windows Runtime API offer support for an amazing array of input devices and input techniques, so be sure to add these features to your applications as you write more sophisticated programs.

For more information about planning for touch input in your applications, visit *http://msdn .microsoft.com* and search for the topics "Touch Interaction Design" and "Responding to User Interaction."

For now, though, you can close Visual Studio. You're finished enhancing Windows 8 apps in this chapter. And congratulations—what you have learned is putting you on a path toward distributing your own applications via the Windows Store, an exciting opportunity described in the final chapter.

Summary

This chapter focused on the design of Windows 8 applications and several features that you can use to enhance the appearance and usability of your programs. You learned how to create an attractive tile for your app on the Windows Start page, and how to create a splash screen for your app that appears when you first start your program. You also learned how to set permissions and capabilities for your app to enhance the security of your program and the systems of users who purchase and use your applications.

The final two topics in this chapter presented material about user interface design with an eye toward future development opportunities. You learned about the Grid App template and some of the strategies that Visual Basic programmers use to work with multiple pages of information. You also learned more about supporting touch input and gestures in your Windows 8 applications. Although much of this support comes automatically when you have a touch-enabled device, there are still important design concepts to consider, including sizing objects appropriately on the screen and determining how the user might be holding or manipulating the touch-enabled device.

In the final chapter, you'll learn more about distributing applications via the Windows Store, and what you can do to enhance your Visual Basic and Visual Studio programming skills.

Chapter 12

Future Development Opportunities and the Windows Store

After completing this chapter, you'll be able to

- Prepare a Visual Basic application for certification and deployment via the Windows Store.

- Locate additional resources for Visual Basic programmers, including helpful web sites, books about software development, and other materials.

IN THIS CHAPTER, YOU'LL LEARN ABOUT the Windows Store, an exciting new distribution point for Windows 8 applications. You'll develop a checklist of items to complete before submitting an application for certification, and you'll learn about the distribution process for apps that are purchased through the Windows Store.

You'll also learn about future development opportunities for programmers of Microsoft Visual Basic, and several of the skill areas that you should build upon the road to becoming a commercial-grade Visual Basic developer. You'll find book and web site recommendations that will help you with your training and research, and you'll review topics that will help you to seek employment as a Visual Basic or Windows developer.

Preparing for the Windows Store

The Windows Store is a new electronic marketplace that allows consumers to search for and acquire Windows applications. The Windows Store is designed to distribute Windows 8 apps, much like Apple's Mac App Store allows consumers to download Mac software and the Windows Phone Marketplace allows consumers to download products for Windows Phone.

The Windows Store allows developers to reach a global marketplace in ways that have been difficult or impossible in the past. Through the Windows Store, Windows apps can be monetized, either by charging for an application or by including advertising in the application. Programs downloaded from the Windows Store are certified and ready to run; once you meet the requirements for preparing an app for the marketplace, the details about downloading and deploying the application are handled by the Store.

Throughout this book, you have been learning how to create Windows 8 apps using Visual Basic and Microsoft Visual Studio 2012. You are on the way to creating an app that can be certified and distributed by the Windows Store. You just need to learn how products are bought and sold in the Store, and you need to complete various work items on a Store checklist to prepare for certification and distribution. The following sections will help you with the process.

Exploring the Store's Features

When you click the Store tile on the Windows 8 Start page, the Windows Store launches and presents its suite of products, organized by category. The following illustration shows what the Windows Store looks like when you first start it. Since the list of featured products is always changing, your screen will look different.

The Spotlight area advertises best-selling items and the top new and free apps. As you scroll or pan to the right, you'll see additional product categories, such as Games, Social, Entertainment, Photo, Music & Video, Sports, and Books & Reference. When you select a category and an item, you'll see an app listing page similar to the following screen:

The app listing page is your chance to make a first impression on potential customers for your product. The application name, description, feature list, age rating, price, and screen shots are all important factors in making a good impression on your audience. As people purchase or download your app, the rating system (based on five possible stars for the highest level of customer satisfaction) is also an important factor in drawing people to your app.

Installing a Windows app from the Store is extremely simple; you just click the Install button and within moments the app will be deployed on your desktop and available for use. A reliable Internet connection is required to download the app and (often) to feed the app data as the program runs.

Pricing and Sales

Windows apps may be distributed free or sold for a price. A setting called a *price tier* sets the fee for the app that you plan to sell. You can set the price tier that you like; tiers start at $1.49 and move up in increments of $.50, to $4.99 USD; higher product prices are available as well. (These prices are the proposed initial settings for the Store. They will likely change over time.)

For the first $25,000 of an app's sales, you will receive 70 percent of the revenues that Microsoft receives for the product. If and when an application receives more than $25,000 in sales, you will receive 80 percent of the revenues. Keep in mind that your product will be sold internationally, and in some countries the amount that Microsoft receives will be reduced to account for taxes required by local laws. The Windows Store has been designed to reach customers in over 200 countries and regions around the world. In some of these markets, the Windows Store will accept payment in the local current of the country or region.

It is also required that you register to be a Windows Store developer before you can sell products through Microsoft's new electronic marketplace. The annual cost for a developer account in the United States is $49 for an individual and $99 for a company. (These annual costs are subject to change and may vary from country to country, but the costs are up-to-date as of late 2012.) You will also need to complete some registration paperwork containing contact information and other details.

Getting Ready for Certification and Deployment

Microsoft recommends that you review the certification requirements carefully for Windows Store apps before you begin serious development on your project, so that you aren't surprised by the necessary steps. For the most part, these steps are simply good development practices that will make your programs robust and high quality. Microsoft is enforcing high standards so that customers come to trust the Windows Store and all of the software distributed through it. We all have a lot riding on the success of the Windows Store.

The Visual Studio IDE contains a Store menu with eight commands pertaining to the Windows Store, as shown in the following illustration:

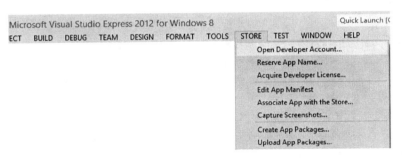

Before you begin serious development on a project that you intend to submit to the Windows Store, you should run the first three commands on the Store menu. The Open Developer Account command will get you signed up with Microsoft as an individual or a company. This enables the submission process and allows you to get more information. The Reserve App Name command lets you reserve a name for your application within the store. You want to do this before you get too far along (and then learn you need to change the name). The Acquire Developer License command lets you get a temporary developer license, which you may have already done during your work in Visual Studio.

Tip A useful blog for developers preparing for the Windows Store is available at *http://blogs.msdn.com/b/windowsstore/.* Here you'll find Microsoft employees and other industry experts explaining key Store concepts and answering pertinent questions. For example, in addition to the Store checklist supplied following, you'll need to fill out a complete package manifest for your project and practice other safe programming practices. You can also find useful information in the MSDN article "Selling apps," at *http://msdn.microsoft.com/en-us/library/windows/apps/br230836.aspx.*

Store Requirements Checklist

The formal certification process begins when you upload your app to the Windows Store. Table 12-1 contains a checklist recommended by Microsoft for developers who are creating Windows 8 apps for the Store. Most of these items are required for certification and will be evaluated when you register with Microsoft and fill out the required submission pages online. The checklist may be updated periodically, but this specification will help you get started. The point is that you need to do some preparation before you get online and submit your app for certification. You should have the necessary information ready, and be sure that it has been proofread carefully.

TABLE 12-1 Windows Store Submission Checklist

Submission Page	Field Name	Description
Name	App Name	Choose a name for your app that is 256 characters or less. Pick a name that will capture your customers' attention. It is best to keep this name short.
Selling Details	Price Tier	Prepare to specify a selling price for your app (or set the price to "free").
	Free trial period	Allow your customer to download the app for a free trial period. If the customer does not buy it in the set period of time, it will stop working.
	Countries/Regions	Identify the market for your product.
	Release Date	Set the app's release date.
	Category	Assign a category for your app so that customers can find it in the Windows Store. There is a helpful list of predefined categories to choose from.
	Accessible App	If your app has been designed to meet Microsoft's accessibility guidelines, indicate that here.
	Minimum DirectX Feature Level	Indicate the video and hardware requirements for your application.
	Minimum System RAM	Indicate how much RAM your app requires. You might want to double-check the basic system requirements for the devices that your app will run on too.
Advanced Features	In-app Offers	Provide information about products that users can purchase from within your app, including what the customer must pay and how long the purchased feature can be used.

Submission Page	Field Name	Description
Ratings	Age Rating	Specify an appropriate age rating for your app using the levels provided.
	Rating Certificates	If you are selling a game, you may need to provide a rating certificate from a ratings board, depending on where you plan to sell your app.
Cryptography	Question 1	Indicate whether your app makes use of cryptography or encryption.
	Question 2	Verify that any use of cryptography is within the allowable limits imposed by the Bureau of Industry and Security in the United States Department of Commerce.
Packages	Package Upload Control	Provide the path to your app's completed package.
Description	Description	Include clear and concise marketing copy that describes your application, its features, and its benefits. Review this information carefully before posting. The description must be 10,000 characters or less.
	App Features	List up to 20 features of your app (optional). Each feature must be 200 characters or less.
	Keywords	List up to seven concise keywords describing your app (optional).
	Description of Update	Provide a description of how this new version of your app updates the previous version. (Leave this blank for the first release of your app.)
	Copyright and Trademark Info	Provide a brief copyright notice (200 characters or less).
	Additional License Terms	Provide legal requirements regarding the use of the application. Must be 10,000 characters or less (optional).
	Screenshots	Provide up to eight quality screen shots of your app as it is running. Each may have a description of up to 200 words. The minimum size of the image must be 1366×766 pixels. You can capture these screens using the Store | Capture Screenshots command in Visual Studio.
	Promotional Images	Include up to four other promotional images for your app (optional).
	Recommended Hardware	Provide up to 11 notes about the hardware requirements for your app (optional).
	App Website	Provide the web site URL for your product.
	Support Contact	Provide a contact URL for customers so that they can get support or ask additional questions. Prepare to be very responsive to customer questions and feedback.
	Privacy Policy	Prepare an appropriate statement about your privacy policy regarding data collected about users.
	In-app Offer Description	Provide information about products that users can purchase from within your app, including what the customer must pay and how long the purchased feature can be used. (This field was indicated previously as well—see "Advanced Features" near the top of this table. Use the same information.)
Notes to Testers	Notes	Give the evaluators at Microsoft additional information about your app so that they can test its functionality. For example, describe hidden features or provide user name and password information if needed.

Future Opportunities and Programming Resources

This book has presented beginning and intermediate Visual Basic 2012 programming techniques with the aim of making you a confident software developer and Windows 8 programmer. As you can see, the techniques that you have learned are preparing you to distribute your creations through the Windows Store, although there is still work to be done to create truly commercial-grade software.

Now that you've experimented with many of the tools and features in Visual Studio Express 2012 for Windows 8, you're ready for more advanced topics and the full breadth of the Visual Studio 2012 development suite.

If you have your sights set on a career in Visual Basic programming, you might want to test your proficiency by preparing for a certified exam in Visual Studio development. You may also wish to upgrade to a full retail version of Visual Studio 2012, such as Visual Studio 2012 Professional Edition. In the following sections, you'll learn about additional resources for Visual Basic programming, including helpful web sites, a source for certification information, and books that you can use to expand your Visual Basic programming skills.

Web Sites for Visual Basic and Windows 8

The web is a boon to programmers and is definitely the fastest mechanism for gathering the latest information about Visual Basic 2012 and related technologies. This section lists several of the web sites that I use to learn about new products and services related to Visual Basic. As you use this list, note that the Internet address and contents of each site change from time to time, so the sites might not appear exactly as I've described them. Considering the constant ebb and flow of the Internet, it's also a good idea to search for "Visual Basic," "Visual Studio 2012," "Windows Store apps," and "Windows 8" occasionally to see what new information is available. (To get the most specific hits, include quotation marks around each search item.) You might also find some useful information if you search early product code names such as "Visual Basic 11."

- ***http://msdn.microsoft.com/en-us/vstudio/*** The Microsoft Visual Studio Developer Center home page is the best overall site for documentation, breaking news, conference information, and product support for Visual Studio 2012. (If you'd like this information in another language, browse to the web site and select the current language at the bottom of the page. You will be directed to a site with other language options.) The Developer Center gives you up-to-date information about the entire Visual Studio product line and lets you know how new operating systems, applications, and programming tools affect Visual Basic development. Features that I like here are the blogs by Visual Basic team members and access to recent videos and downloads.

Note Remember that you can also access MSDN resources quickly from the Visual Studio Start Page within the Visual Studio IDE. The Start Page loads updated articles and news content each time you start Visual Studio, so its contents are always changing.

- *http://msdn.microsoft.com/en-us/windows/apps/*   The Windows Dev Center for Windows Store apps is the best corporate web site for Windows 8 programming documentation and learning resources. You can download Visual Studio 2012 here, read the developer's guides, and attend a virtual Windows development camp online. Look for the "C# and VB Roadmap" link and other information about Visual Basic programming for Windows 8.

- *http://shop.oreilly.com/category/browse-subjects/programming/visual-basic.do*
  This is the O'Reilly Media web site for Visual Basic programming books. Here you'll find the most recent titles for Visual Studio 2012 and more. Be sure to check the .NET & Windows Programming category as well.

- *http://www.microsoft.com/learning/en/us/training/format-books.aspx*   The Microsoft Learning web site offers numerous books on Visual Studio programming from Microsoft Press. Check here for new books about Visual Basic, Microsoft Visual C#, Microsoft Visual C++, and supporting database and web programming technologies. You can also download freebies, learn about certification examinations, and send e-mail to Microsoft Press.

- *http://social.msdn.microsoft.com/Forums/en-US/*   This site of technical forums for Microsoft products and technologies offers opportunities to interact with Microsoft employees and your software development peers. The forums reward bloggers by giving them points for asking and answering questions, allowing developers to demonstrate their expertise and help fellow programmers. You'll find this site to be tremendously useful if you are stuck on a problem or want to ask a general question.

Video on the Web

The web has seen an explosion of video content. There are several sites that have videos related to Visual Basic and programming. If you have a few minutes and a high-speed Internet connection, videos can be a great way to quickly learn something new. If you are the type of person that learns best by visualizing, check out these sites:

- *http://msdn.microsoft.com/en-us/vstudio/cc136611*   The Visual Basic Learning Center has a "How Do I" videos section with videos that are specific to Visual Basic. These videos cover a variety of areas, including Visual Basic techniques, Windows, Office, and LINQ.

- *http://channel9.msdn.com/*   Channel 9 is a Microsoft site that hosts videos, Twitter feeds, and discussions about programming. It has a learning center that has online training videos. Some of the training includes Visual Studio, Windows, SQL Server, and Windows Phone.

Books About Visual Basic and Visual Studio

Books about Visual Basic and Visual Studio programming provide in-depth sources of information and self-paced training that web sites can supplement but not replace. As you seek to expand your Visual Basic and Visual Studio programming skills, I recommend that you consult the following sources of printed information (listed here by category and date of publication). Note that this isn't a complete bibliography of Visual Studio titles, but it is a list that's representative of the books available in English at the time of the initial release of Visual Studio 2012. I also list books related to Windows 8, database and LINQ programming, and general books about software development and computer science.

Visual Basic Programming

- *Microsoft Visual Basic 2012 Step by Step,* by Michael Halvorson (Microsoft Press, 2013). This book provides a general introduction to writing Windows 8 apps, traditional Windows desktop apps (i.e. Windows Forms), console applications, and web applications using the newest version of Visual Basic. It picks up where this book leaves off and emphasizes the unique features of Visual Basic 2012 Professional Edition and Premium Edition. The book also includes an introduction to writing Visual Basic programs for Windows Phone 8.

- *Visual Basic 2012 Programmer's Reference,* by Rod Stephens (Wrox, 2012). This book is a well-organized reference to Visual Basic 2012 program statements, functions, and features. However, it limits coverage of Windows 8 apps to just one chapter.

- *Professional Visual Basic 2012 and .NET 4.5,* by Bill Sheldon et al. (Wrox, 2013). Coverage of more advanced Visual Basic programming topics such as data access with ADO.NET, security, ASP.NET web programming, Windows workflow, and threading.

- *XAML Developer Reference,* by Mamta Dalal and Ashish Ghoda (Microsoft Press, 2011). This book's nine chapters cover XAML basics as well as more advanced XAML techniques such as using resources and styles, managing layout on the page, data binding, graphics, and animation.

Windows Programming

- *Build Windows 8 Apps with Microsoft Visual C# and Visual Basic Step by Step,* by Luca Regnicoli, Paolo Pialorsi, and Roberto Brunetti (Microsoft Press, 2012). Intermediate to advanced .NET development skills, including more on the Windows 8 design guidelines. Includes some useful examples in Visual Basic 2012.

- *Essential Windows Phone 7.5: Application Development with Silverlight,* by Shawn Wildermuth (Addison Wesley, 2011). Although Windows Phone 8 is expected to be released around the end of 2012, this book provides a very useful introduction to writing Windows Phone applications with the version of Phone that was current while this book was being completed. It provides useful XAML examples, as well as some C# examples.

- *Microsoft Expression Blend 4 Step by Step*, by Elena Kosinska and Chris Leeds (Microsoft Press, 2011). This book will help you learn more about Blend, enabling you to create better-looking user interfaces for Windows 8 apps.

Database Programming and LINQ

- *Microsoft ADO.NET 4 Programming Step by Step*, by Tim Patrick (Microsoft Press, 2010). Examples in Visual Basic and C# make this an essential database programming title for Visual Studio programmers.

- *Programming Microsoft LINQ in Microsoft .NET Framework 4*, by Paolo Pialorsi and Marco Russo (Microsoft Press, 2010). This is a great source of in-depth information about the LINQ technology included with Visual Studio 2010. It is still useful with Visual Studio 2012.

Web Programming with Visual Basic

- *Beginning ASP.NET 4.5 in VB*, by Matthew MacDonald (Apress, 2012). If you have a full retail version of Visual Studio, you can write apps for the web using a technology known as ASP.NET. This book provides an excellent introduction to the topic.

General Books About Programming and Computer Science

- *Code Complete, Second Edition*, by Steve McConnell (Microsoft Press, 2004). I list this book first because it is one of my favorite resources for teaching yourself programming.

- *Code*, by Charles Petzold (Microsoft Press, 2000). An excellent introduction to what really happens in a computer. For both programmers and a general audience.

- *Writing Secure Code, Second Edition*, by Michael Howard and David LeBlanc (Microsoft Press, 2003). This is a general book that focuses on security issues throughout the entire development process—from designing secure applications, to writing robust code that can withstand repeated attacks, to testing applications for security flaws.

- *Software Project Survival Guide*, by Steve McConnell (Microsoft Press, 1997). This book provides general concepts and strategies you can use to plan and organize the development process, including design, management, quality assurance, testing, and archiving tasks. It's a great book for newcomers and seasoned project managers alike.

- *Data Structures and Algorithms Using Visual Basic .NET*, by Michael McMillan (Cambridge University Press, 2005). As a college professor, I can't help but recommend a more academic-oriented book that brings something from the discipline of computer science to the profession of Visual Basic programming. This book presents a discussion of arrays, linked lists, hash tables, dictionaries, trees, graphs, sorting, and searching, with examples in the Visual Basic programming language.

It is especially important that as a self-taught programmer you acquire a library of general programming books over time that can help you with more theoretical (and non-language-dependent) topics such as fundamental algorithms, data structures, sorting, searching, compression, random numbers, advanced mathematics, networking, and compilers. The books listed in this chapter are only the beginning, and many can be found in bookstores that sell used programming books.

Summary

Chapter 12 explored future development opportunities for Visual Basic programmers, including building applications for the Windows Store. You've learned how the Windows Store operates, and about some of the requirements you'll need to satisfy to post items for sale or distribution. Although the process is involved, the upside is significant: software developers who sell products on the Windows Store have the potential to reach millions of customers worldwide.

In addition to discussing the requirements for apps in the Windows Store, this chapter also covered additional resources for Visual Basic programmers who want to develop commercial-grade skills. The world of professional Visual Basic programming literally awaits you—you can delve into advanced work with databases, Internet data, user interface design, Windows Phone programming, and working with the many touch-enabled devices that are now entering the marketplace. I wish you the best of luck as you continue your programming with Visual Basic!

Index

Symbols

+ (addition) operator, 170, 174
= (assignment operator), 151–152
/> (closing bracket), 128
/ (division) operator, 170, 174
^ (exponentiation) operator, 170, 172–174
\ (integer division) operator, 170, 172, 174
* (multiplication) operator, 170, 174
– (negation) operator, 174
< (opening angle bracket), 128
& (string concatenation) operator, 55, 170, 172, 200, 262
- (subtraction) operator, 170, 174

A

Abs(n) method, System.Math class, 223
Add Existing Item dialog box, 181
addition operator, 170, 174
Adobe Elements, 294
Adobe Illustrator, 294
advanced operators, 172–173
alphanumeric order for arrays, 263
Always Show Solution check box, 9, 31
animation. *See* storyboards
Animation workspace. Blend, 108
applications. *See also* controls; *See also* Blend for Visual Studio
  button objects
    adding, 44
    setting Content property for, 48
  capabilities for, 299–302
  deploying release build for, 61–62
  event handlers, creating, 51–54
  hierarchical interface for, 302
  hub design for, 302
  opening using Search tool, 283
  overview, 36
  permissions for, 299–302
  projects, creating, 37–39
  reserving names for in Windows Store, 318
  running from IDE, 56–58
  security for in Windows 8, 299
  splash screens for, 294–299
  text boxes
    adding, 44–45
    for web addresses, 46–48
    moving and resizing, 43
  tile-based layout for, 178–179
  tiles for Start Page
    adding live content to, 286
    dimensions for, 283, 284
    matching color to application, 289–290
    overview, 282
    PNG format, 286
  touch input for
    built-in for Windows 8, 310
    design implications of, 313
    resize gesture, 311–312
    slide gesture, 311
    tap gesture, 310
    zoom gesture, 311–312
  user interface, creating, 39–42
  web view objects
    adding, 45–46
    properties of, setting, 49–50
App.xaml file, 13, 129, 130–131, 132
App.xaml.vb file, 39, 129–132
Array.Clear() method, 263
Array.Copy() method, 263
Array.Find() method, 263
Array.Reverse() method, 263–265

Z

X

About the Author

 MICHAEL HALVORSON is the author or co-author of more than 35 books, including *Microsoft Visual Basic 2010 Step by Step, Learn Microsoft Visual Basic Now,* and *Microsoft Visual Basic 6.0 Professional Step by Step.* Halvorson has been the recipient of numerous nonfiction writing awards, including the Computer Press Best How-to Book Award (Software category) and the Society for Technical Communication Excellence Award (Writing category). Halvorson earned a bachelor's degree in Computer Science from Pacific Lutheran University and master's and doctoral degrees in History from the University of Washington. He was employed at Microsoft Corporation from 1985 to 1993, and has been an advocate for Visual Basic programming since the product's original debut at Windows World in 1991. Halvorson is currently an associate professor at Pacific Lutheran University. You can learn more about his books and ideas at *http://www.michaelhalvorsonbooks.com.*

What do you think of this book?

We want to hear from you!

To participate in a brief online survey, please visit:

microsoft.com/learning/booksurvey

Tell us how well this book meets your needs—what works effectively, and what we can do better. Your feedback will help us continually improve our books and learning resources for you.

Thank you in advance for your input!

CPSIA information can be obtained at www.ICGtesting.com
Printed in the USA
BVOW021418160113

310781BV00007B/44/P